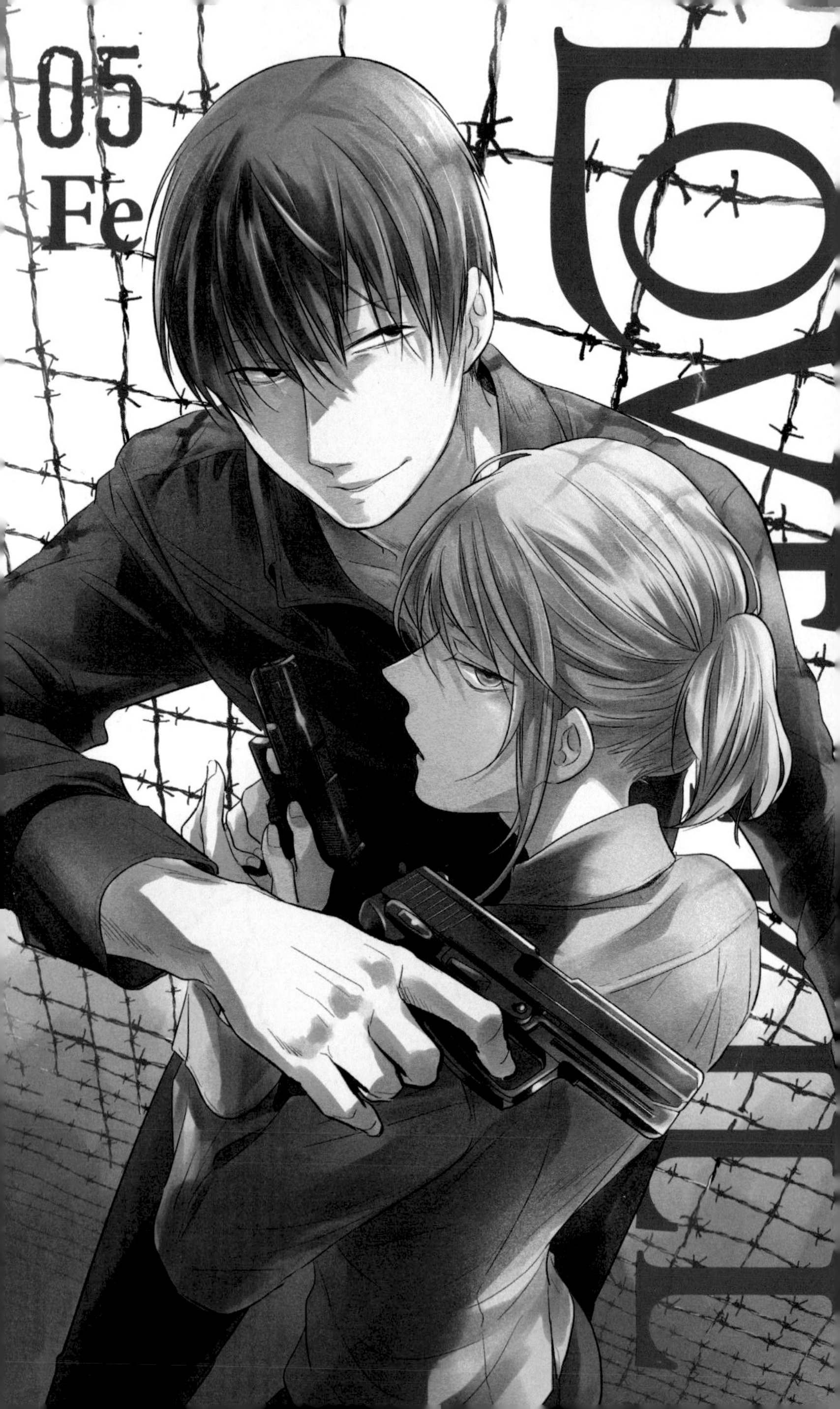
05
Fe

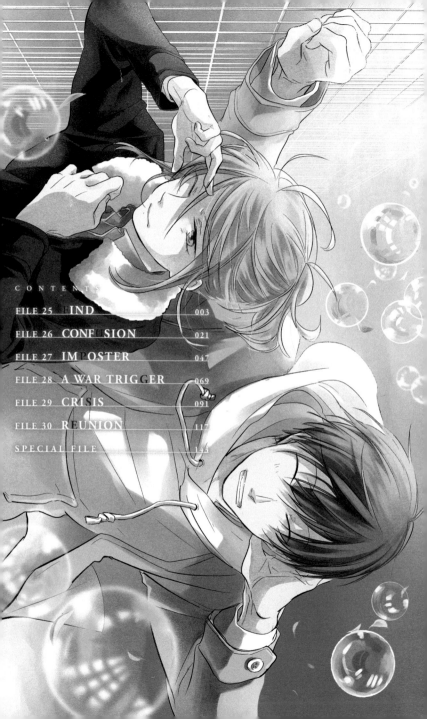

CONTENTS

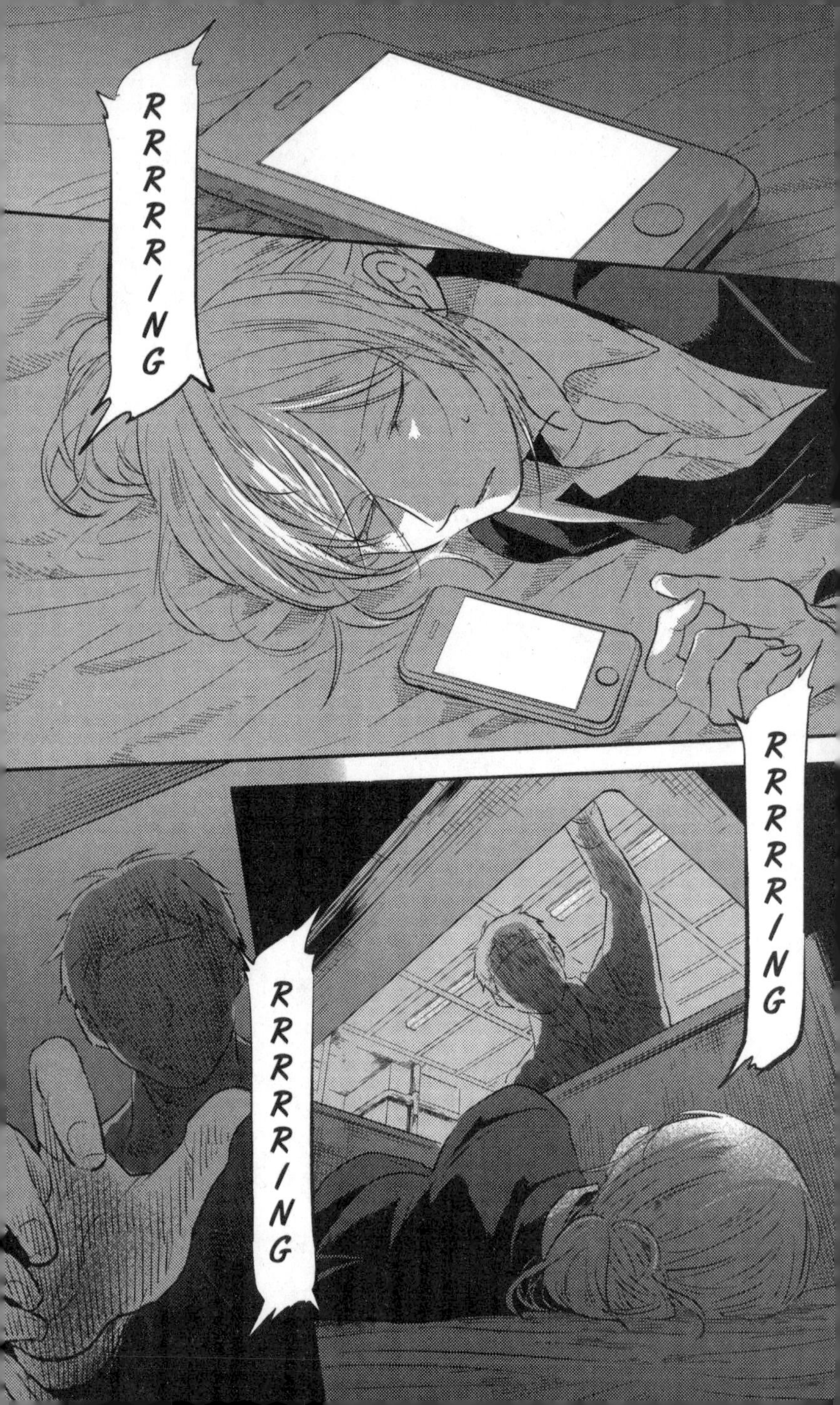
RRRRRING
RRRRRING
RRRRRING

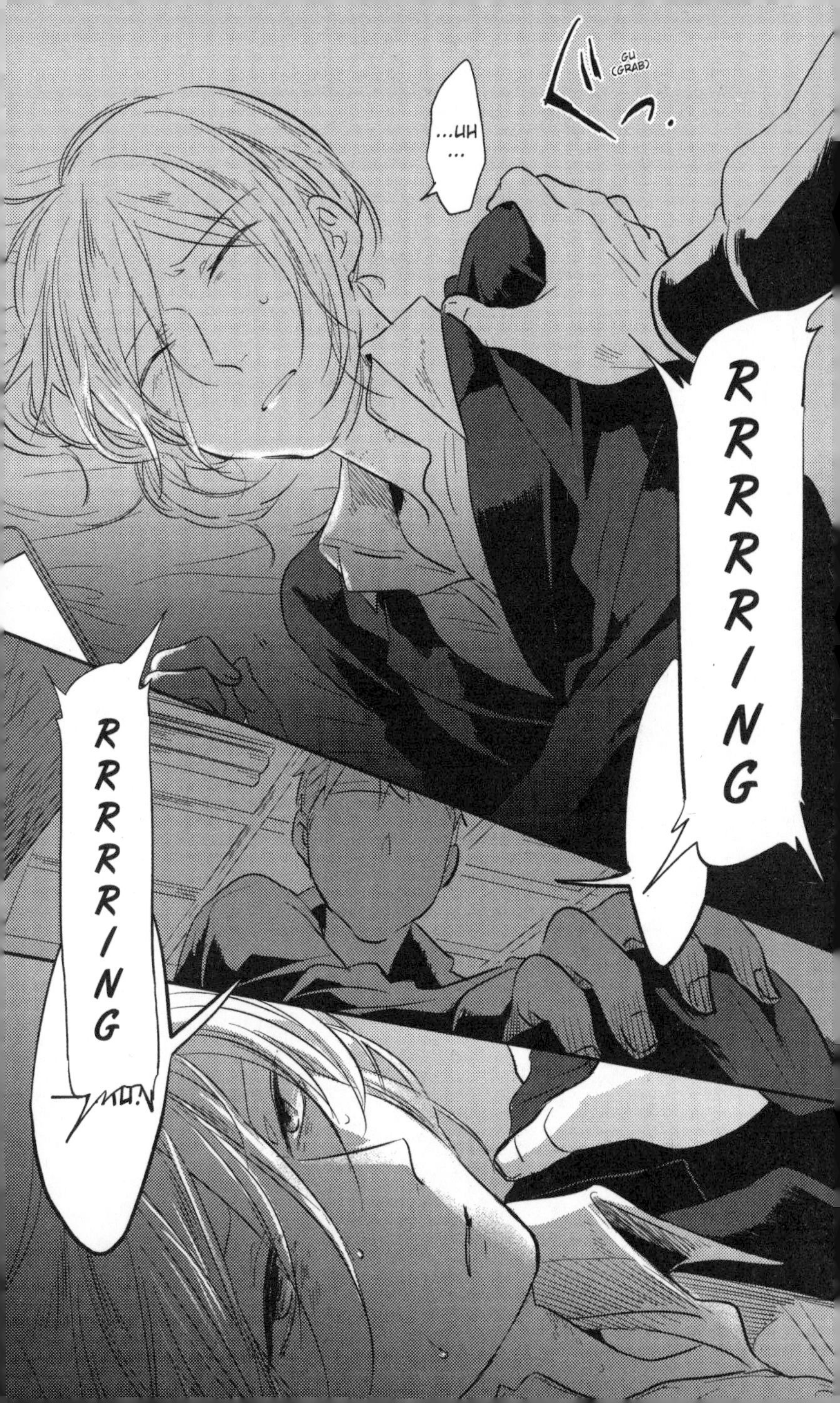
GU (GRAB)
...UH ...
RRRRRING
RRRRRING

FILE 25 FIND

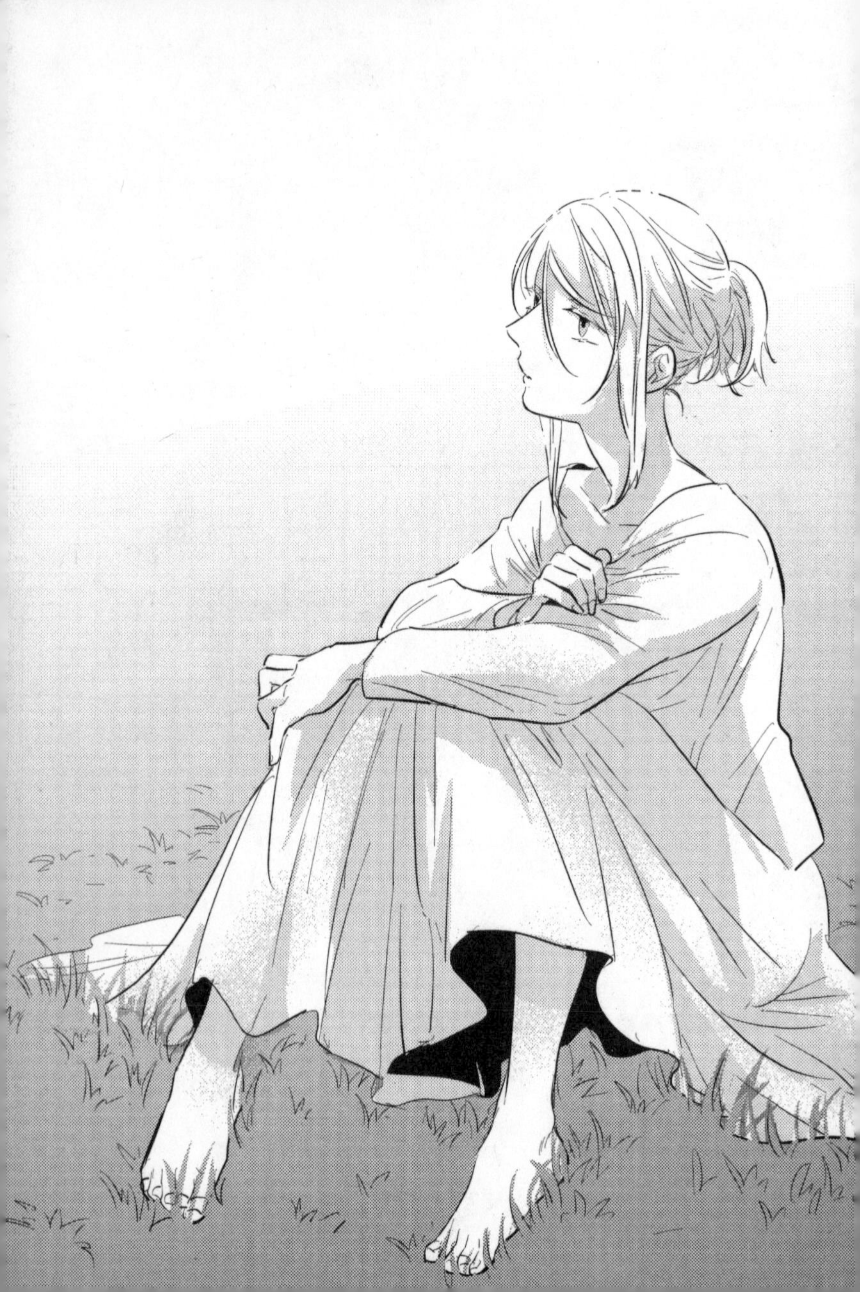

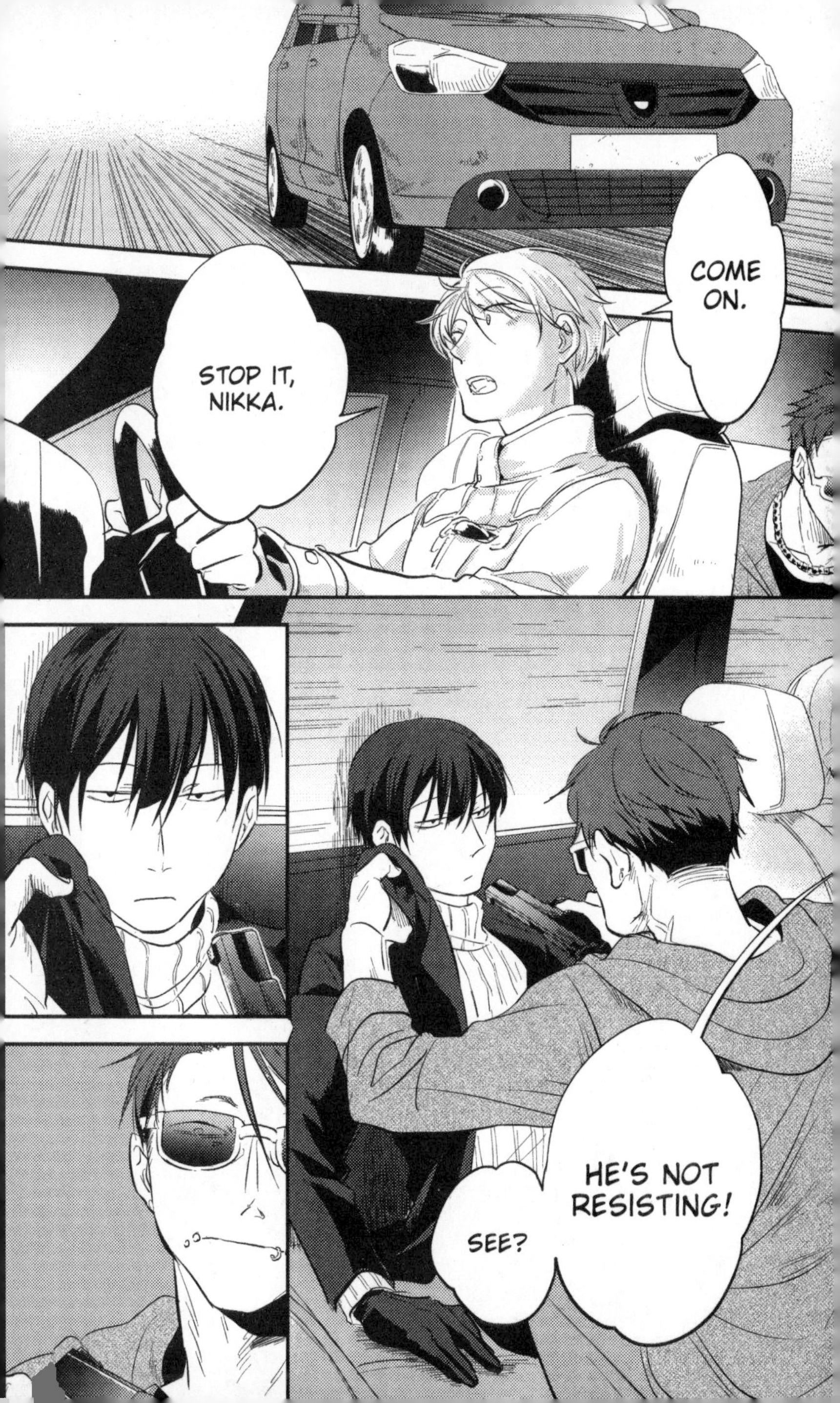
COME ON.
STOP IT, NIKKA.
HE'S NOT RESISTING!
SEE?

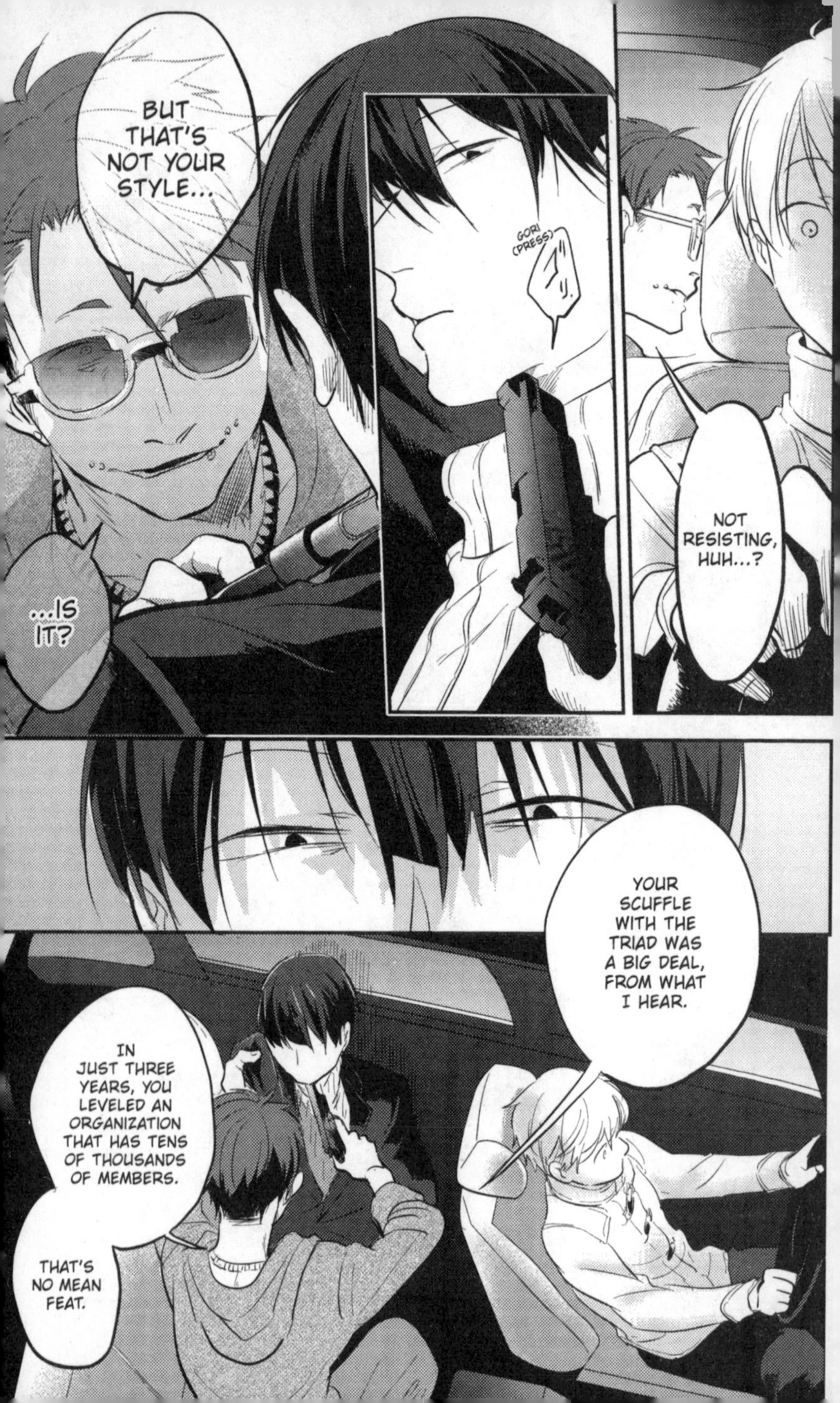
NOT RESISTING, HUH...?
GORI (PRESS)
BUT THAT'S NOT YOUR STYLE...
...IS IT?
YOUR SCUFFLE WITH THE TRIAD WAS A BIG DEAL, FROM WHAT I HEAR.
IN JUST THREE YEARS, YOU LEVELED AN ORGANIZATION THAT HAS TENS OF THOUSANDS OF MEMBERS.
THAT'S NO MEAN FEAT.

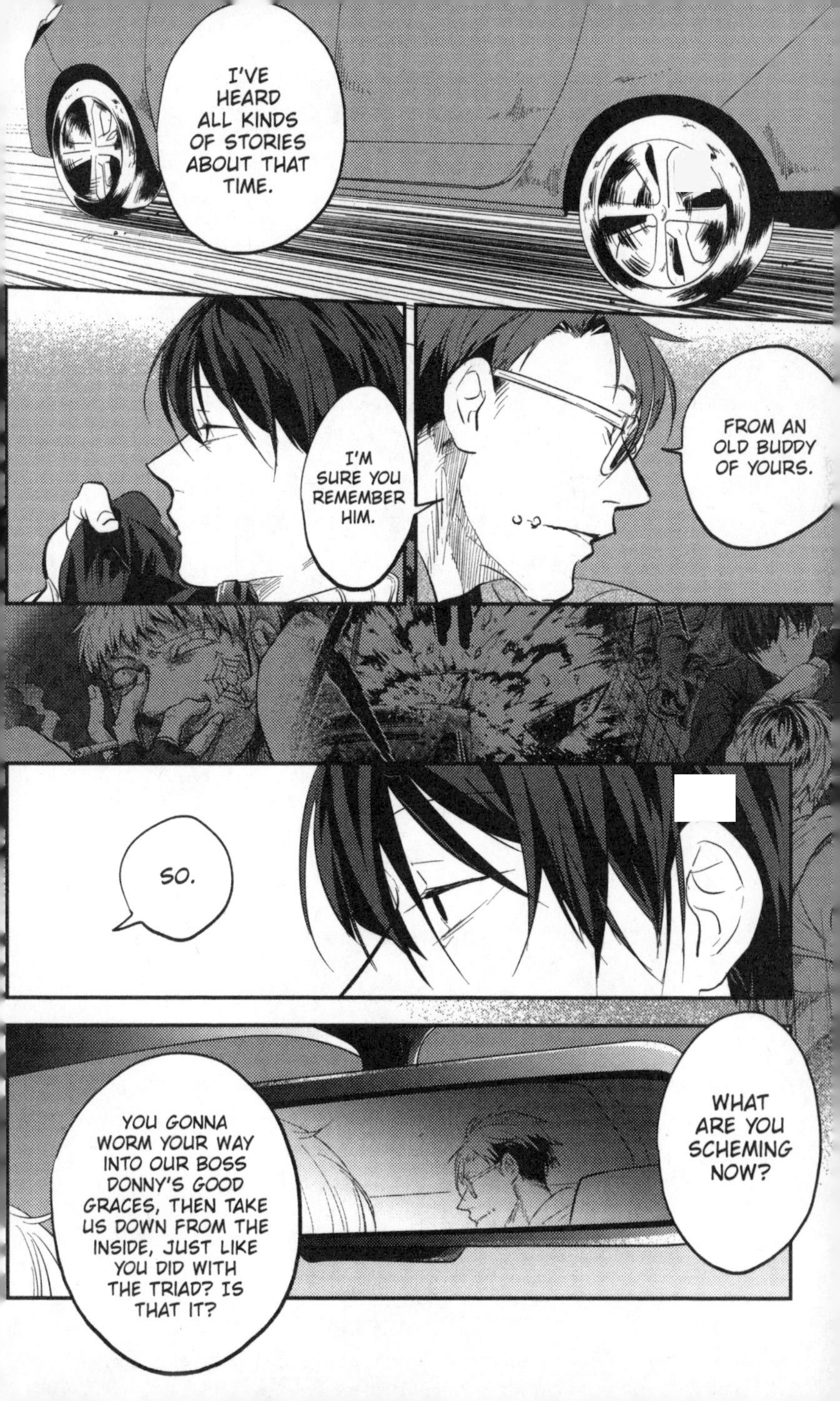
I'VE HEARD ALL KINDS OF STORIES ABOUT THAT TIME.
FROM AN OLD BUDDY OF YOURS.
I'M SURE YOU REMEMBER HIM.
SO.
WHAT ARE YOU SCHEMING NOW?
YOU GONNA WORM YOUR WAY INTO OUR BOSS DONNY'S GOOD GRACES, THEN TAKE US DOWN FROM THE INSIDE, JUST LIKE YOU DID WITH THE TRIAD? IS THAT IT?

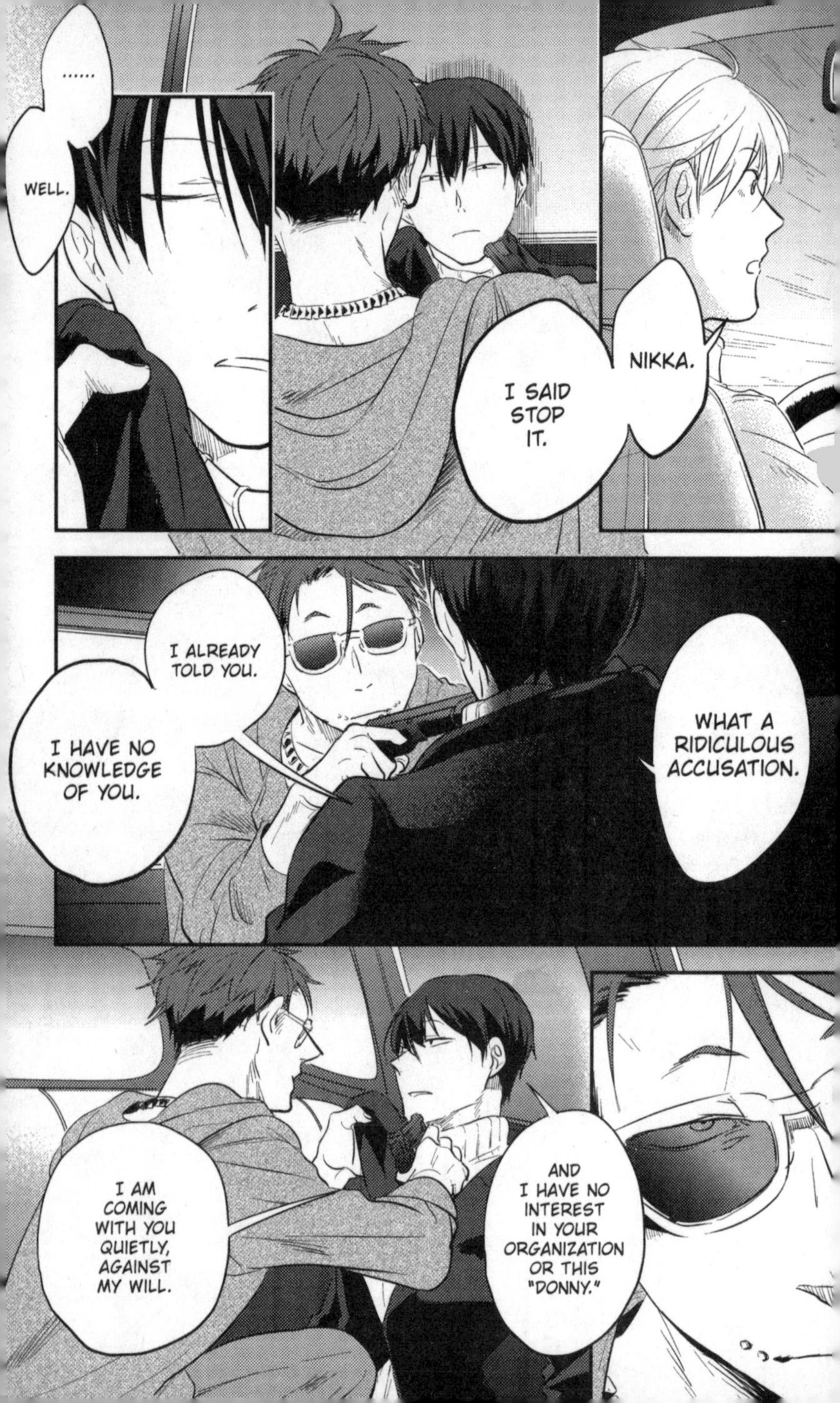
NIKKA.
I SAID STOP IT.
......
WELL.
WHAT A RIDICULOUS ACCUSATION.
I ALREADY TOLD YOU.
I HAVE NO KNOWLEDGE OF YOU.
AND I HAVE NO INTEREST IN YOUR ORGANIZATION OR THIS "DONNY."
I AM COMING WITH YOU QUIETLY, AGAINST MY WILL.

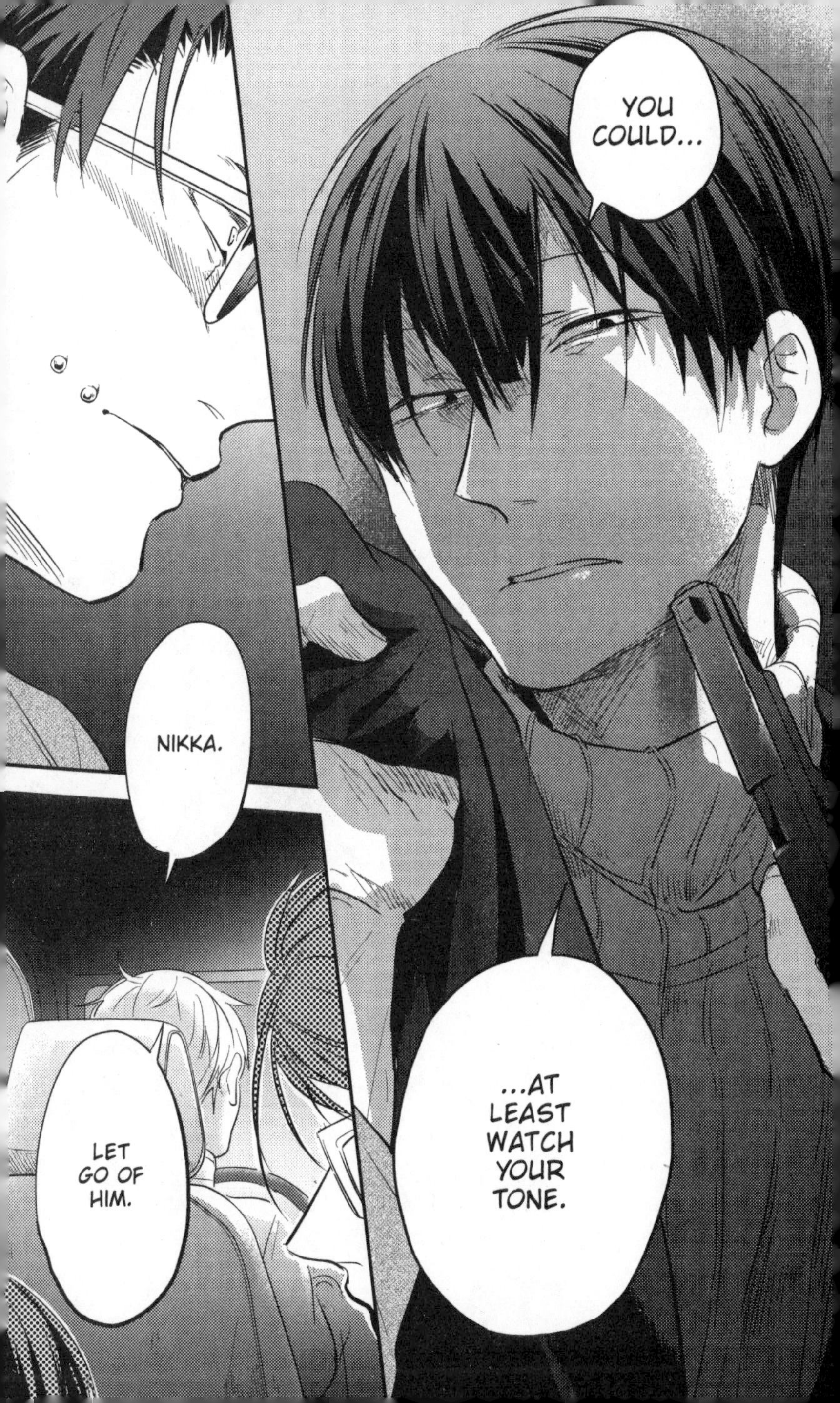
YOU COULD...
...AT LEAST WATCH YOUR TONE.
NIKKA.
LET GO OF HIM.

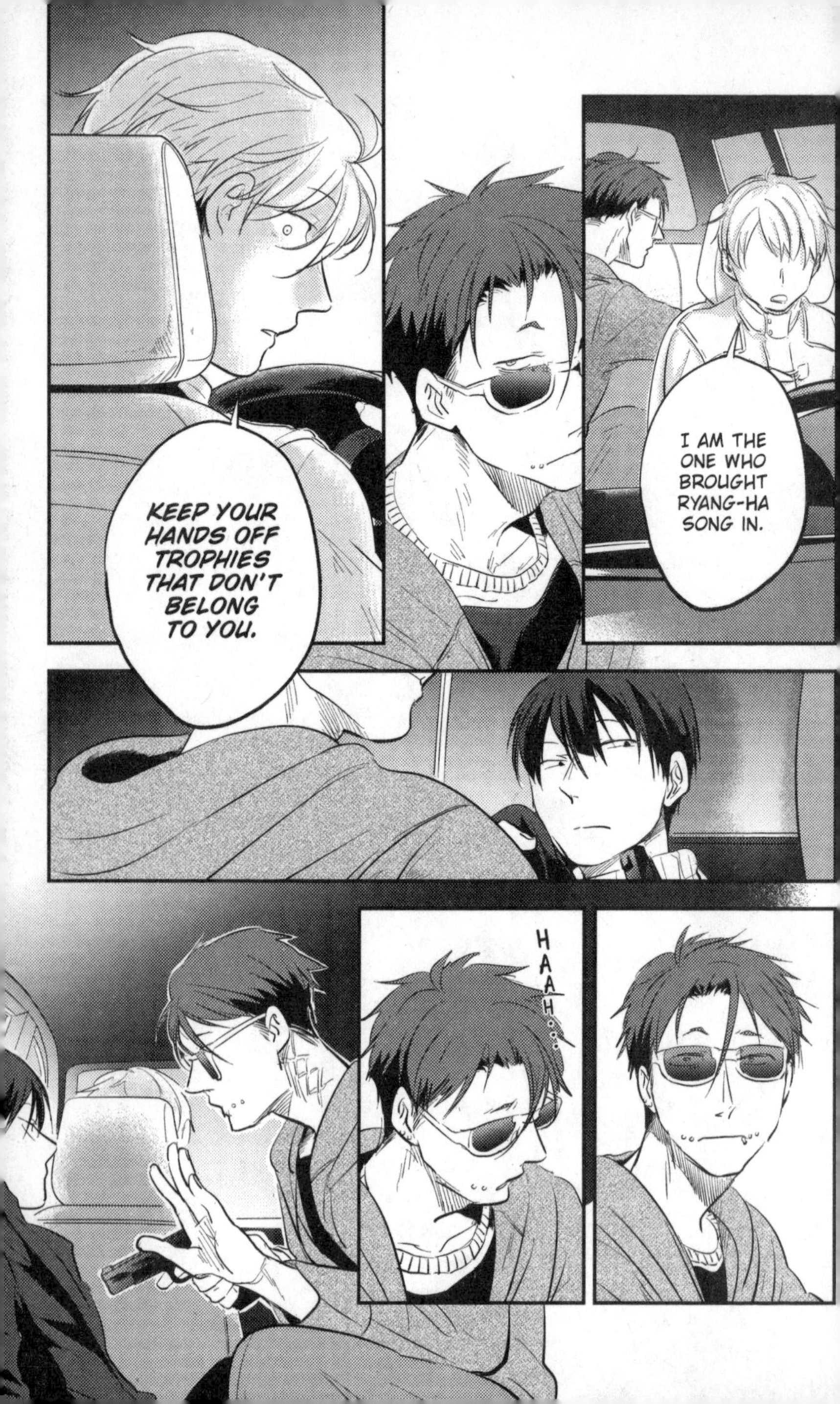
I AM THE ONE WHO BROUGHT RYANG-HA SONG IN.
KEEP YOUR HANDS OFF TROPHIES THAT DON'T BELONG TO YOU.
HAAH...

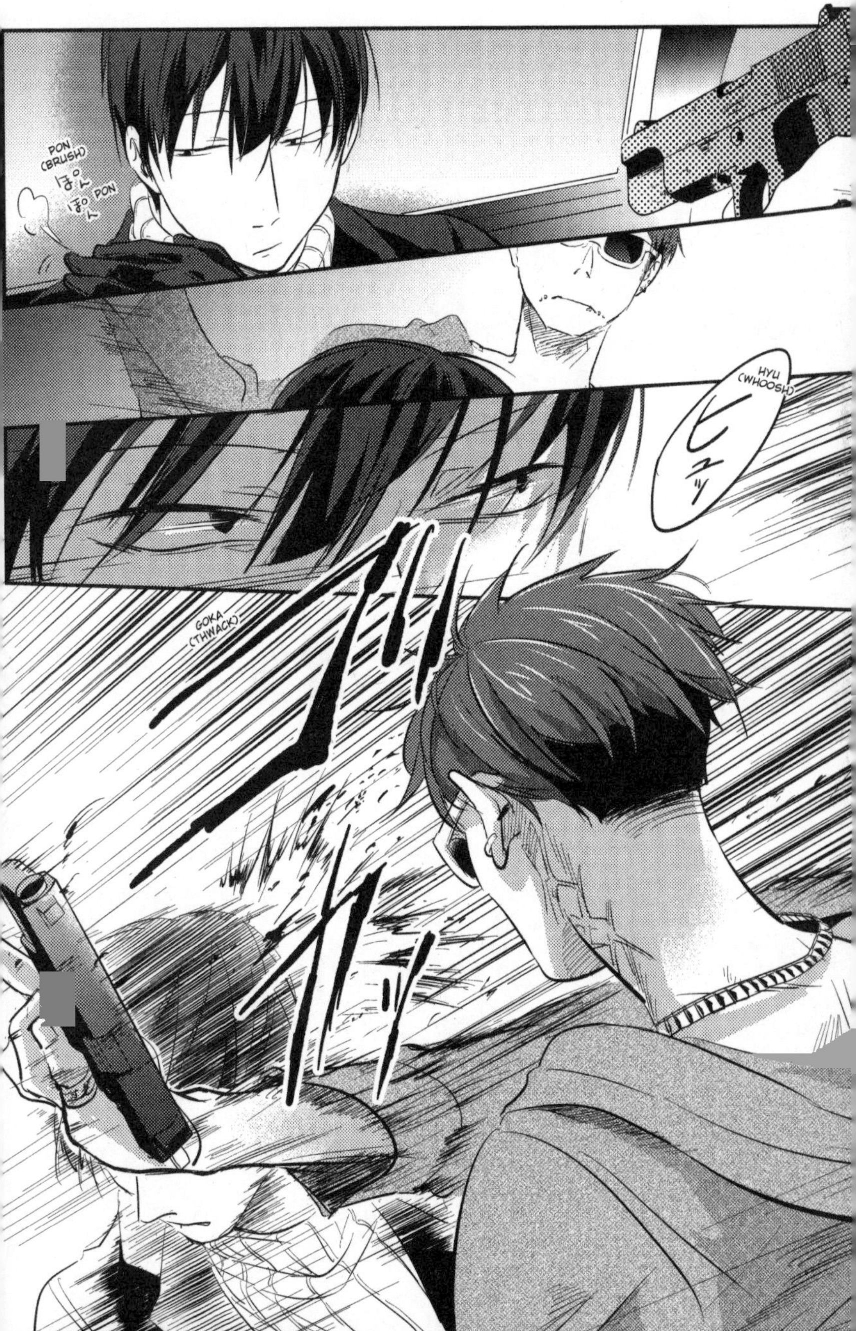

PON (BRUSH)
ぽん
ぽん
PON
HYU (WHOOSH)
ヒュッ
GOKA (THWACK)

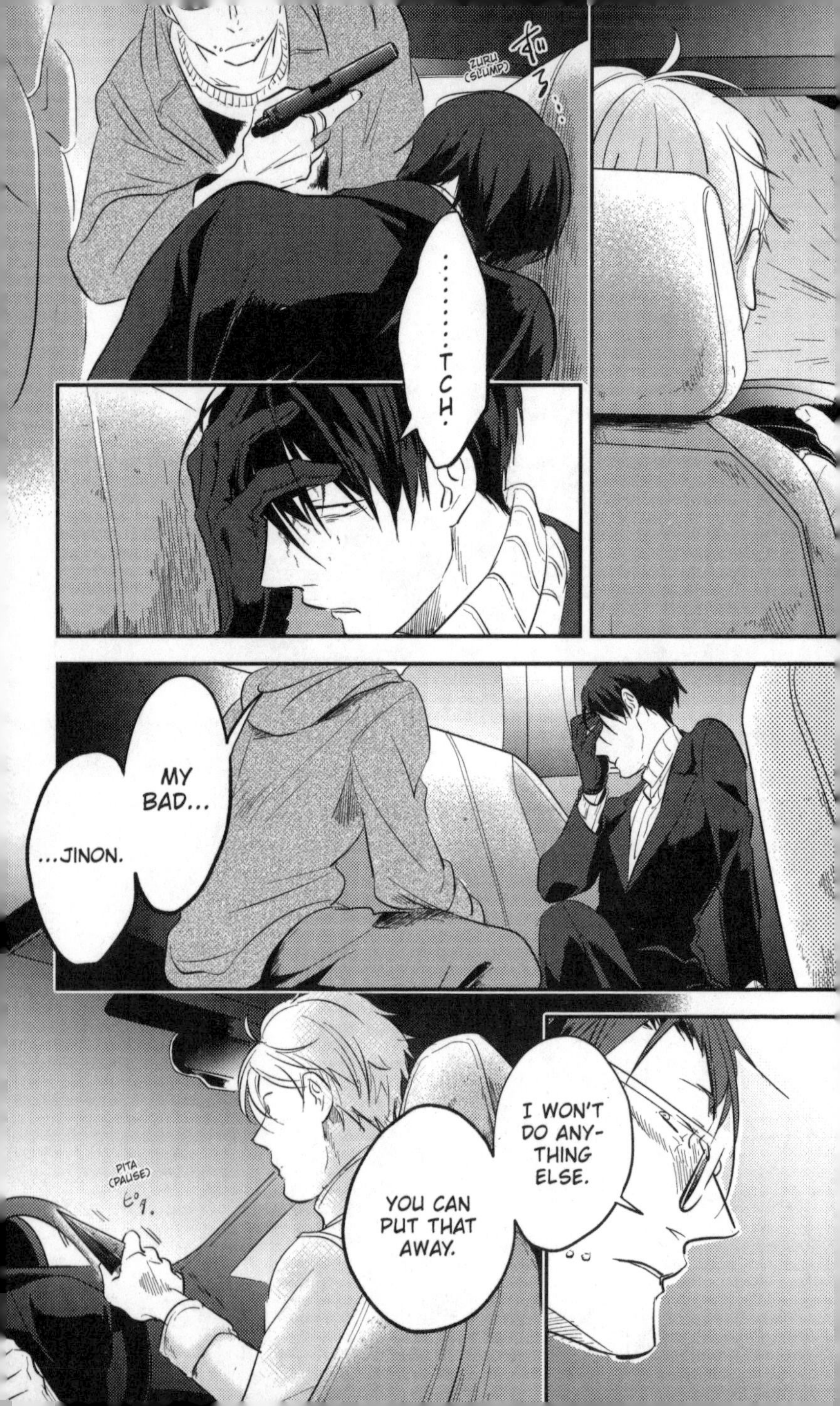
ZURU (SLUMP)
......TCH.
MY BAD...
...JINON.
I WON'T DO ANY-THING ELSE.
YOU CAN PUT THAT AWAY.
PITA (PAUSE)

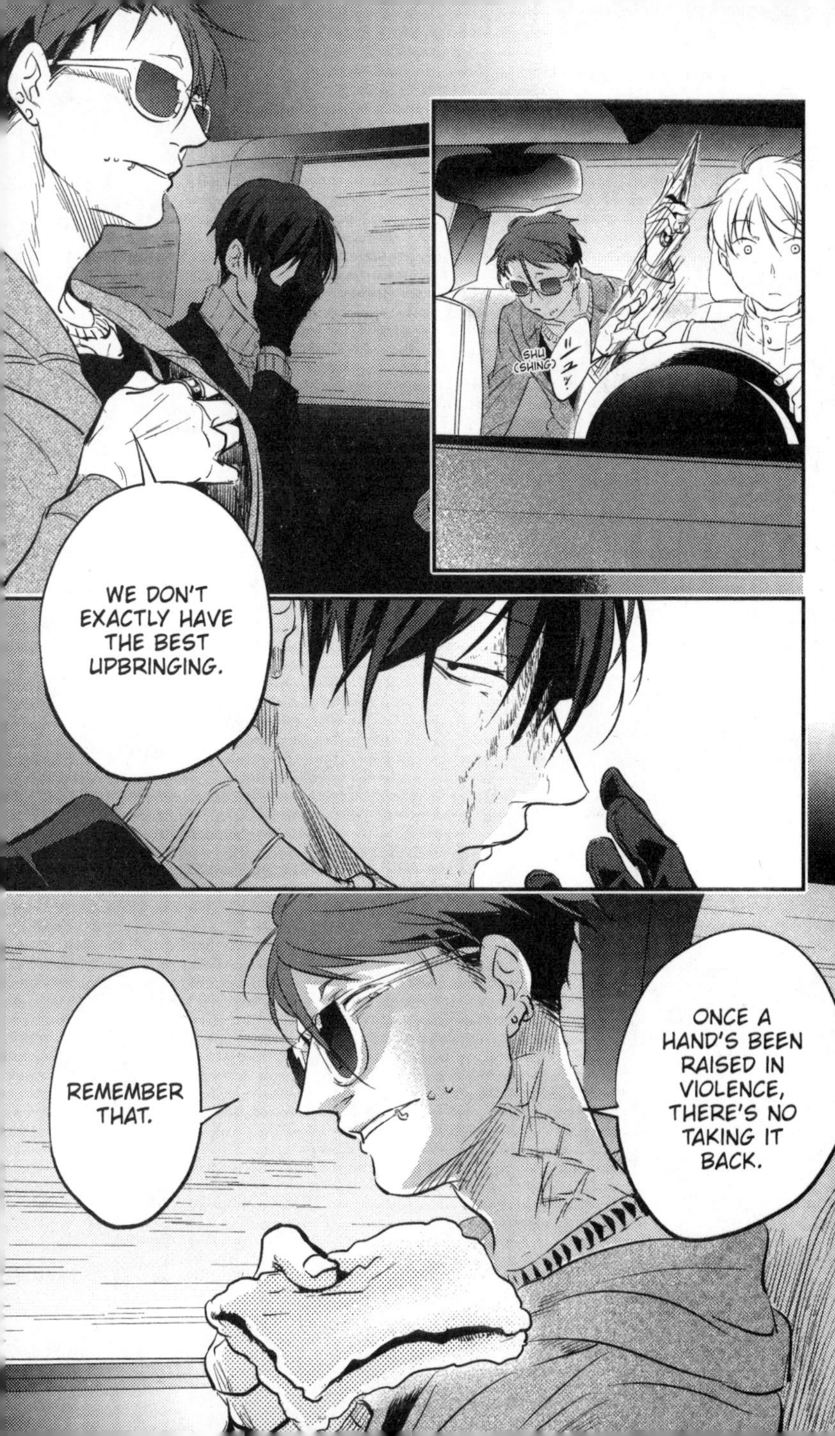
SHU (SHING)
WE DON'T EXACTLY HAVE THE BEST UPBRINGING.
ONCE A HAND'S BEEN RAISED IN VIOLENCE, THERE'S NO TAKING IT BACK.
REMEMBER THAT.

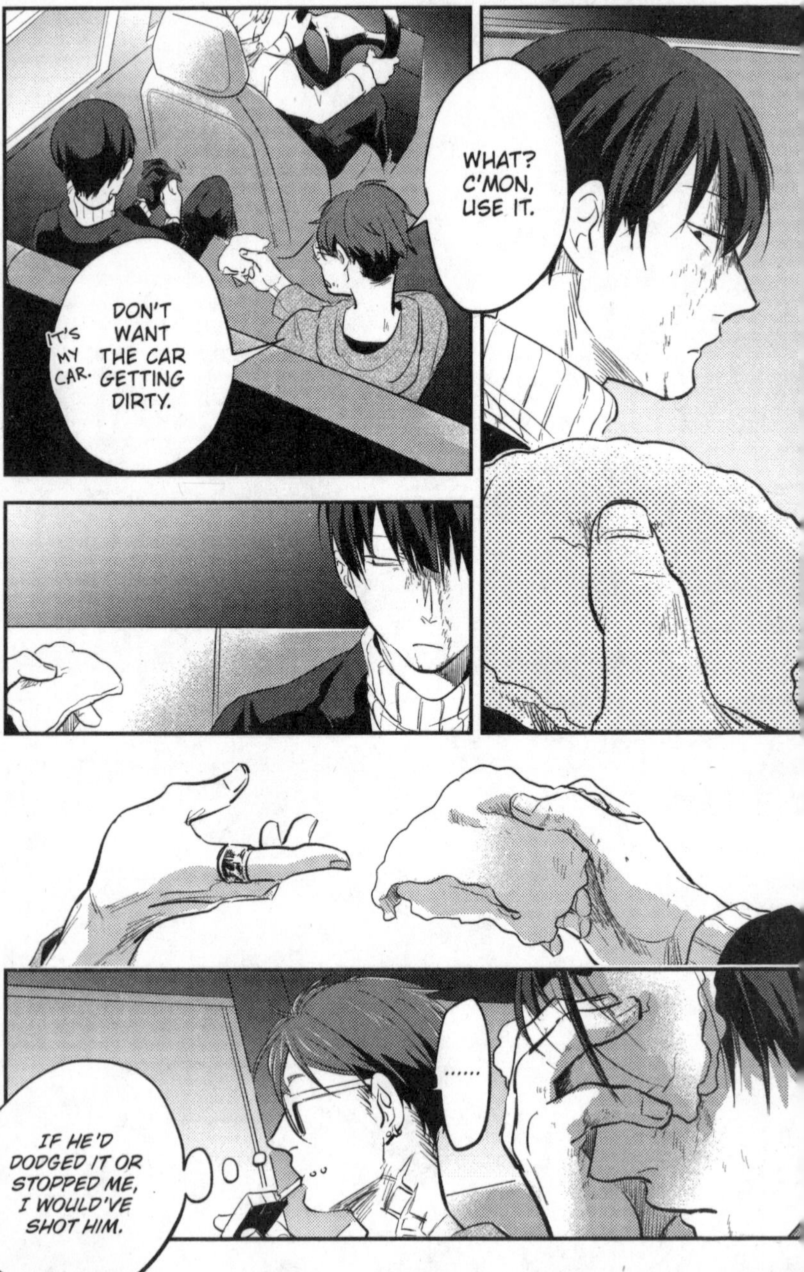
WHAT? C'MON, USE IT.
DON'T WANT THE CAR GETTING DIRTY.
IT'S MY CAR.
......
IF HE'D DODGED IT OR STOPPED ME, I WOULD'VE SHOT HIM.

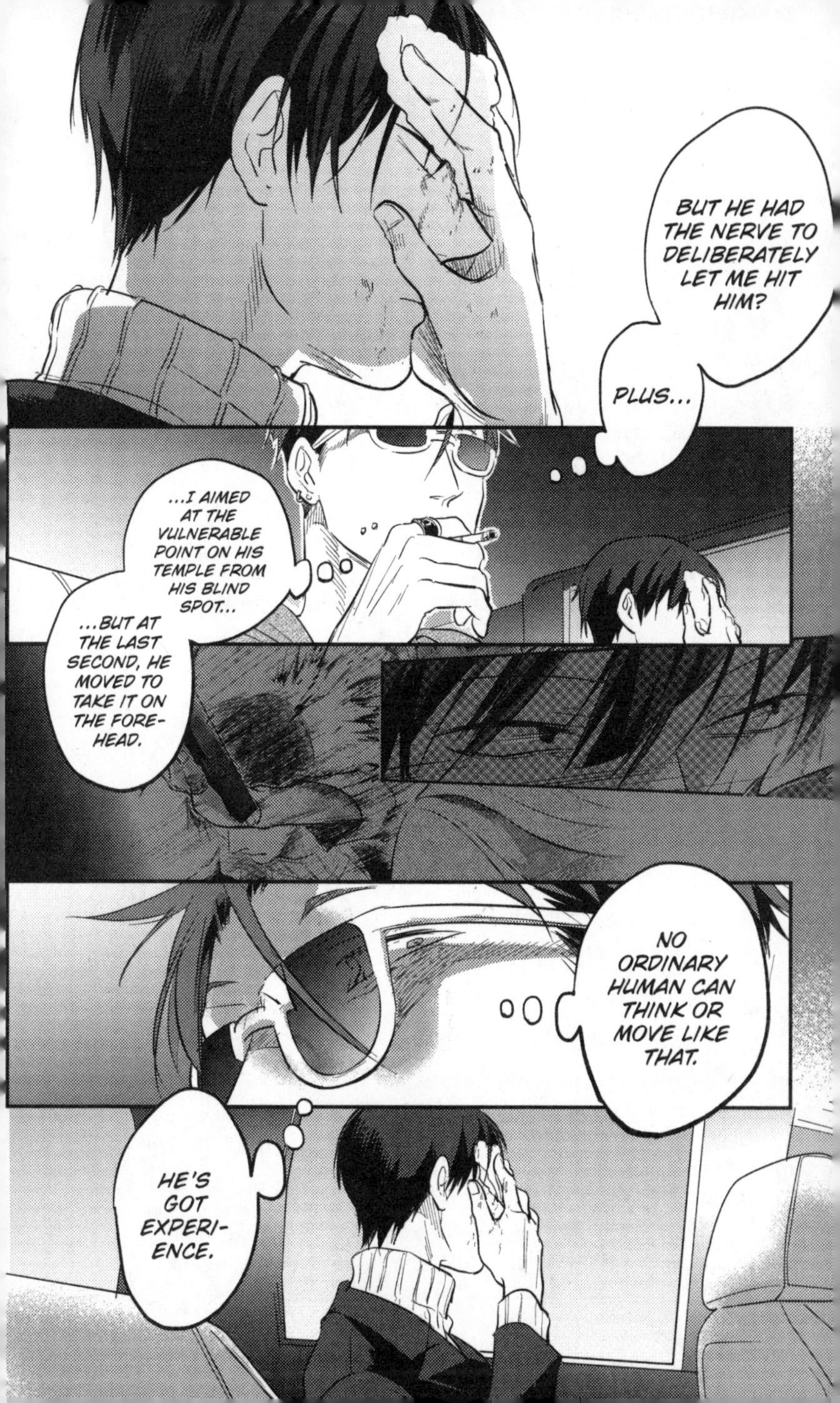
BUT HE HAD THE NERVE TO DELIBERATELY LET ME HIT HIM?
PLUS...
...I AIMED AT THE VULNERABLE POINT ON HIS TEMPLE FROM HIS BLIND SPOT...
...BUT AT THE LAST SECOND, HE MOVED TO TAKE IT ON THE FORE-HEAD.
NO ORDINARY HUMAN CAN THINK OR MOVE LIKE THAT.
HE'S GOT EXPERI-ENCE.

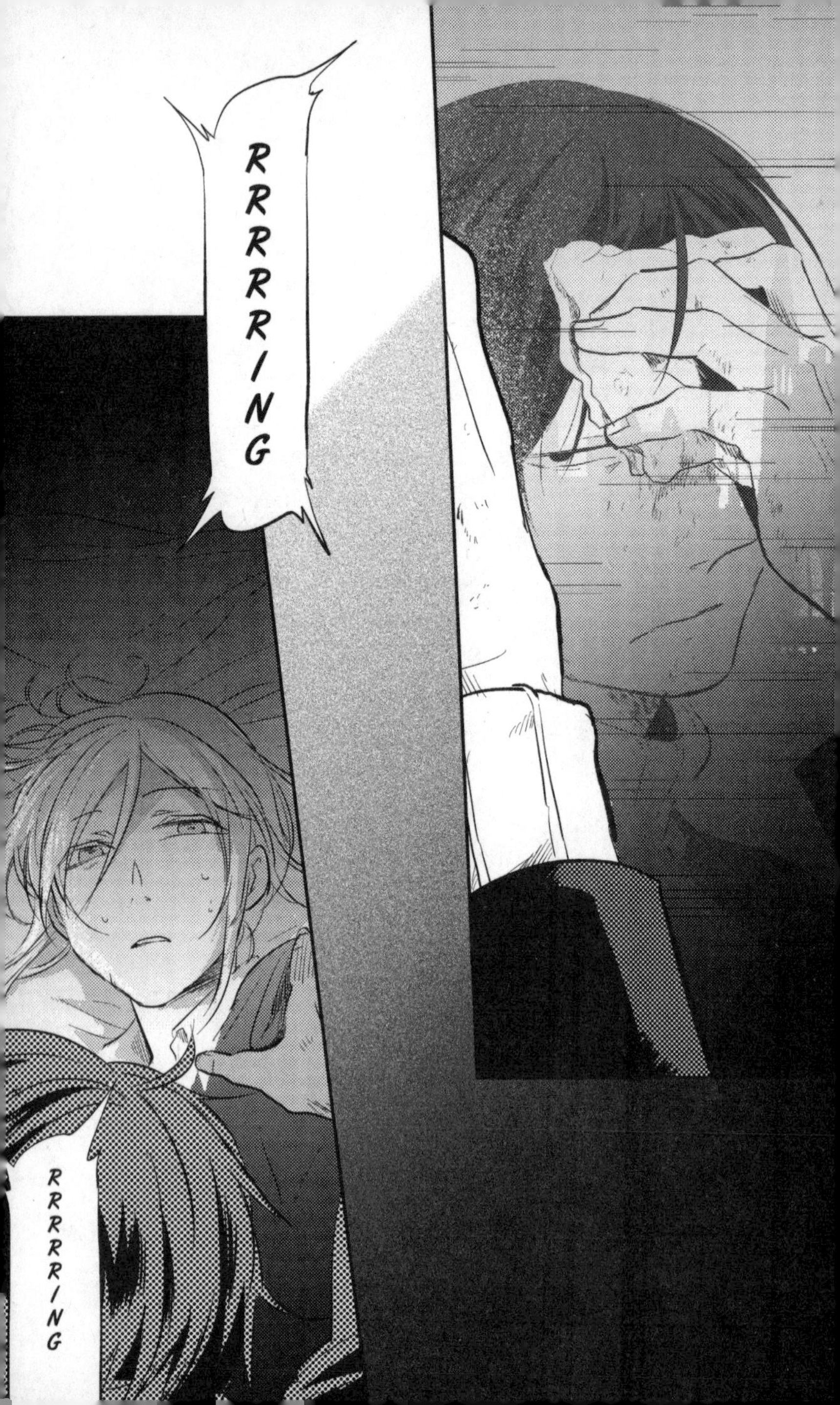
RRRRRING
RRRRRING

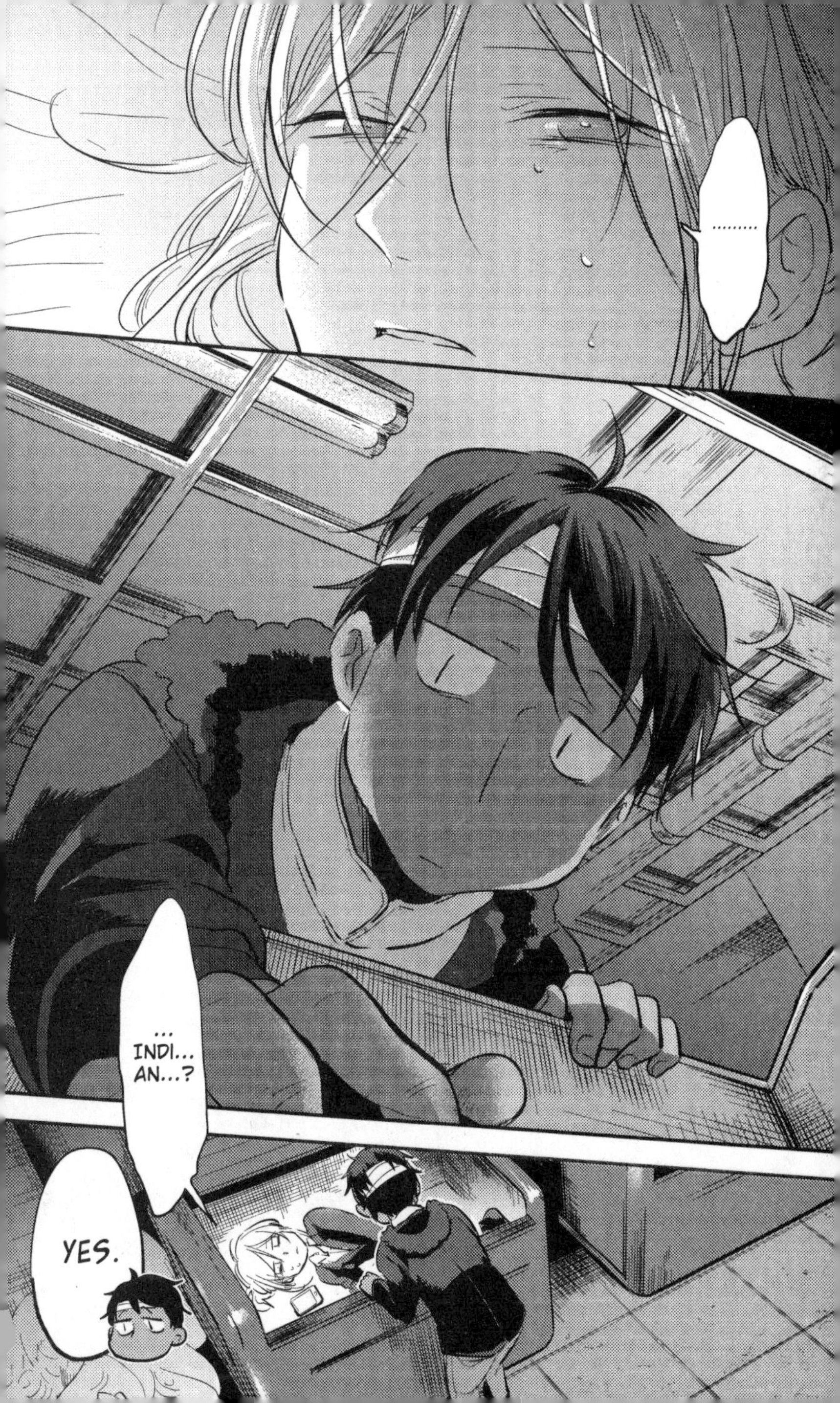
....
... INDI... AN...?
YES.

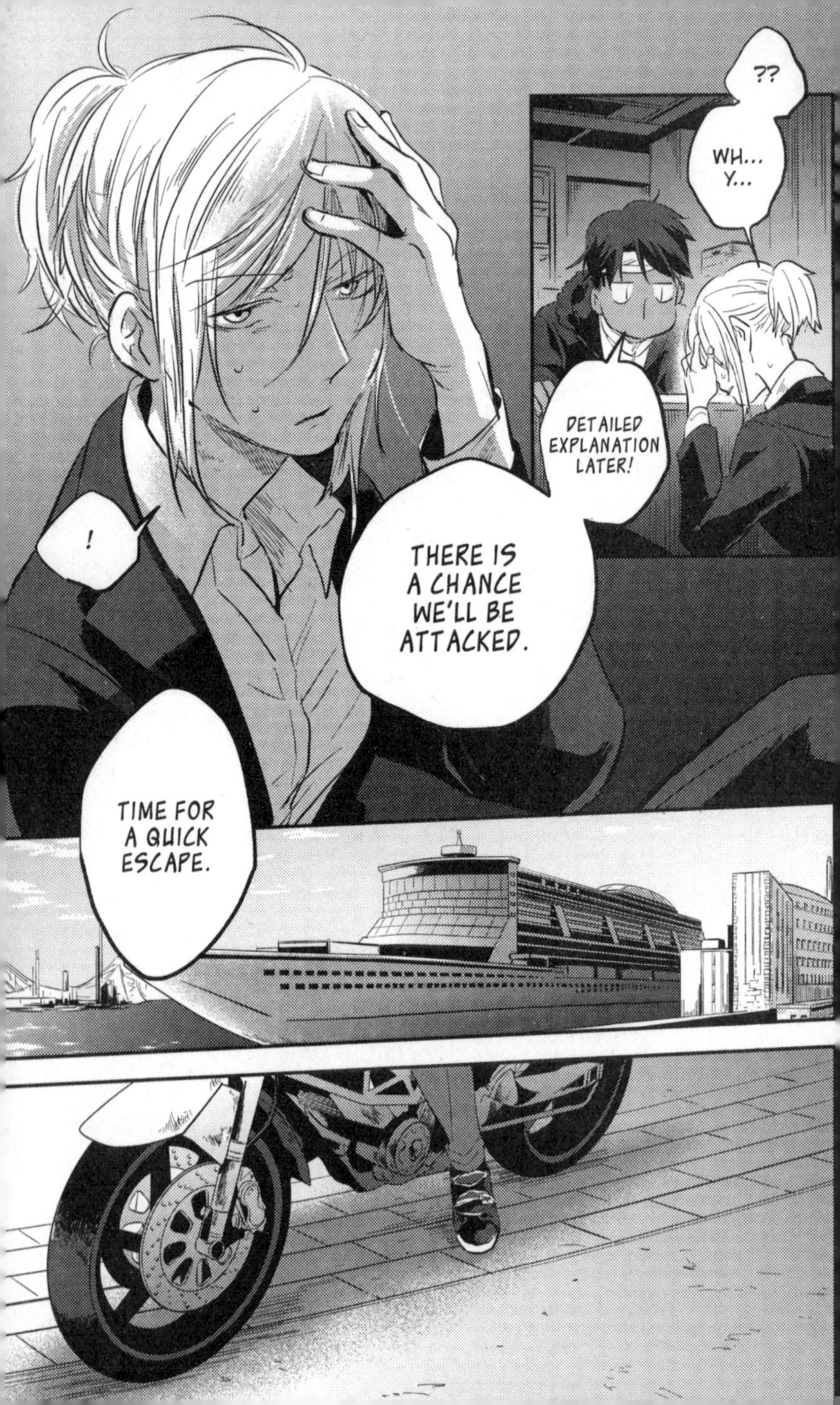
??
WH... Y...
DETAILED EXPLANATION LATER!
!
THERE IS A CHANCE WE'LL BE ATTACKED.
TIME FOR A QUICK ESCAPE.

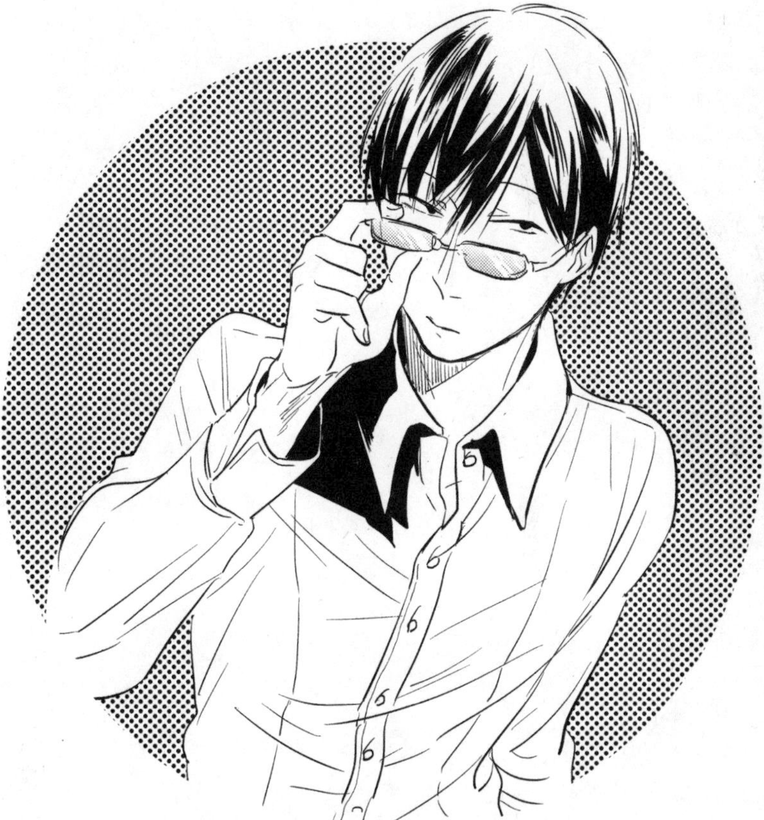

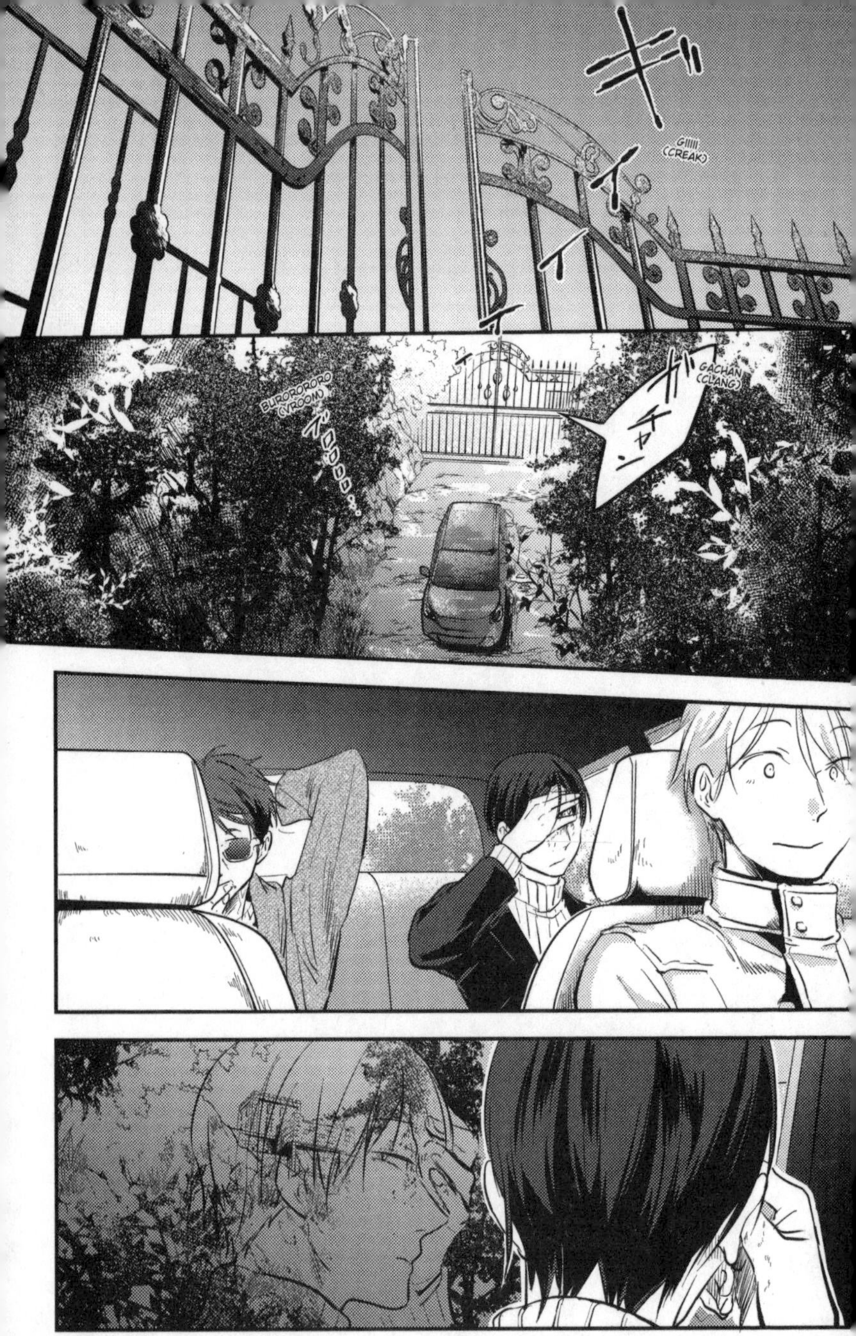
GIIIII (CREAK)
GACHAN (CLANG)
BURORORORO (VROOM)

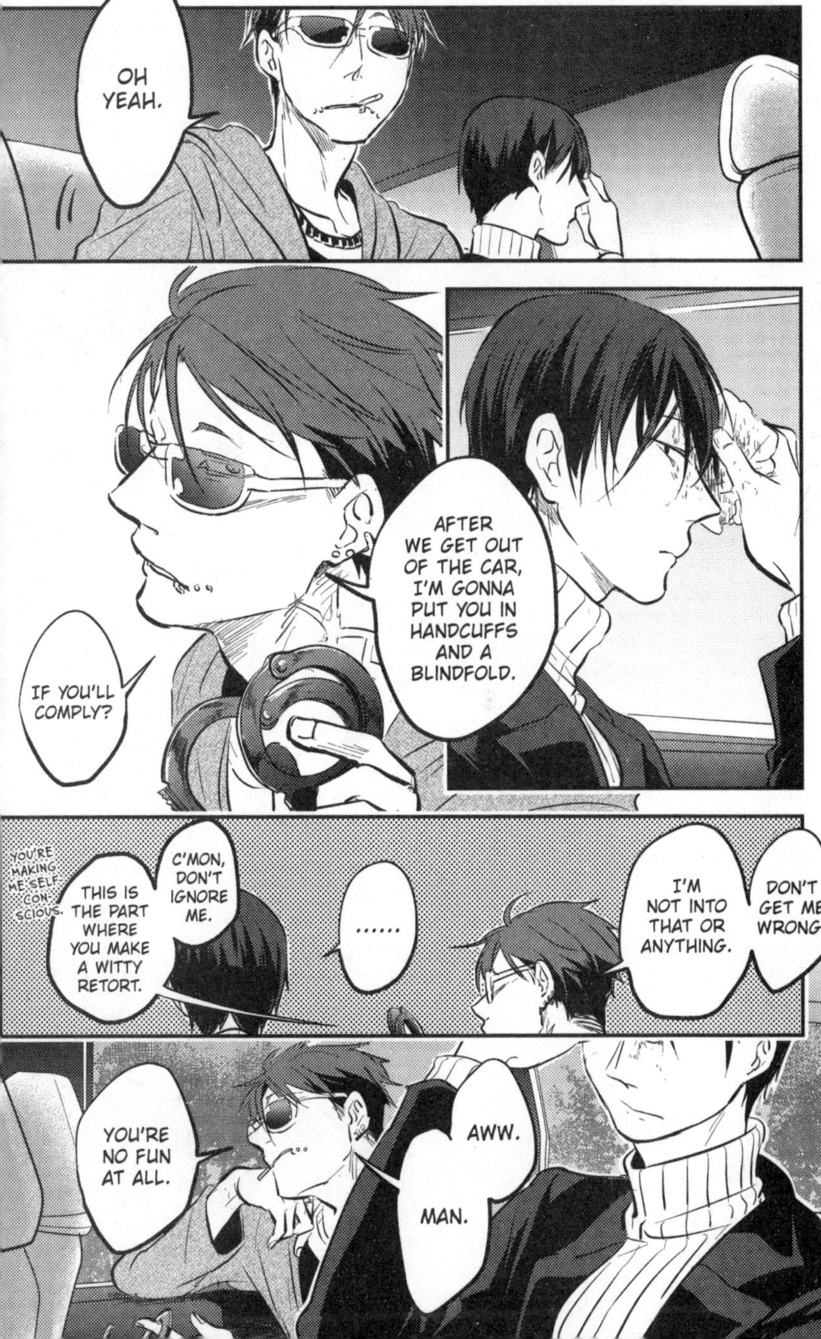
OH YEAH.
AFTER WE GET OUT OF THE CAR, I'M GONNA PUT YOU IN HANDCUFFS AND A BLINDFOLD.
IF YOU'LL COMPLY?
DON'T GET ME WRONG.
I'M NOT INTO THAT OR ANYTHING.
......
C'MON, DON'T IGNORE ME.
THIS IS THE PART WHERE YOU MAKE A WITTY RETORT.
YOU'RE MAKING ME SELF-CONSCIOUS.
AWW.
MAN.
YOU'RE NO FUN AT ALL.

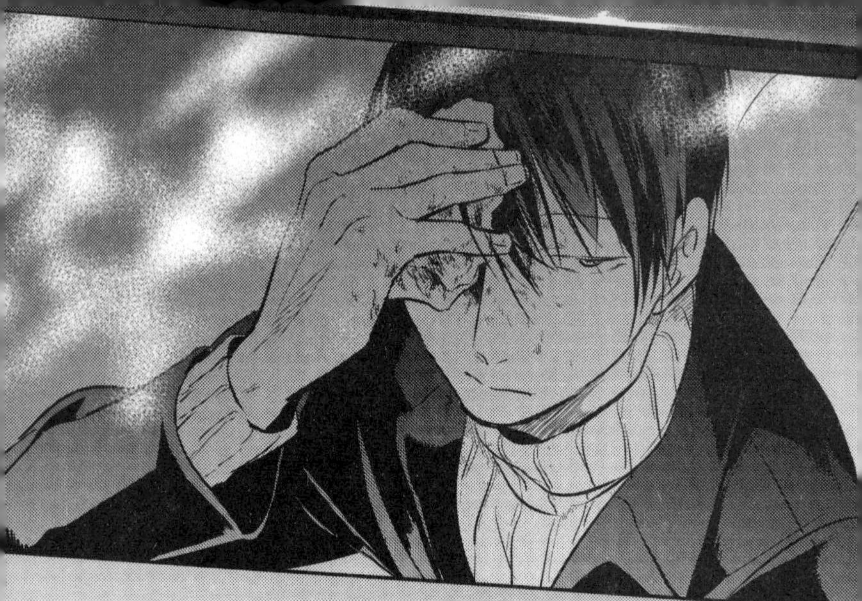

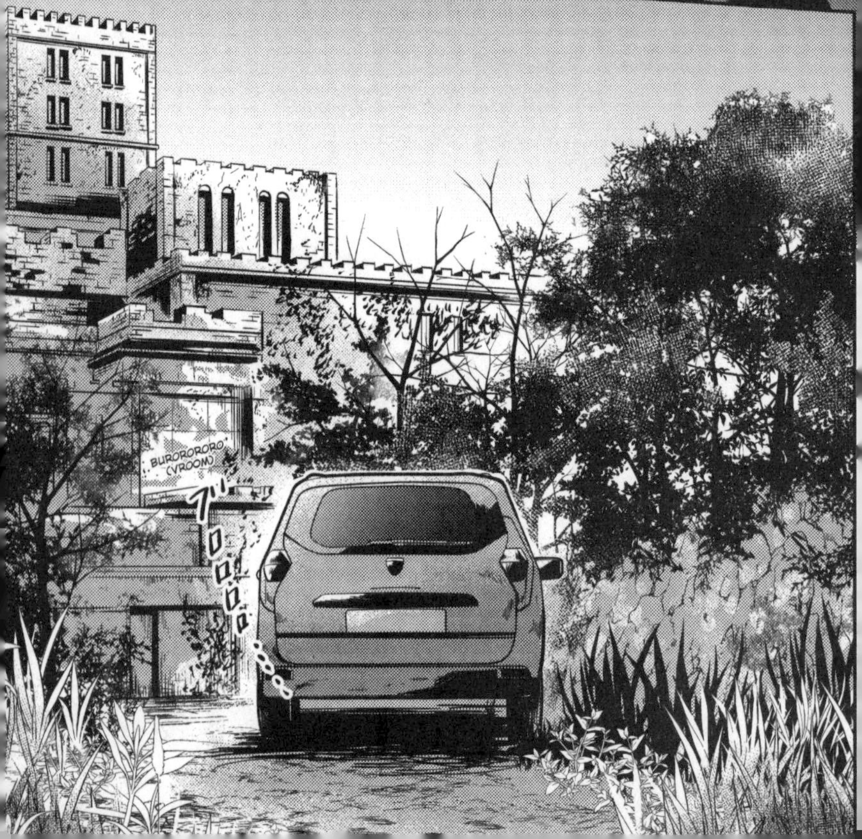
ブロロロロ…
BURORORORO (VROOM)

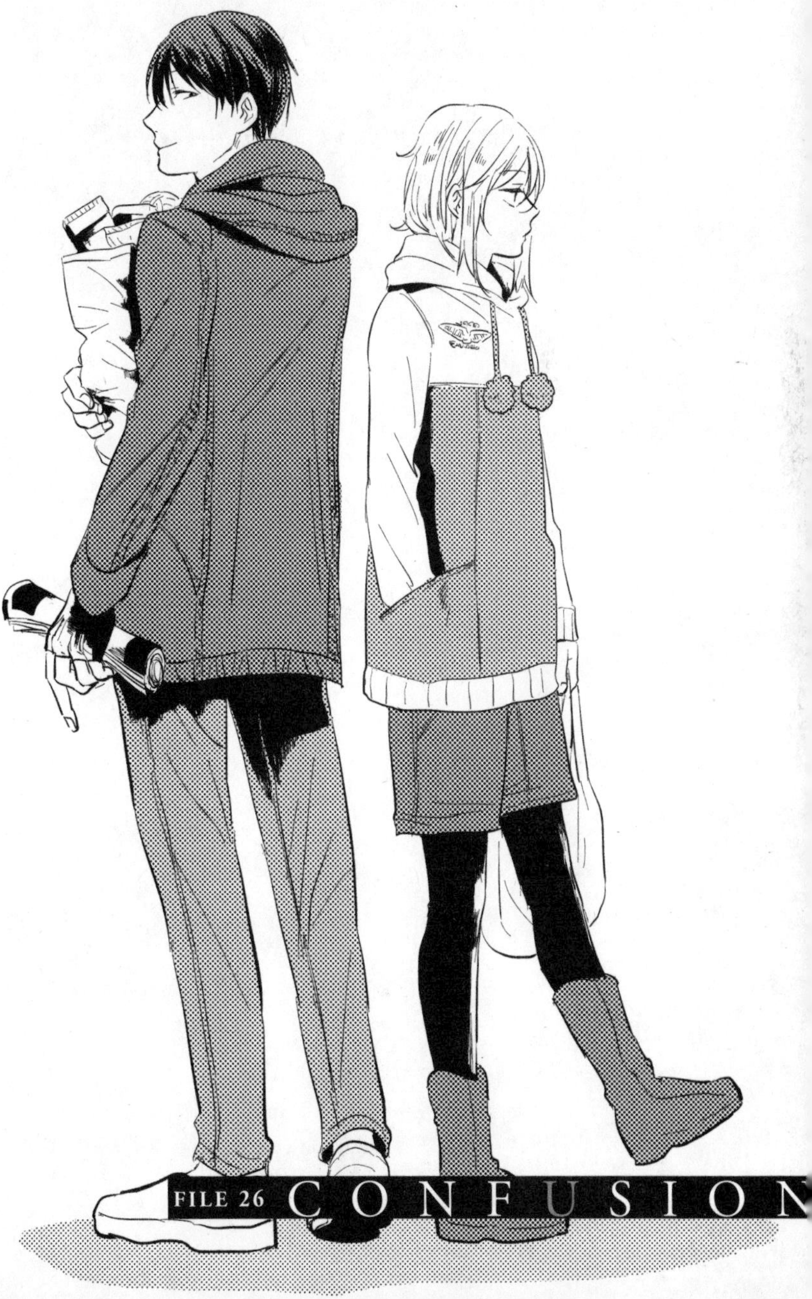
FILE 26
CONFUSION

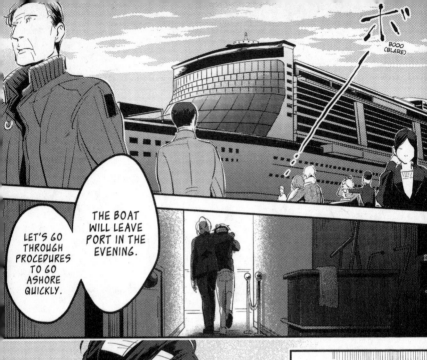

BOOO
(BLARE)

THE BOAT WILL LEAVE PORT IN THE EVENING.

LET'S GO THROUGH PROCEDURES TO GO ASHORE QUICKLY.

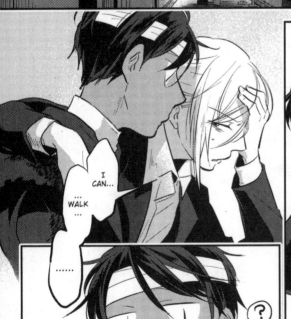

I CAN...

... WALK ...

......

?

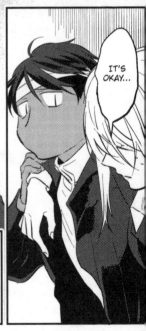

IT'S OKAY...

25

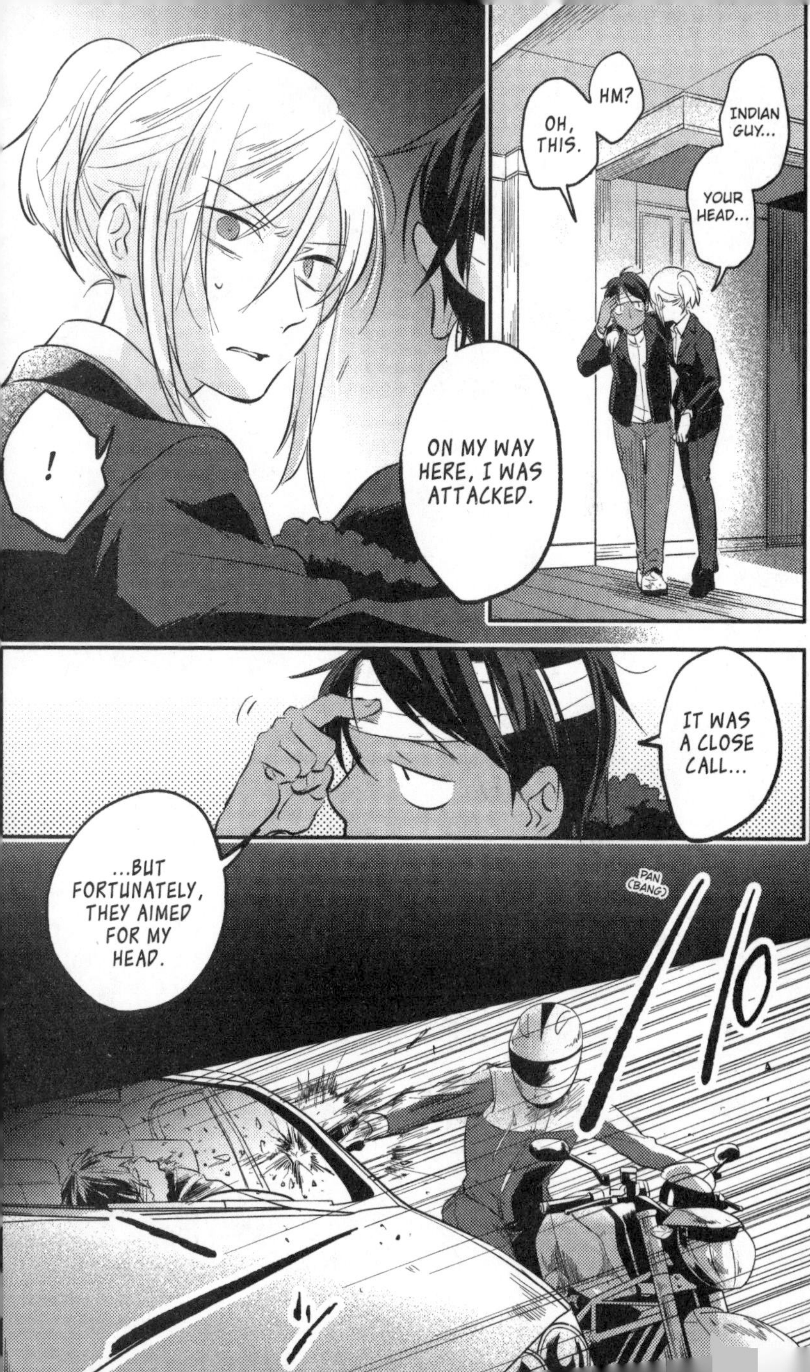
INDIAN GUY...
YOUR HEAD...
HM?
OH, THIS.
ON MY WAY HERE, I WAS ATTACKED.
!
IT WAS A CLOSE CALL...
...BUT FORTUNATELY, THEY AIMED FOR MY HEAD.
PAN (BANG)

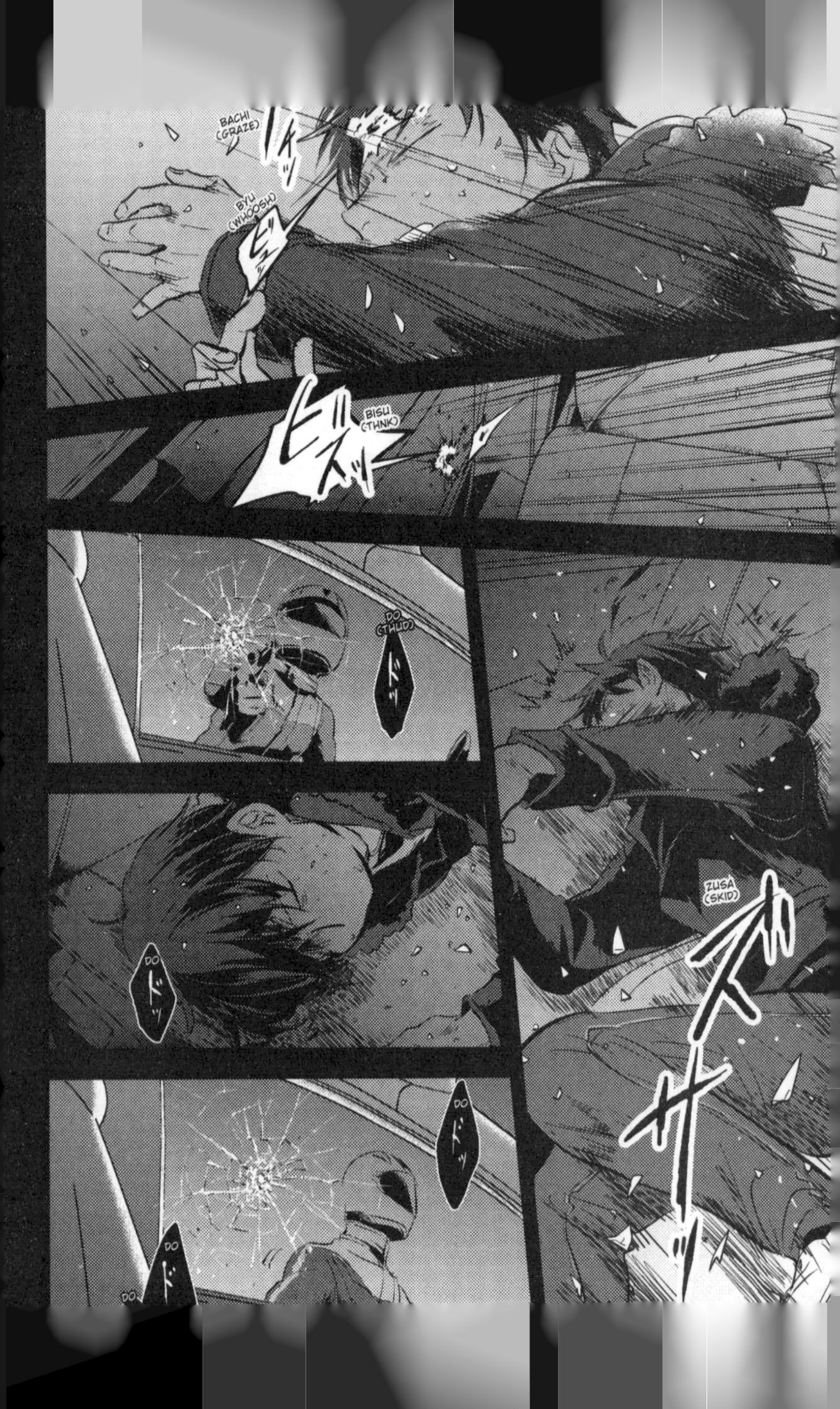

BACHI (GRAZE)
BYU (WHOOSH)
BISU (THNK)
ZUSA (SKID)
DO (THUD)
DO
DO
DO
DO

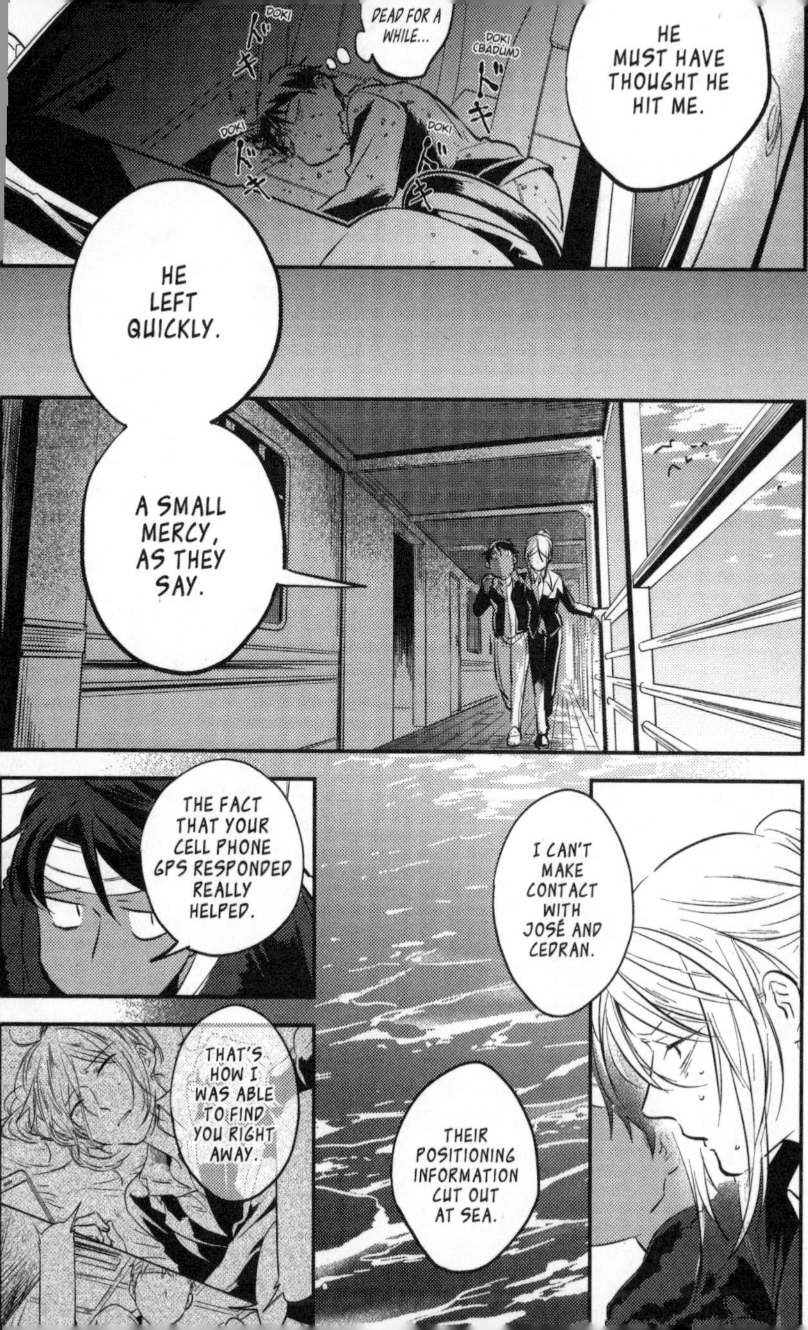
HE MUST HAVE THOUGHT HE HIT ME.
DOKI (BADUM)
ドキ
DEAD FOR A WHILE...
DOKI
ドキ
DOKI
ドキ
DOKI
ドキ
HE LEFT QUICKLY.
A SMALL MERCY, AS THEY SAY.
I CAN'T MAKE CONTACT WITH JOSÉ AND CEDRAN.
THEIR POSITIONING INFORMATION CUT OUT AT SEA.
THE FACT THAT YOUR CELL PHONE GPS RESPONDED REALLY HELPED.
THAT'S HOW I WAS ABLE TO FIND YOU RIGHT AWAY.

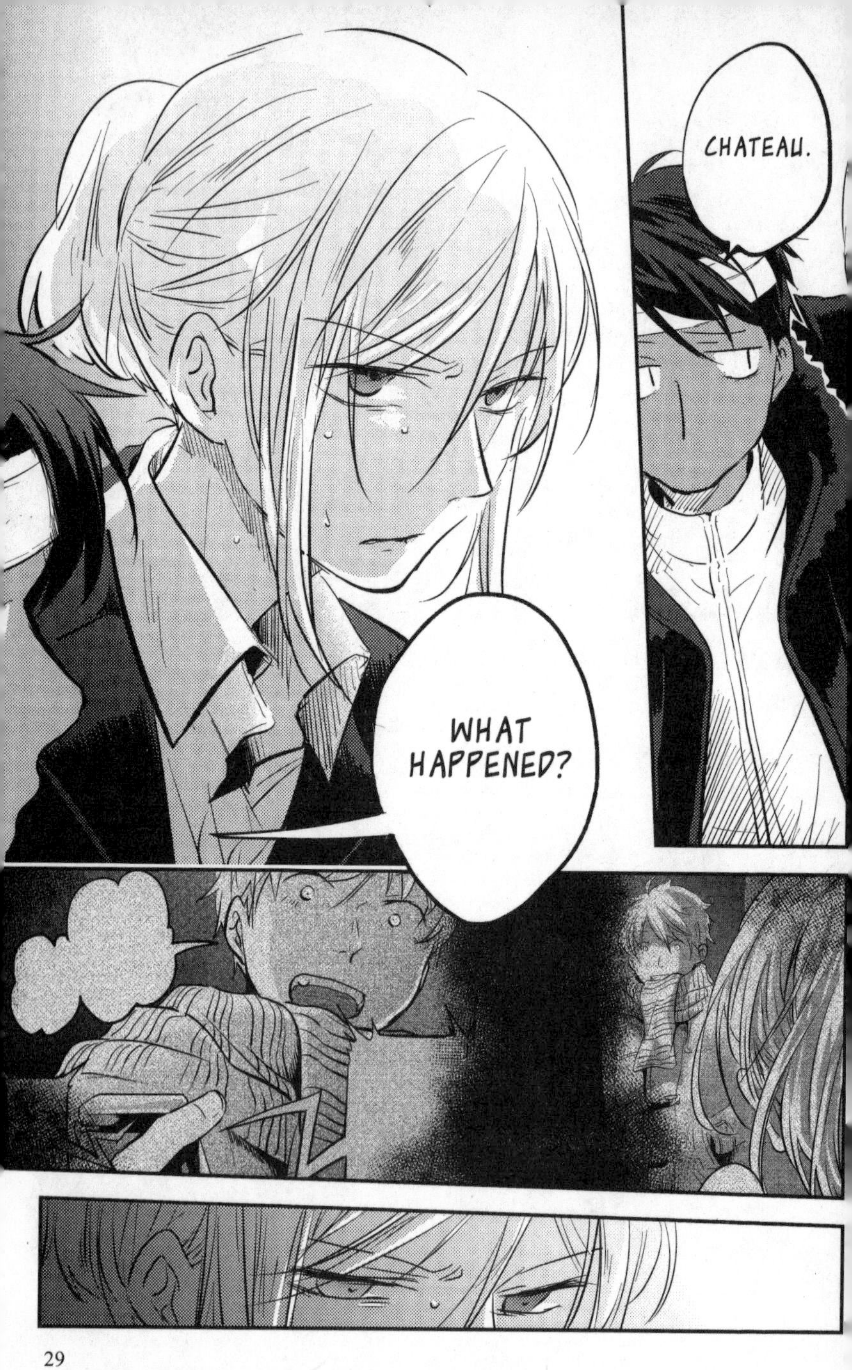
CHATEAU.
WHAT HAPPENED?

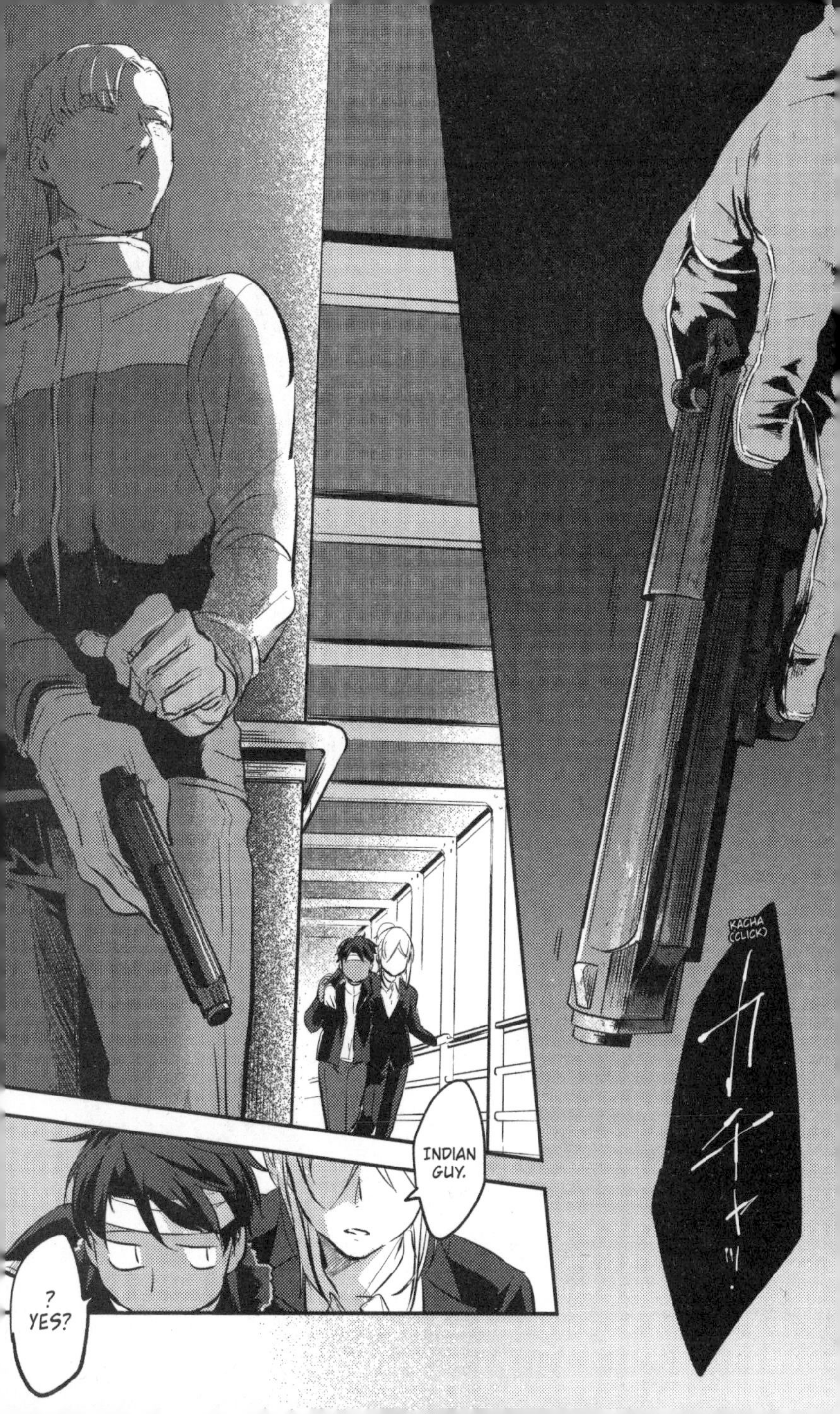
KACHA (CLICK)
カチャッ
INDIAN GUY.
? YES?

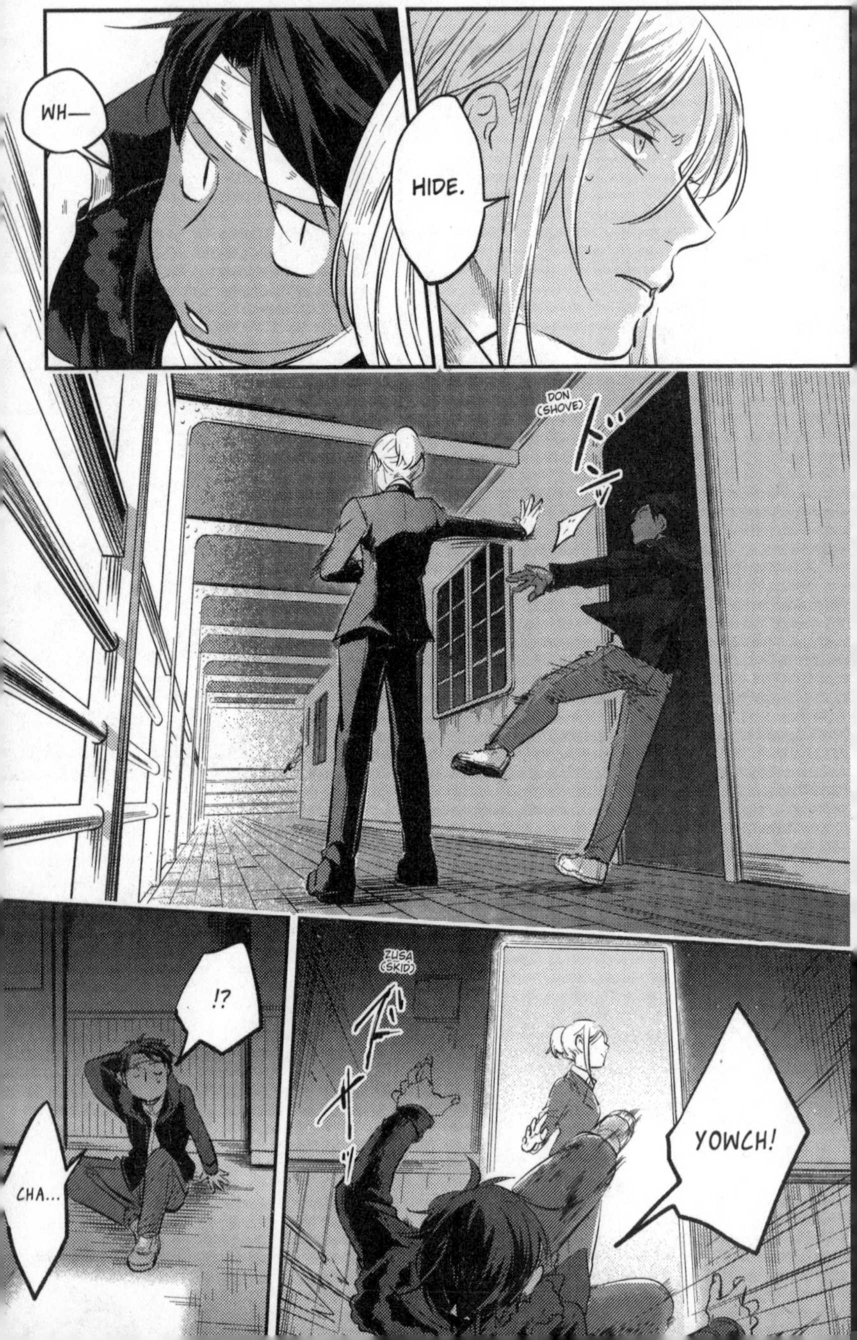
HIDE.
WH—
DON (SHOVE)
ZUSA (SKID)
YOWCH!
!?
CHA...

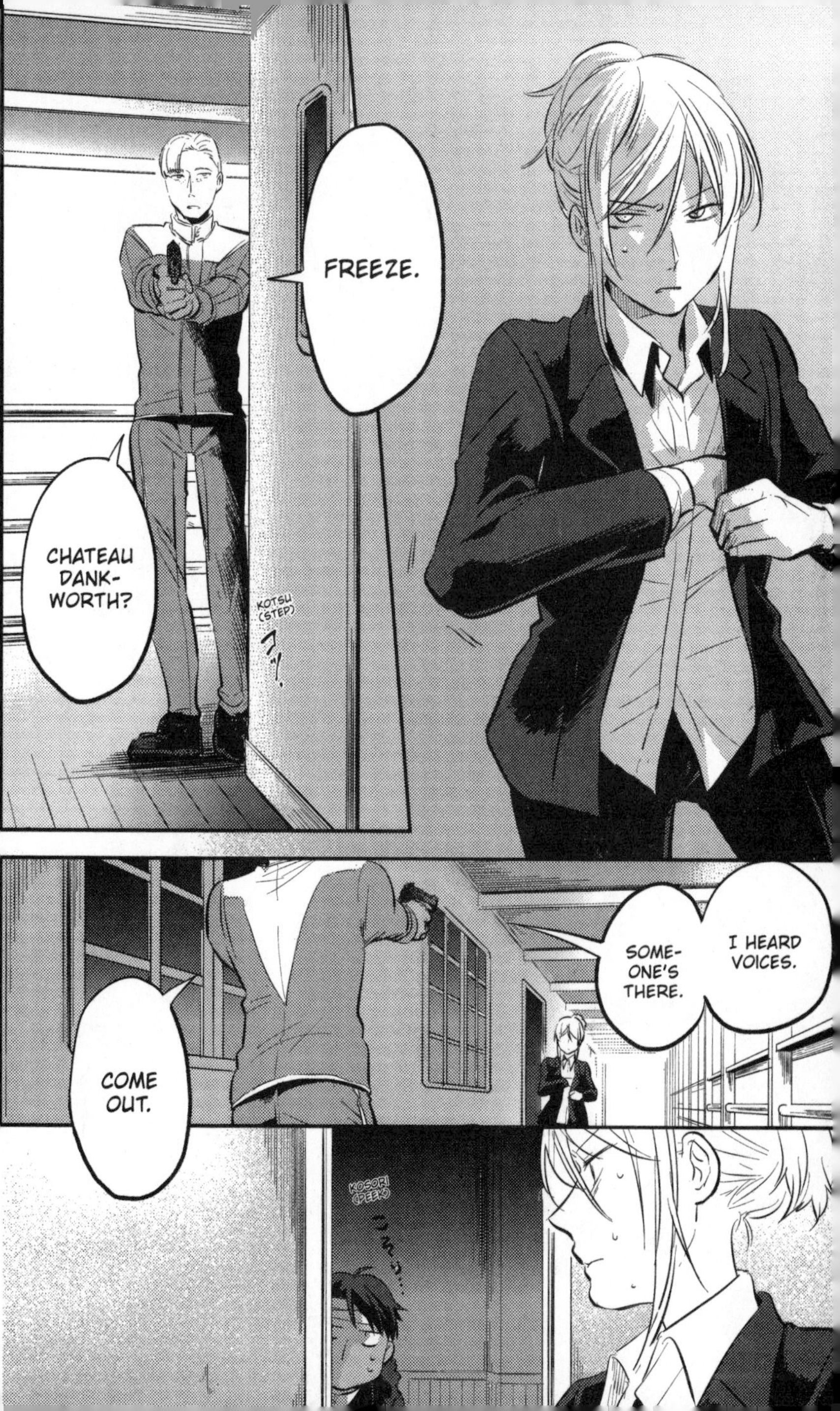
FREEZE.
CHATEAU DANK-WORTH?
KOTSU (STEP)
I HEARD VOICES.
SOME-ONE'S THERE.
COME OUT.
KOSORI (PEEK)

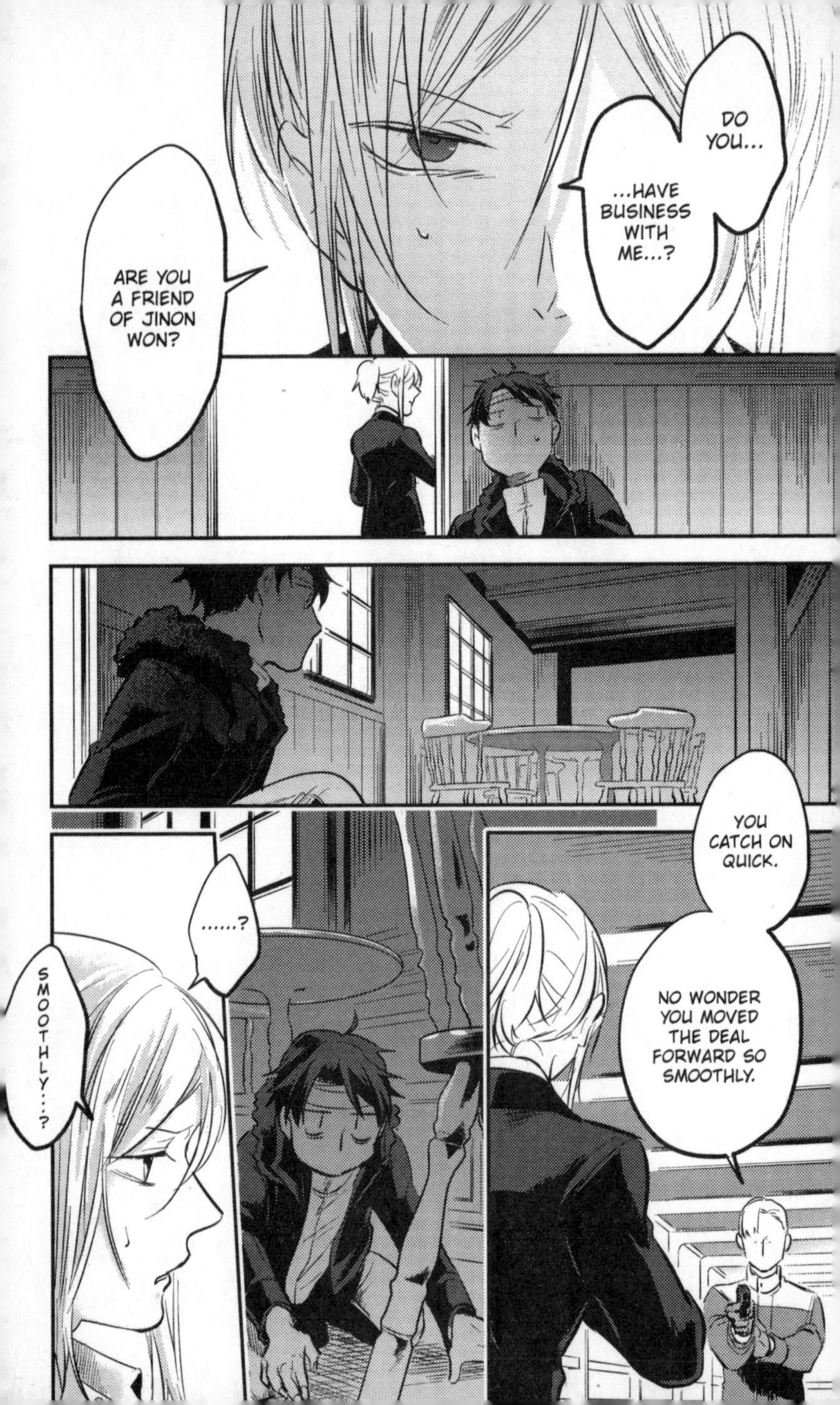
DO YOU...
...HAVE BUSINESS WITH ME...?
ARE YOU A FRIEND OF JINON WON?
YOU CATCH ON QUICK.
NO WONDER YOU MOVED THE DEAL FORWARD SO SMOOTHLY.
......?
SMOOTHLY...?

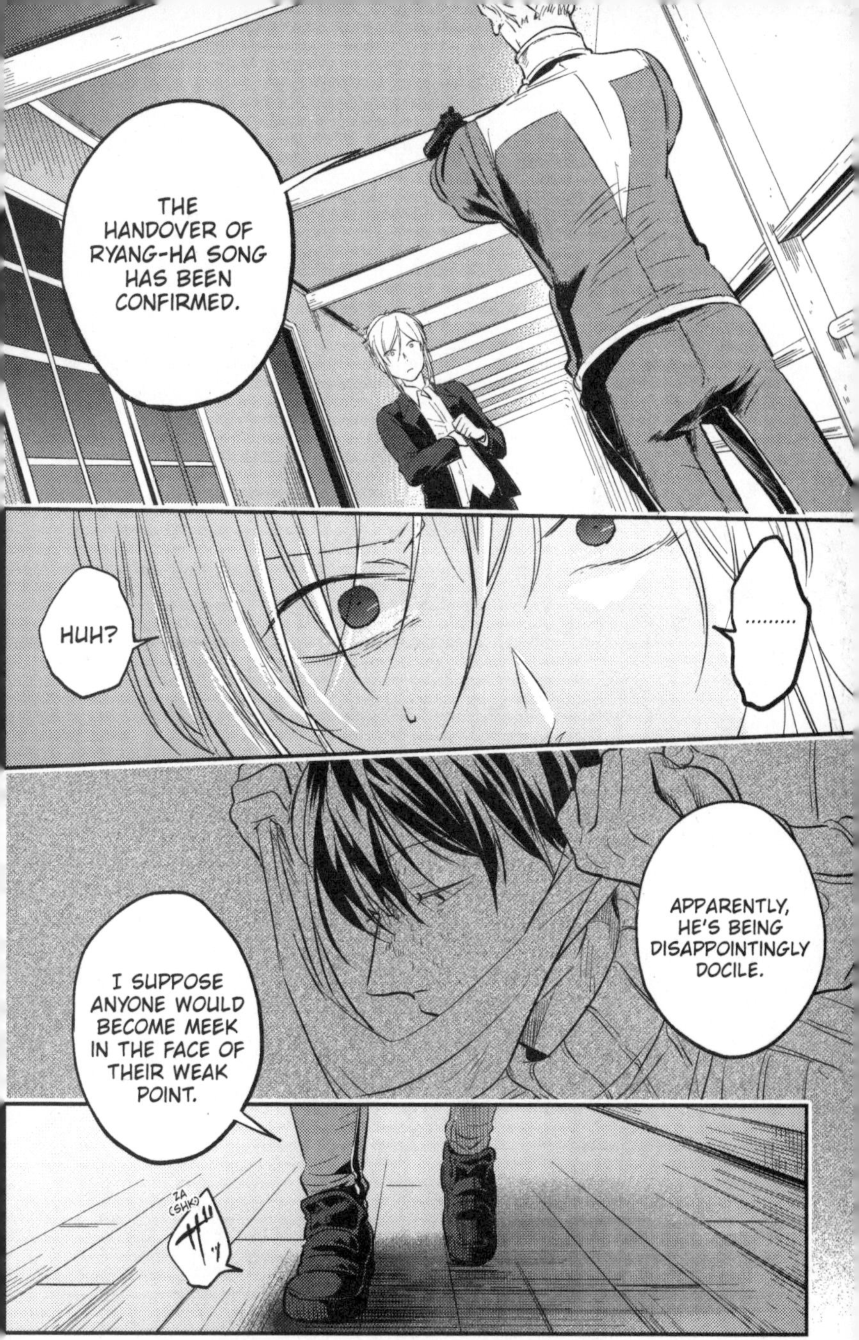
THE HANDOVER OF RYANG-HA SONG HAS BEEN CONFIRMED.
....
HUH?
APPARENTLY, HE'S BEING DISAPPOINTINGLY DOCILE.
I SUPPOSE ANYONE WOULD BECOME MEEK IN THE FACE OF THEIR WEAK POINT.
ZA (SHK)

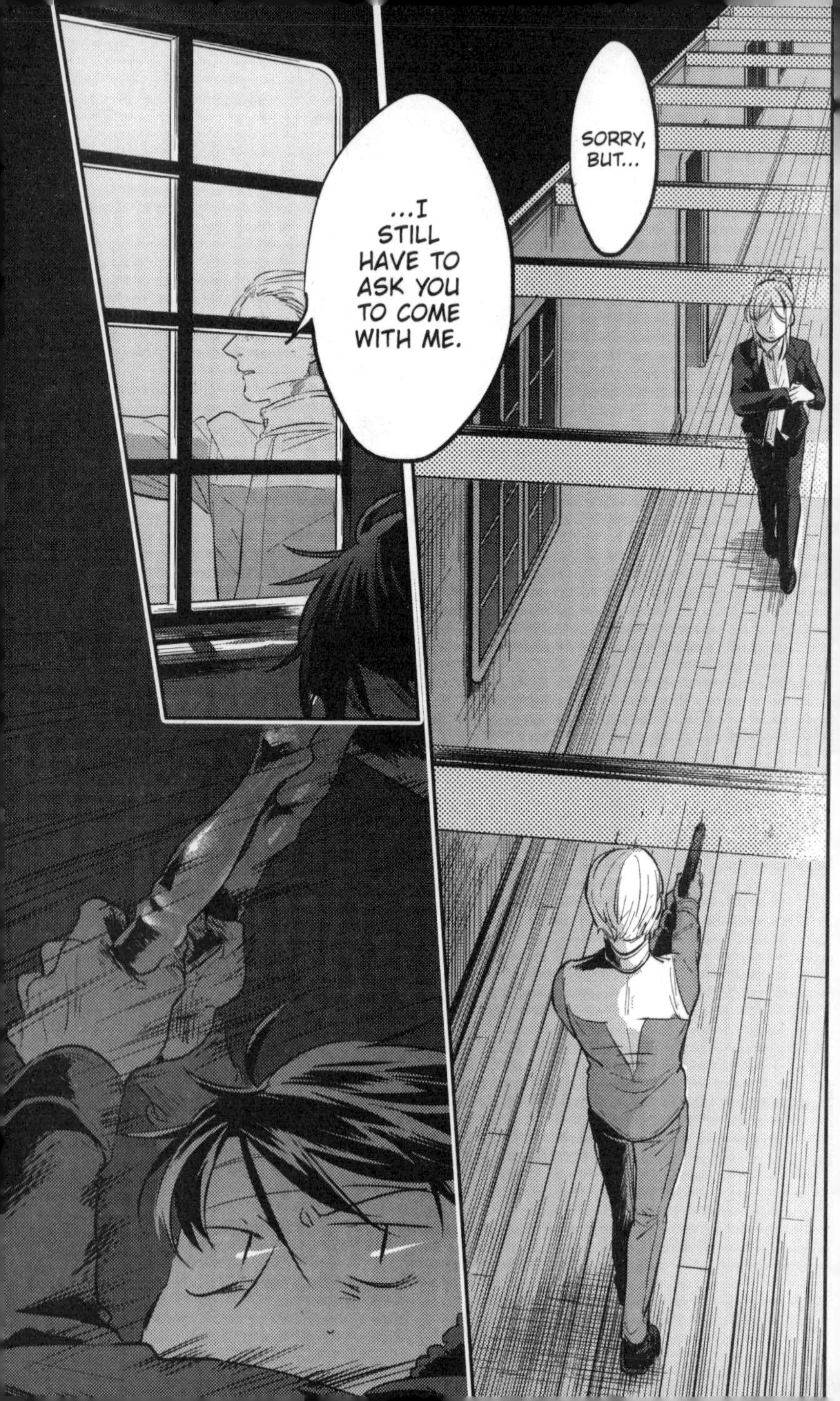
SORRY, BUT...
...I STILL HAVE TO ASK YOU TO COME WITH ME.

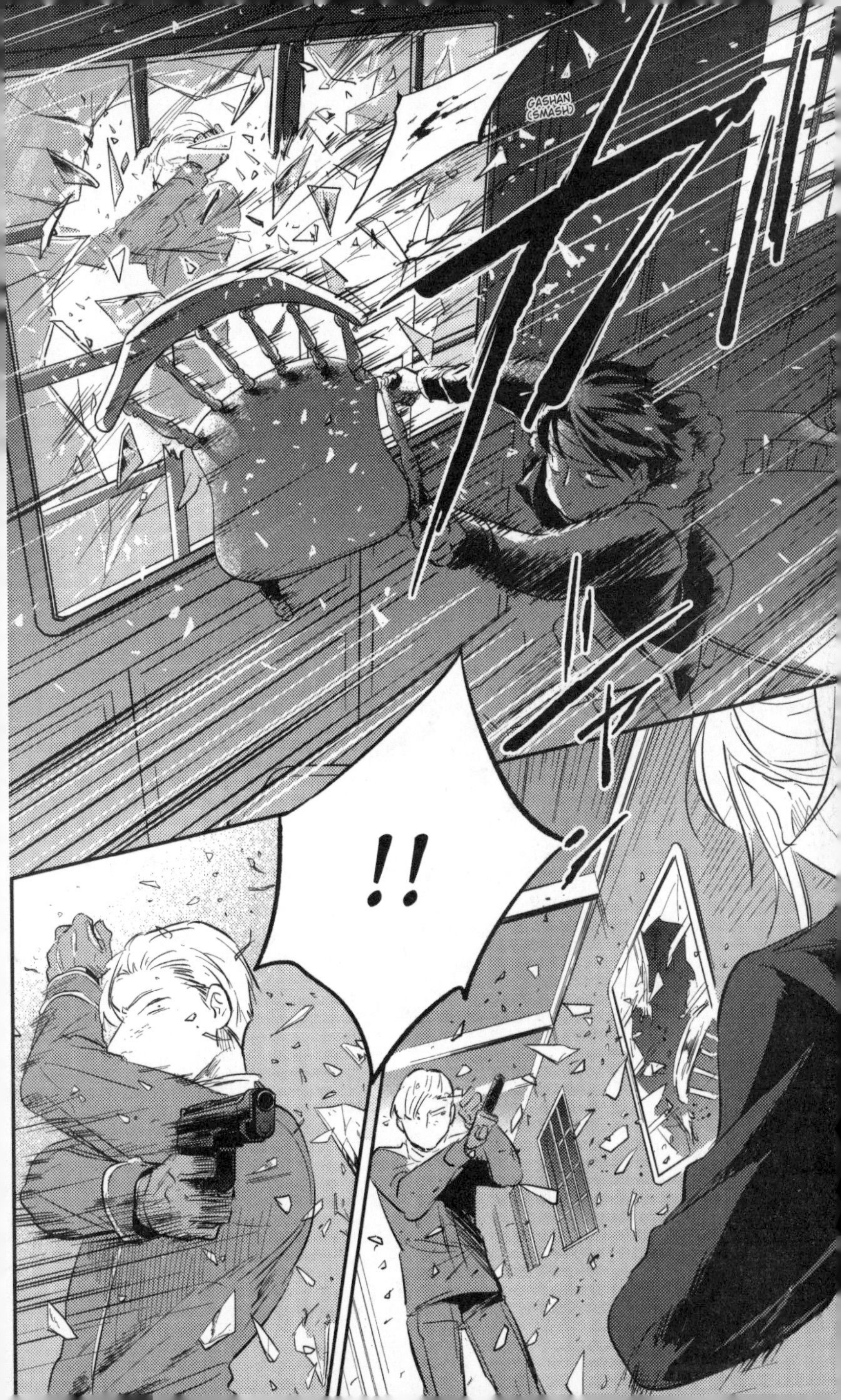
CASHAN (SMASH)
!!

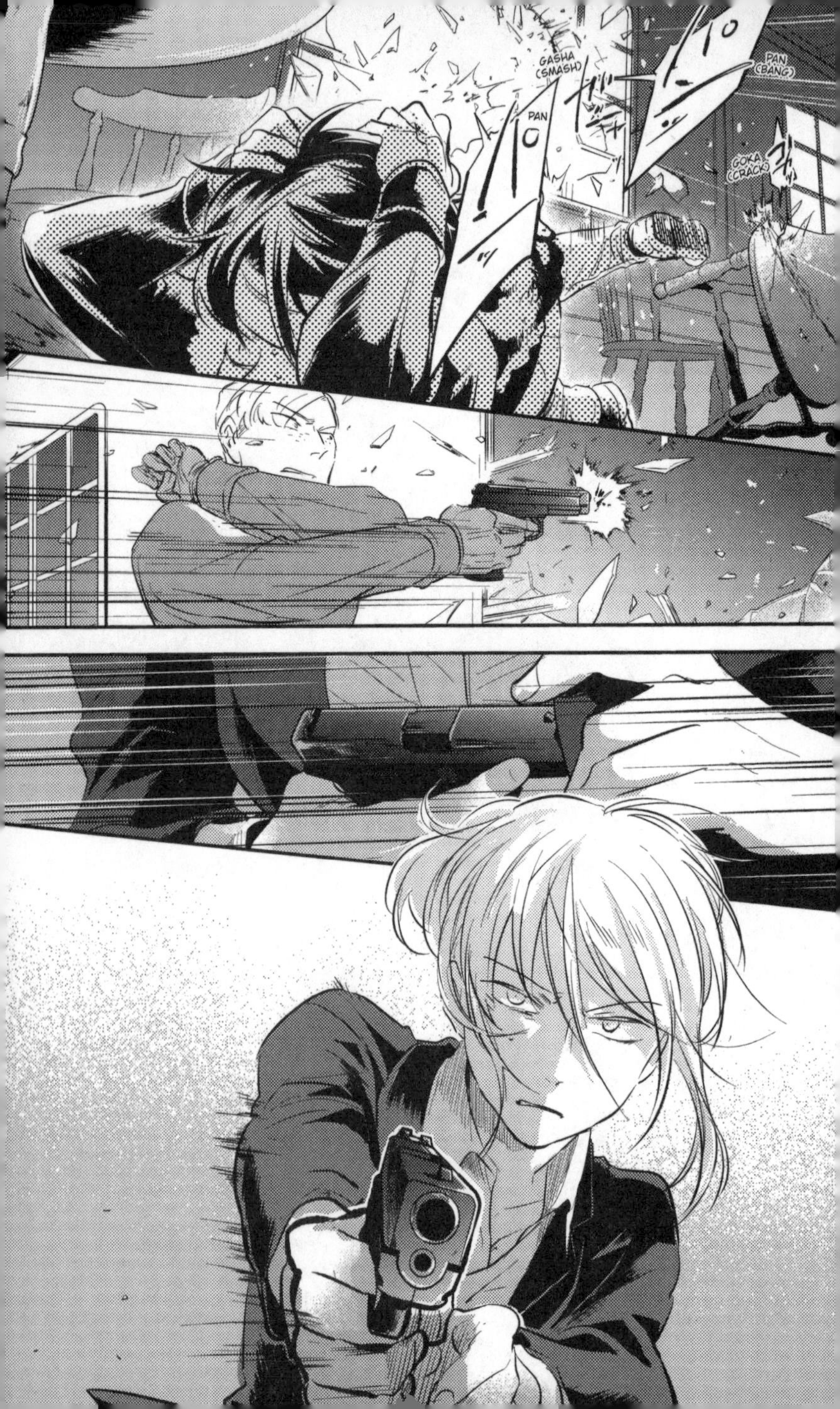
PAN
(BANG)
GOKA
(CRACK)
GASHA
(SMASH)
PAN

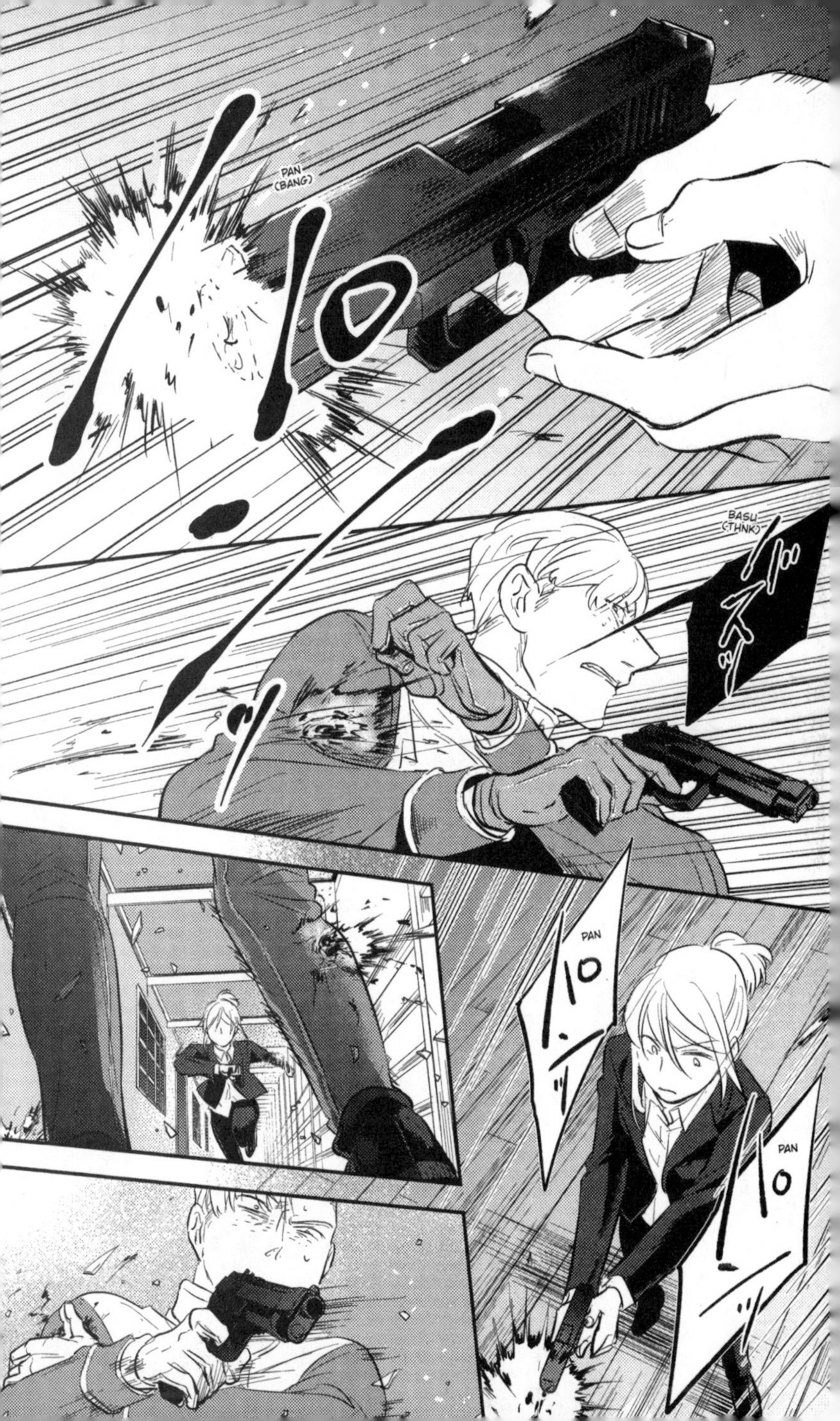
PAN
(BANG)
BASU
(THNK)
PAN
PAN

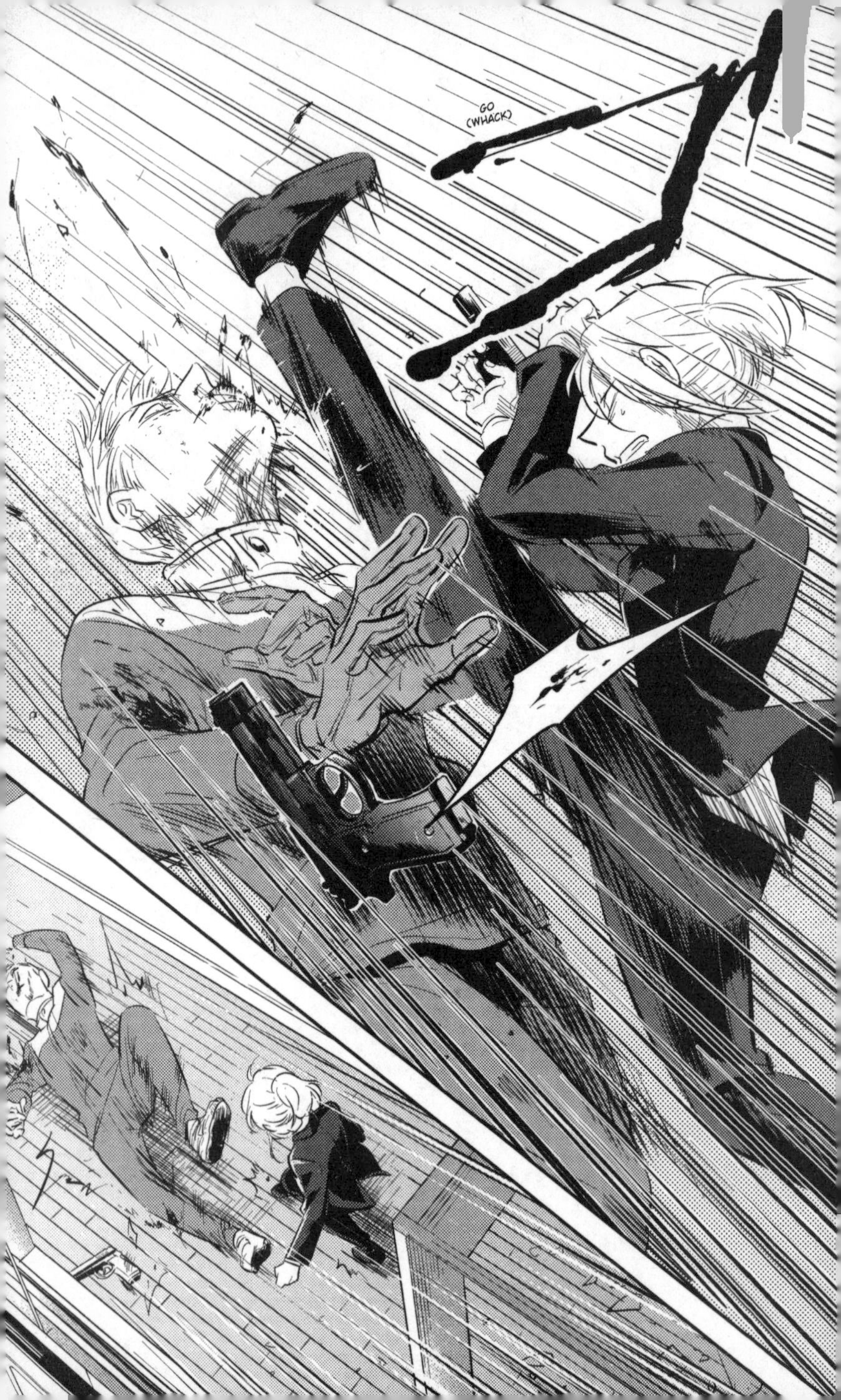
GO
(WHACK)

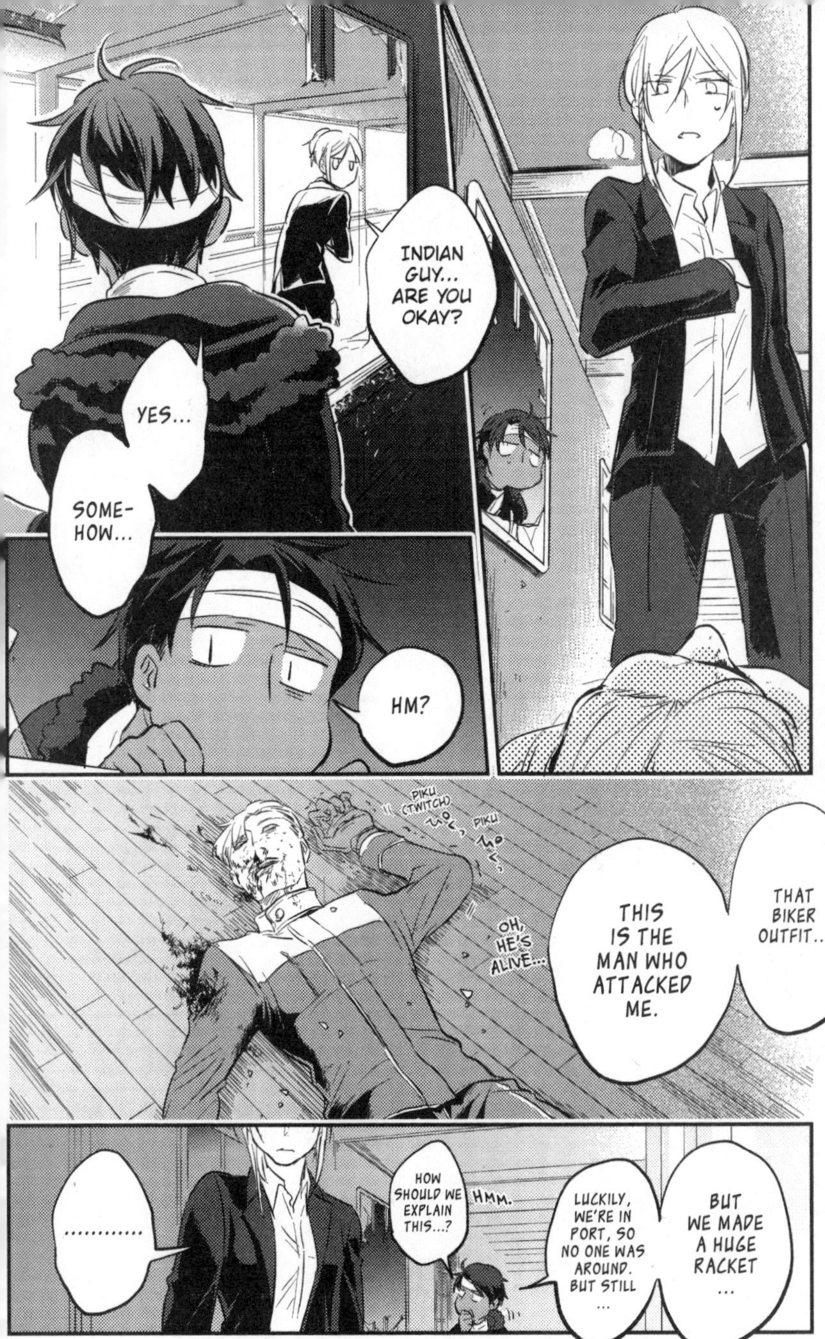

INDIAN GUY... ARE YOU OKAY?
YES...
SOME-HOW...
HM?
THAT BIKER OUTFIT...
THIS IS THE MAN WHO ATTACKED ME.
OH, HE'S ALIVE...
PIKU (TWITCH)
PIKU
BUT WE MADE A HUGE RACKET...
LUCKILY, WE'RE IN PORT, SO NO ONE WAS AROUND. BUT STILL...
HMM.
HOW SHOULD WE EXPLAIN THIS...?
....

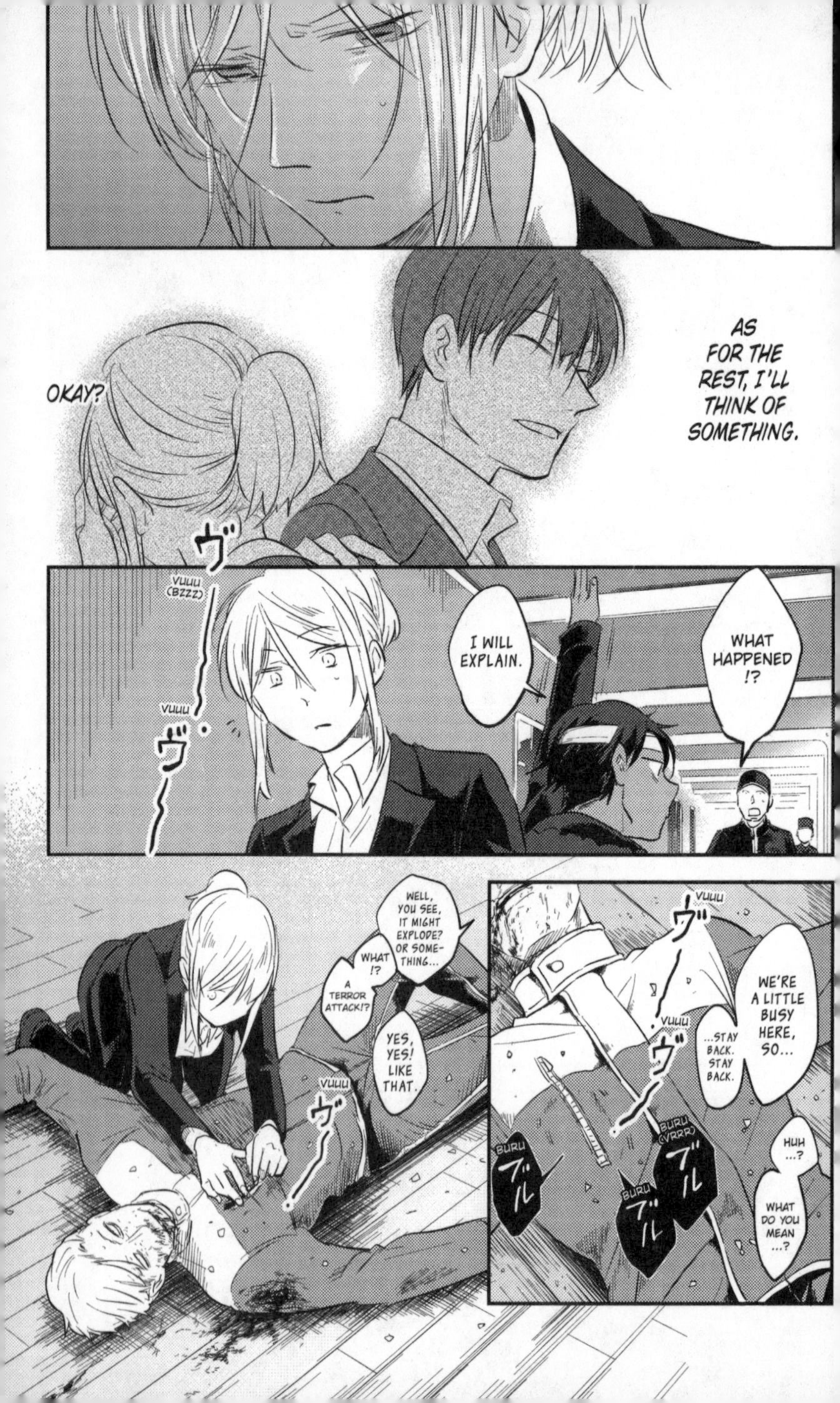
AS FOR THE REST, I'LL THINK OF SOMETHING.
OKAY?
WHAT HAPPENED!?
I WILL EXPLAIN.
ヴ VUUU (BZZZ)
VUUU ヴ
ヴ VUUU
WE'RE A LITTLE BUSY HERE, SO...
...STAY BACK. STAY BACK.
VUUU ヴ
HUH...?
WHAT DO YOU MEAN...?
BURU (VRRR) ブル
BURU ブル
BURU ブル
WELL, YOU SEE, IT MIGHT EXPLODE? OR SOME-THING...
WHAT!?
A TERROR ATTACK!?
YES, YES! LIKE THAT.
VUUU ヴ

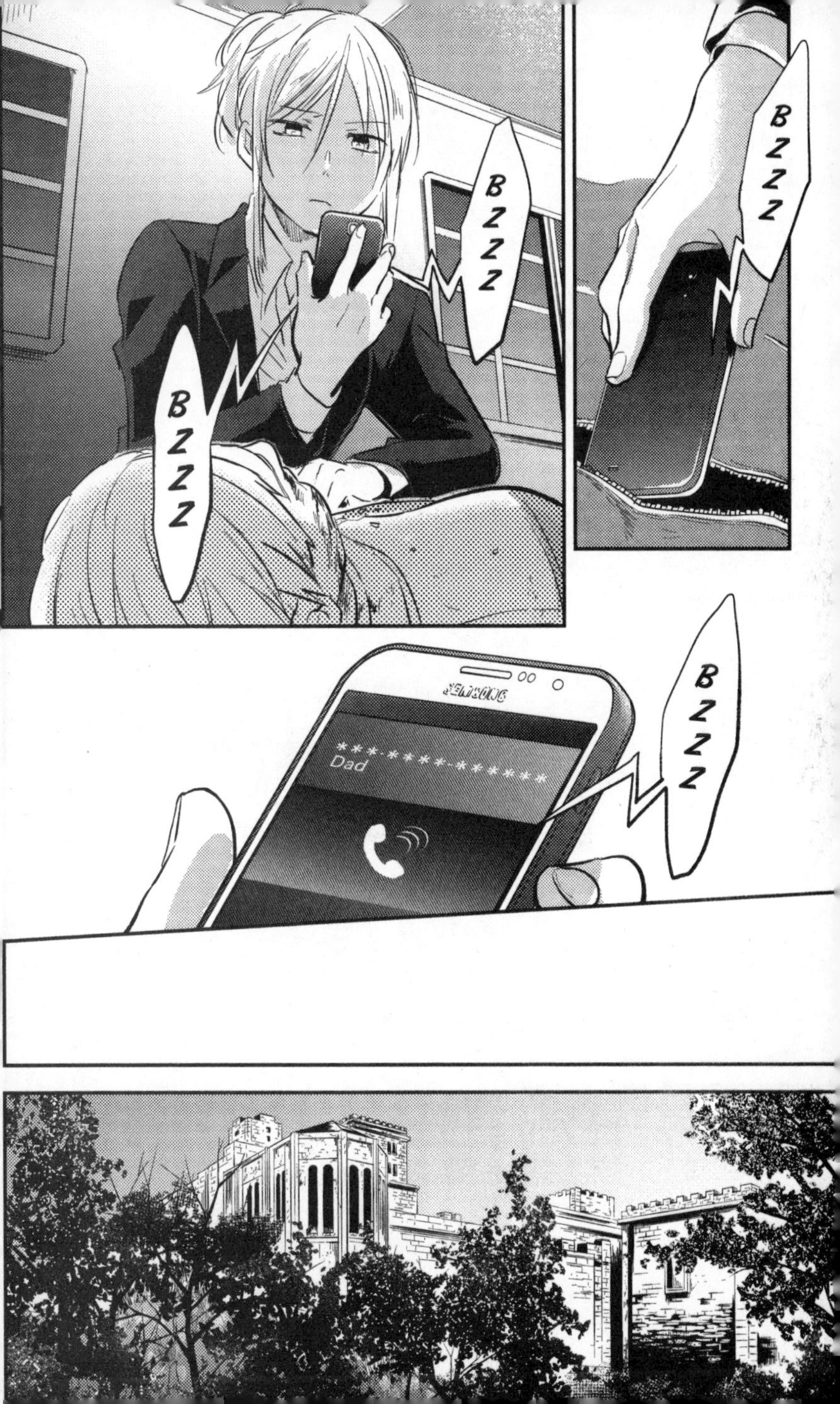
BZZZ
BZZZ
BZZZ
-*-******
Dad
BZZZ

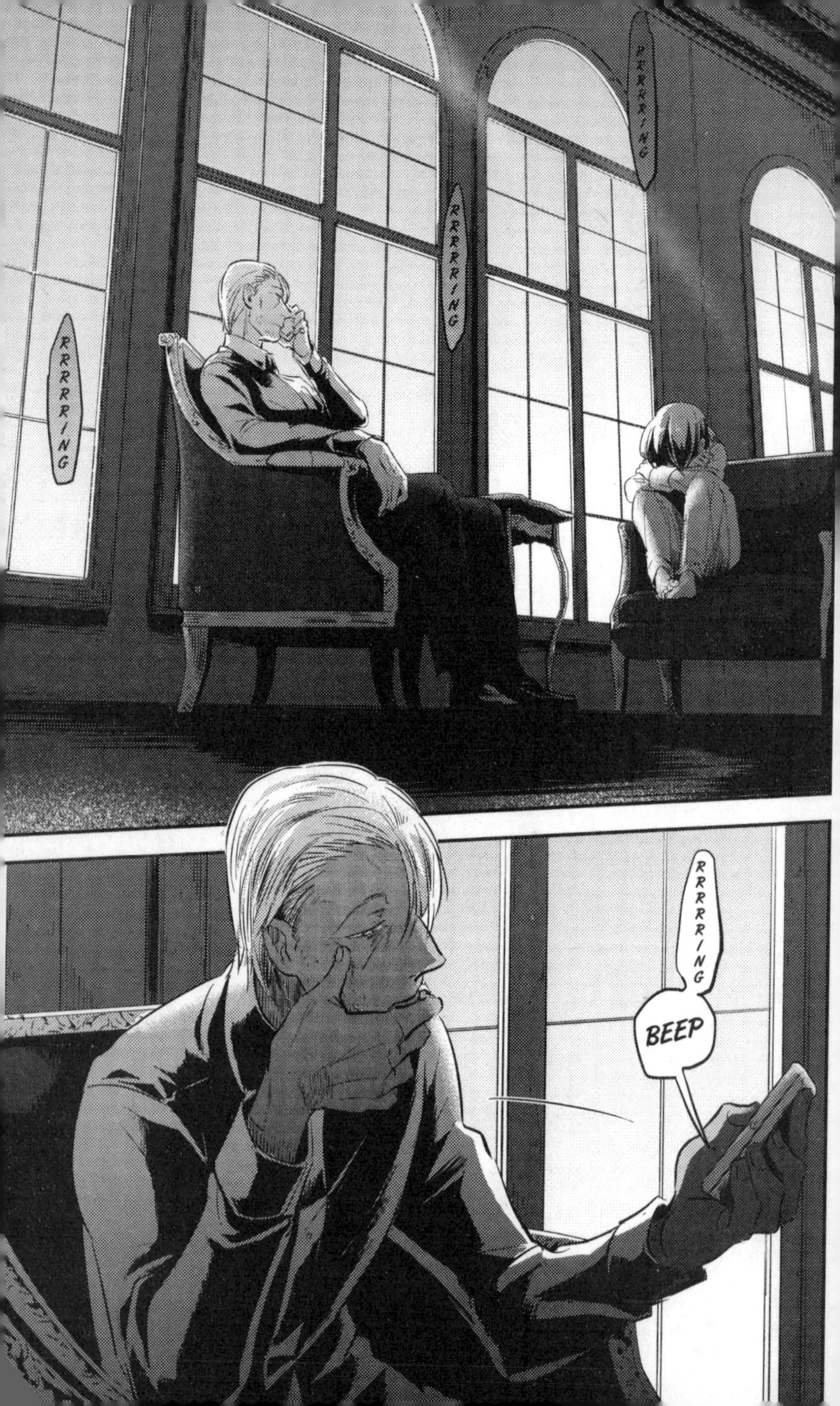
RRRRRING
RRRRRING
RRRRRING
RRRRRING
BEEP

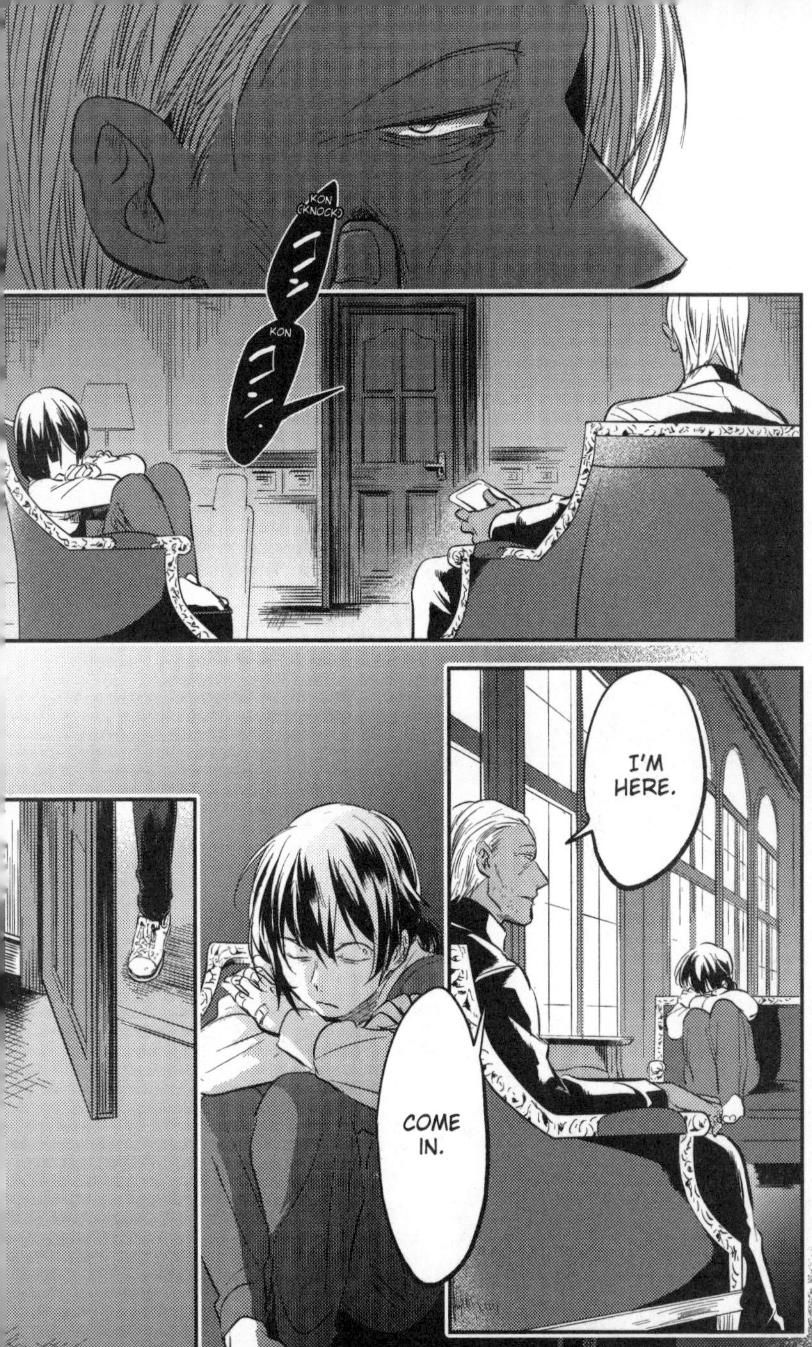
KON (KNOCK)
KON
I'M HERE.
COME IN.

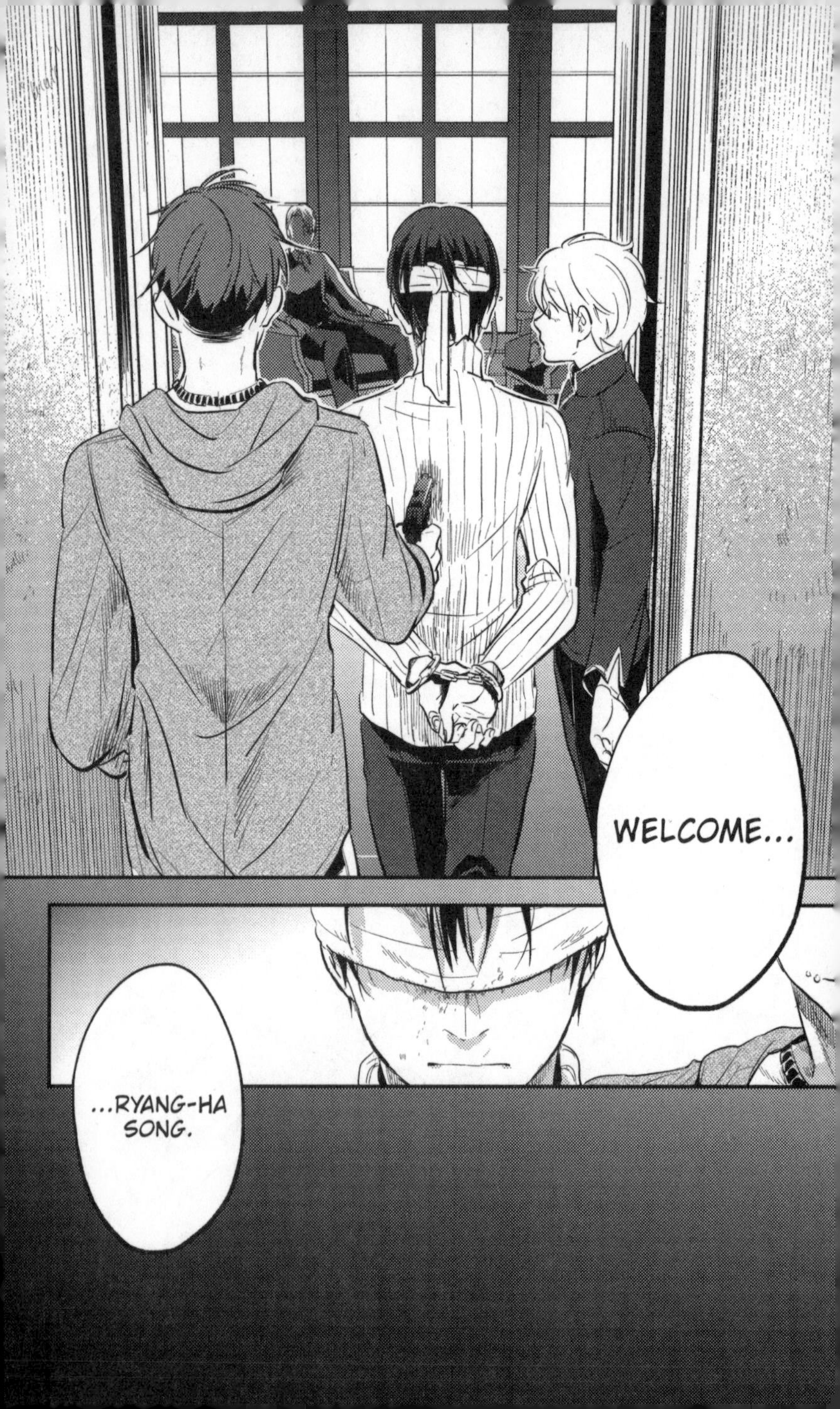
WELCOME...
...RYANG-HA SONG.

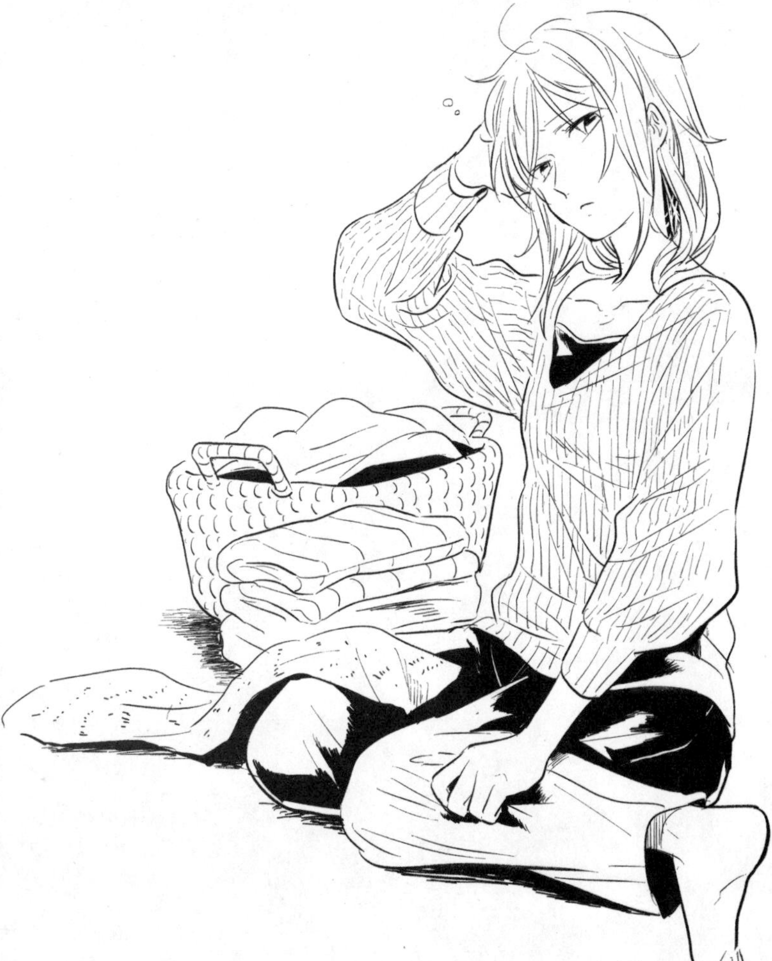

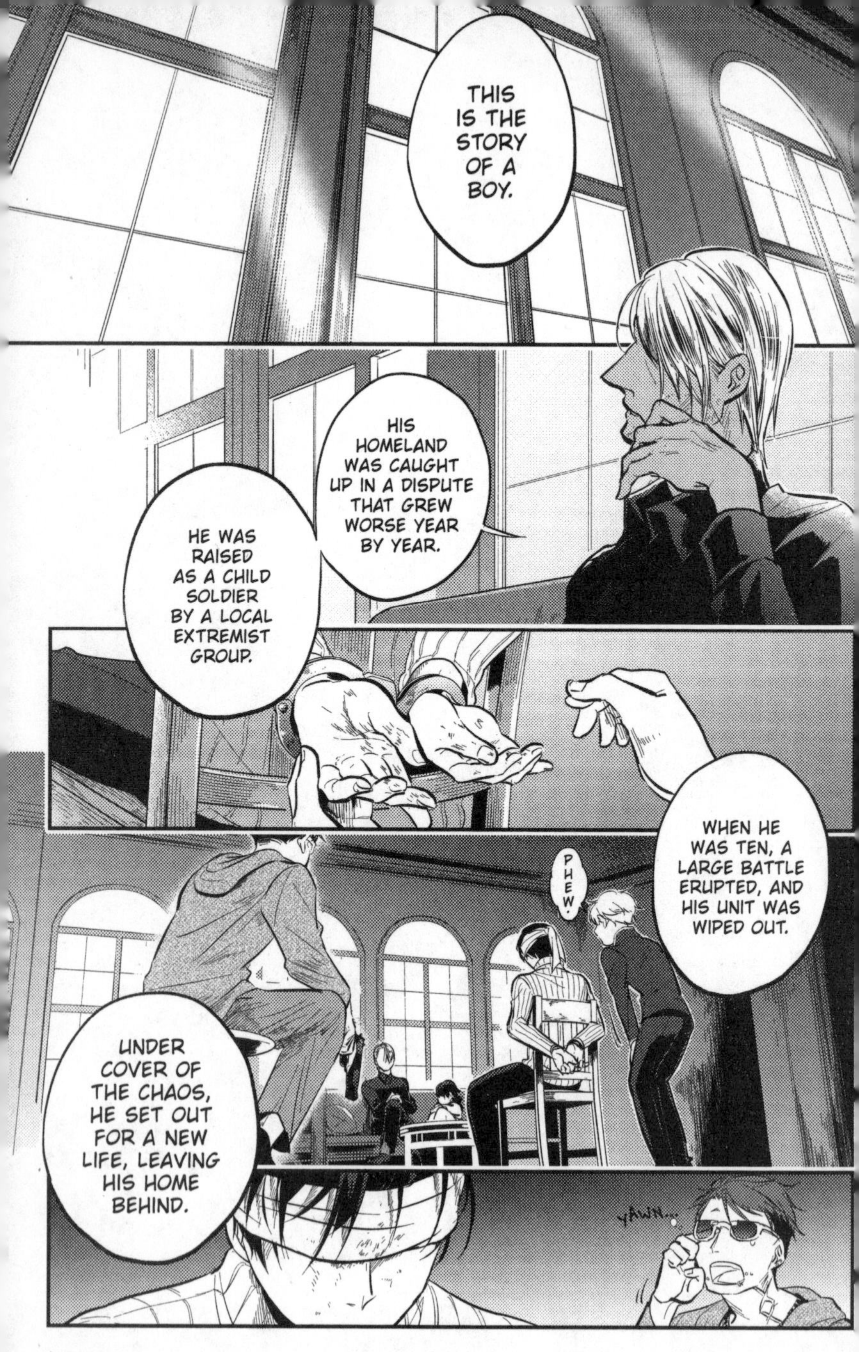
THIS IS THE STORY OF A BOY.
HIS HOMELAND WAS CAUGHT UP IN A DISPUTE THAT GREW WORSE YEAR BY YEAR.
HE WAS RAISED AS A CHILD SOLDIER BY A LOCAL EXTREMIST GROUP.
WHEN HE WAS TEN, A LARGE BATTLE ERUPTED, AND HIS UNIT WAS WIPED OUT.
PHEW.
UNDER COVER OF THE CHAOS, HE SET OUT FOR A NEW LIFE, LEAVING HIS HOME BEHIND.
YAWN...

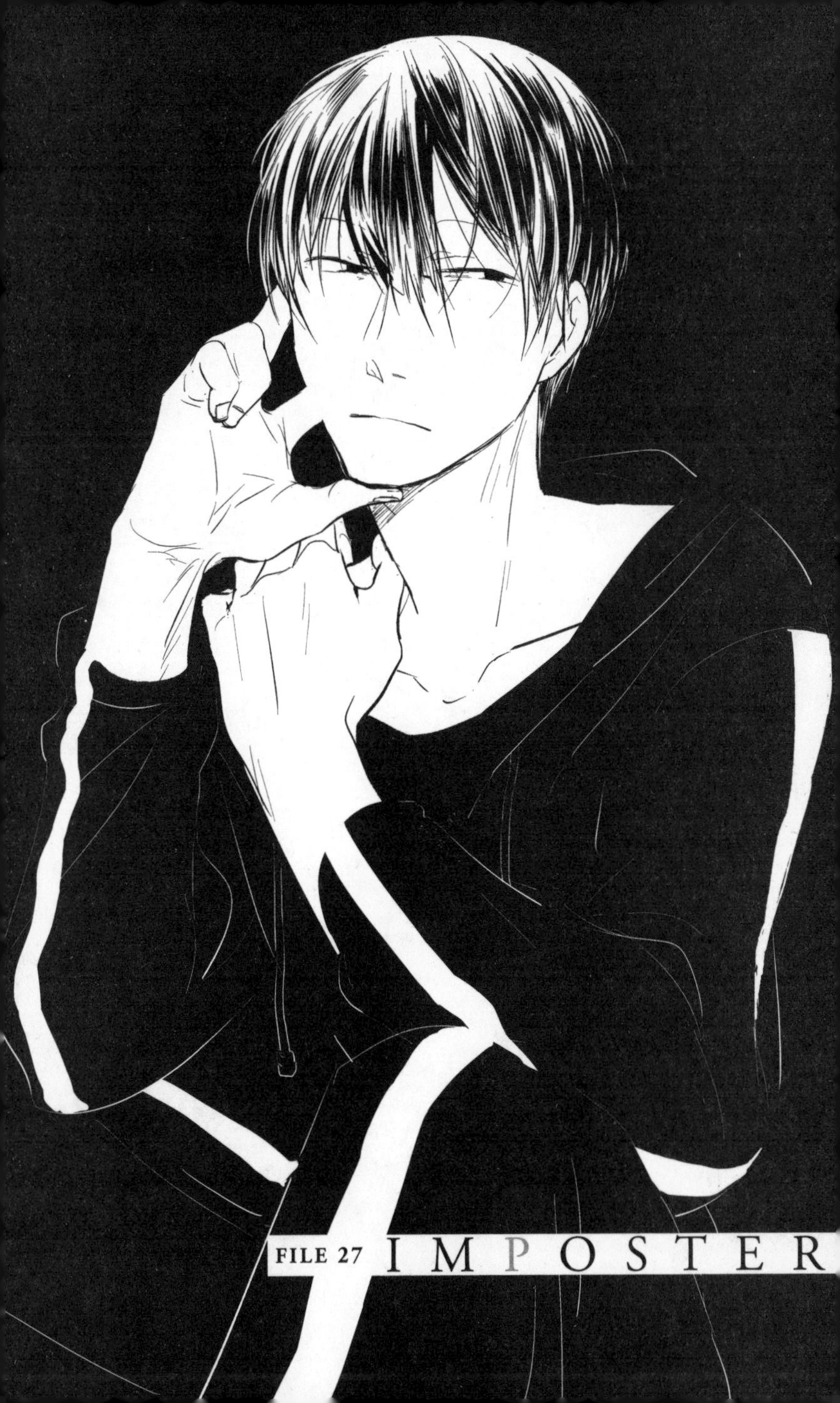
FILE 27 IMPOSTER

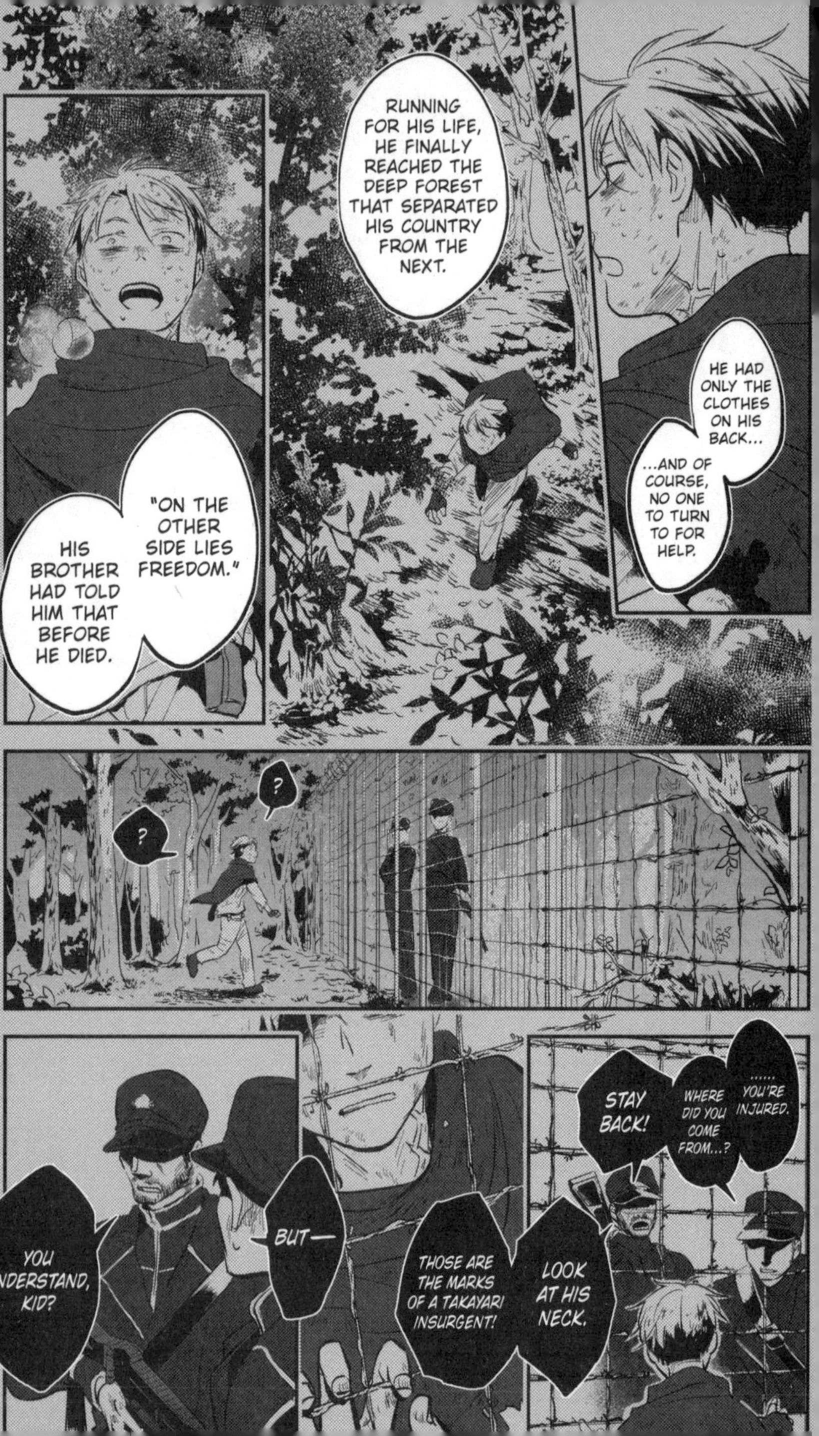
HE HAD ONLY THE CLOTHES ON HIS BACK...
...AND OF COURSE, NO ONE TO TURN TO FOR HELP.
RUNNING FOR HIS LIFE, HE FINALLY REACHED THE DEEP FOREST THAT SEPARATED HIS COUNTRY FROM THE NEXT.
"ON THE OTHER SIDE LIES FREEDOM."
HIS BROTHER HAD TOLD HIM THAT BEFORE HE DIED.
?
?
......YOU'RE INJURED.
WHERE DID YOU COME FROM...?
STAY BACK!
LOOK AT HIS NECK.
THOSE ARE THE MARKS OF A TAKAYARI INSURGENT!
BUT—
YOU UNDERSTAND, KID?

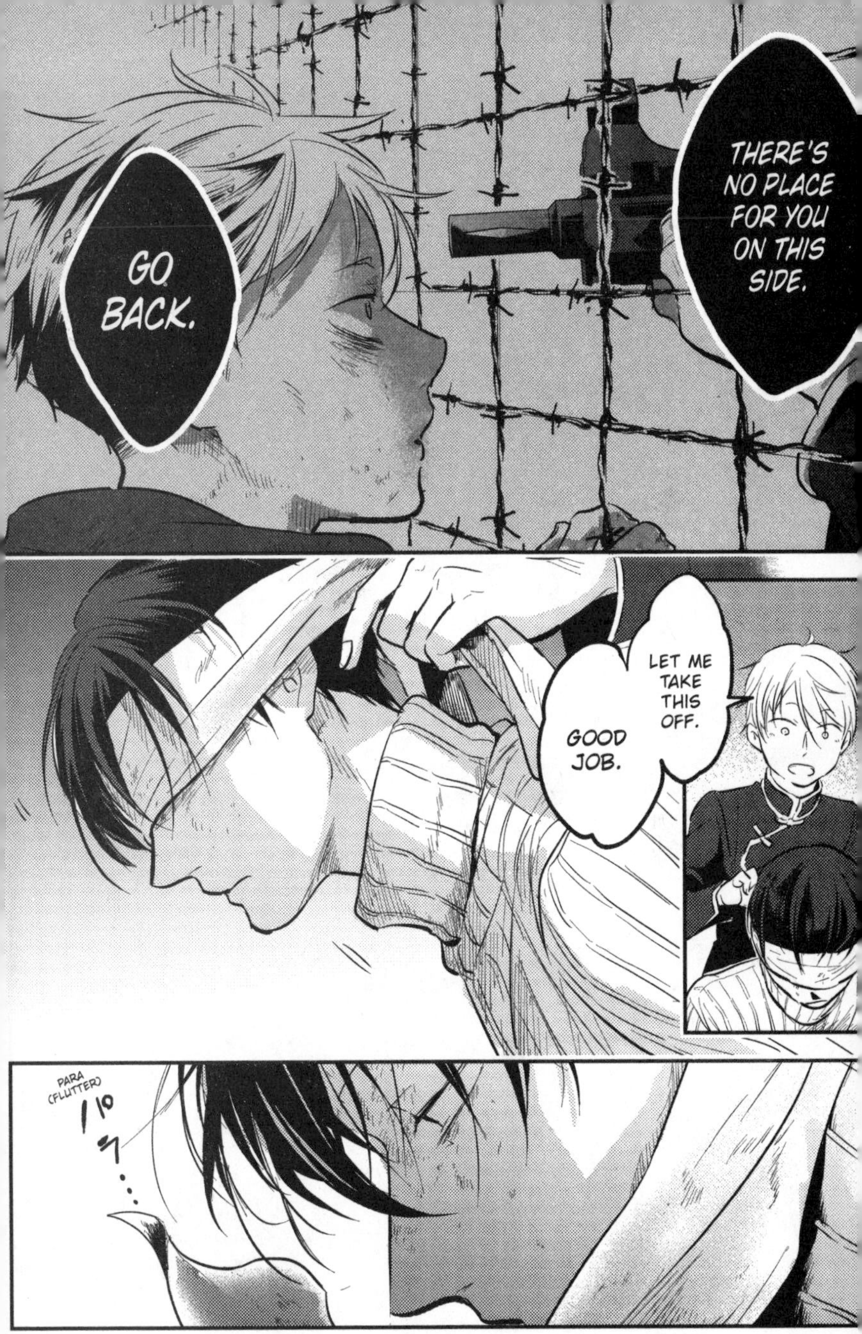
THERE'S NO PLACE FOR YOU ON THIS SIDE.
GO BACK.
LET ME TAKE THIS OFF.
GOOD JOB.
PARA (FLUTTER)
パラ…

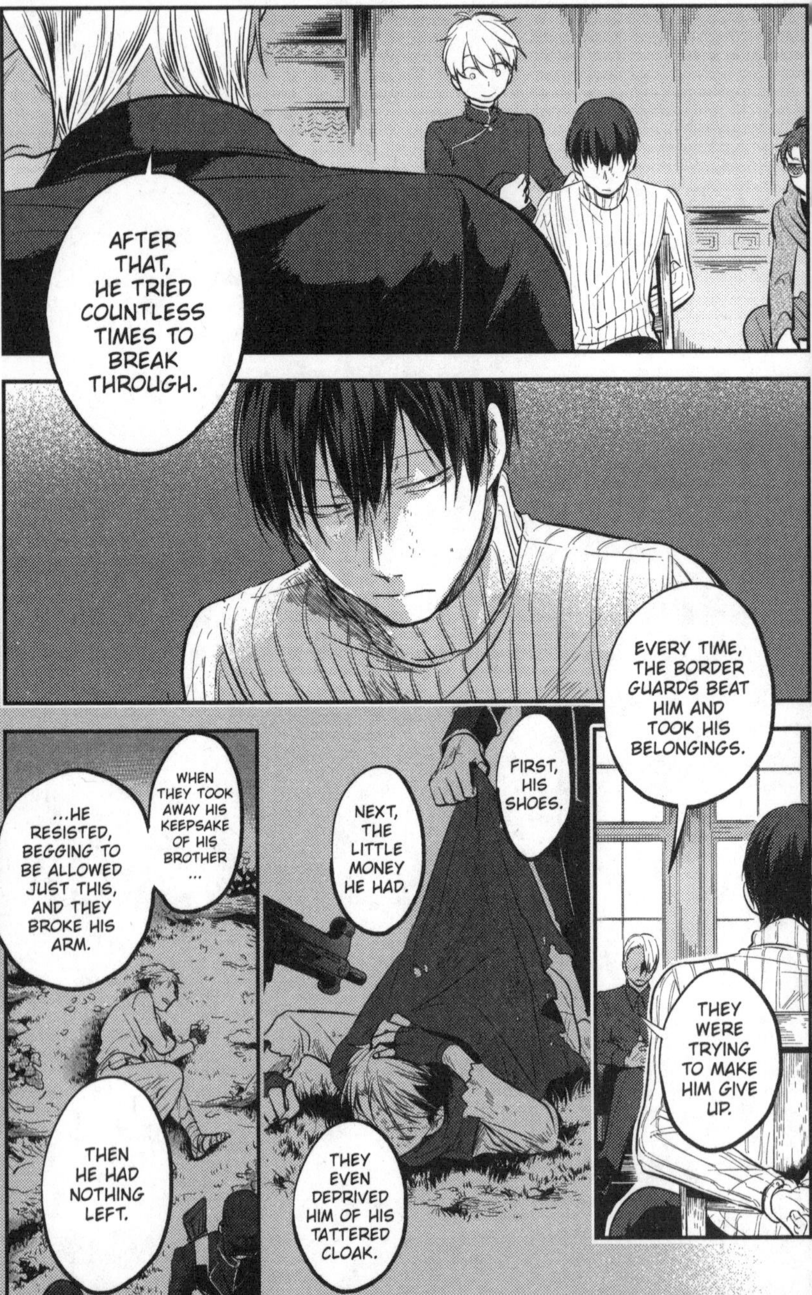
AFTER THAT, HE TRIED COUNTLESS TIMES TO BREAK THROUGH.
EVERY TIME, THE BORDER GUARDS BEAT HIM AND TOOK HIS BELONGINGS.
THEY WERE TRYING TO MAKE HIM GIVE UP.
FIRST, HIS SHOES.
NEXT, THE LITTLE MONEY HE HAD.
THEY EVEN DEPRIVED HIM OF HIS TATTERED CLOAK.
WHEN THEY TOOK AWAY HIS KEEPSAKE OF HIS BROTHER ...
...HE RESISTED, BEGGING TO BE ALLOWED JUST THIS, AND THEY BROKE HIS ARM.
THEN HE HAD NOTHING LEFT.

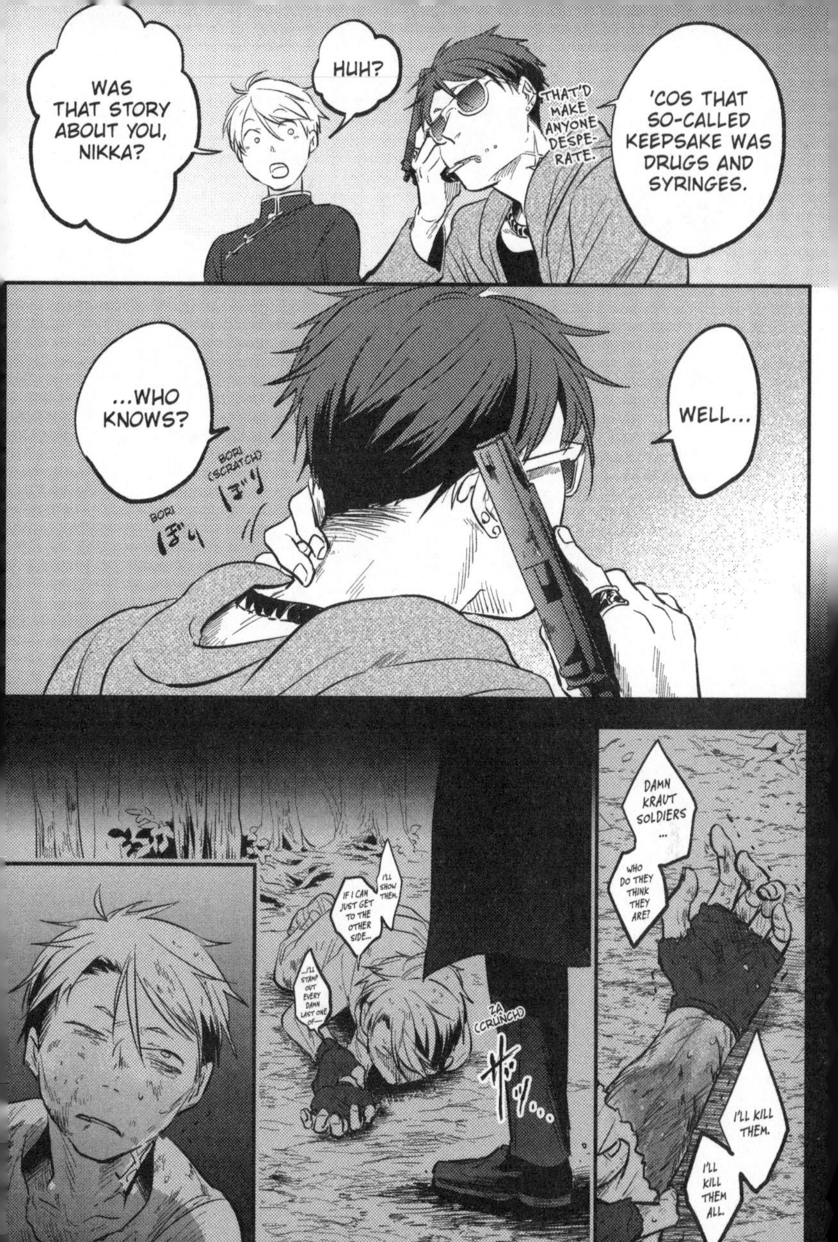
'COS THAT SO-CALLED KEEPSAKE WAS DRUGS AND SYRINGES.
THAT'D MAKE ANYONE DESPE-RATE.
HUH?
WAS THAT STORY ABOUT YOU, NIKKA?
WELL...
BORI (SCRATCH)
BORI
...WHO KNOWS?
DAMN KRAUT SOLDIERS...
WHO DO THEY THINK THEY ARE?
I'LL KILL THEM.
I'LL KILL THEM ALL.
I'LL SHOW THEM.
IF I CAN JUST GET TO THE OTHER SIDE...
...I'LL STAMP OUT EVERY DAMN LAST ONE OF—
ZA (CRUNCH)

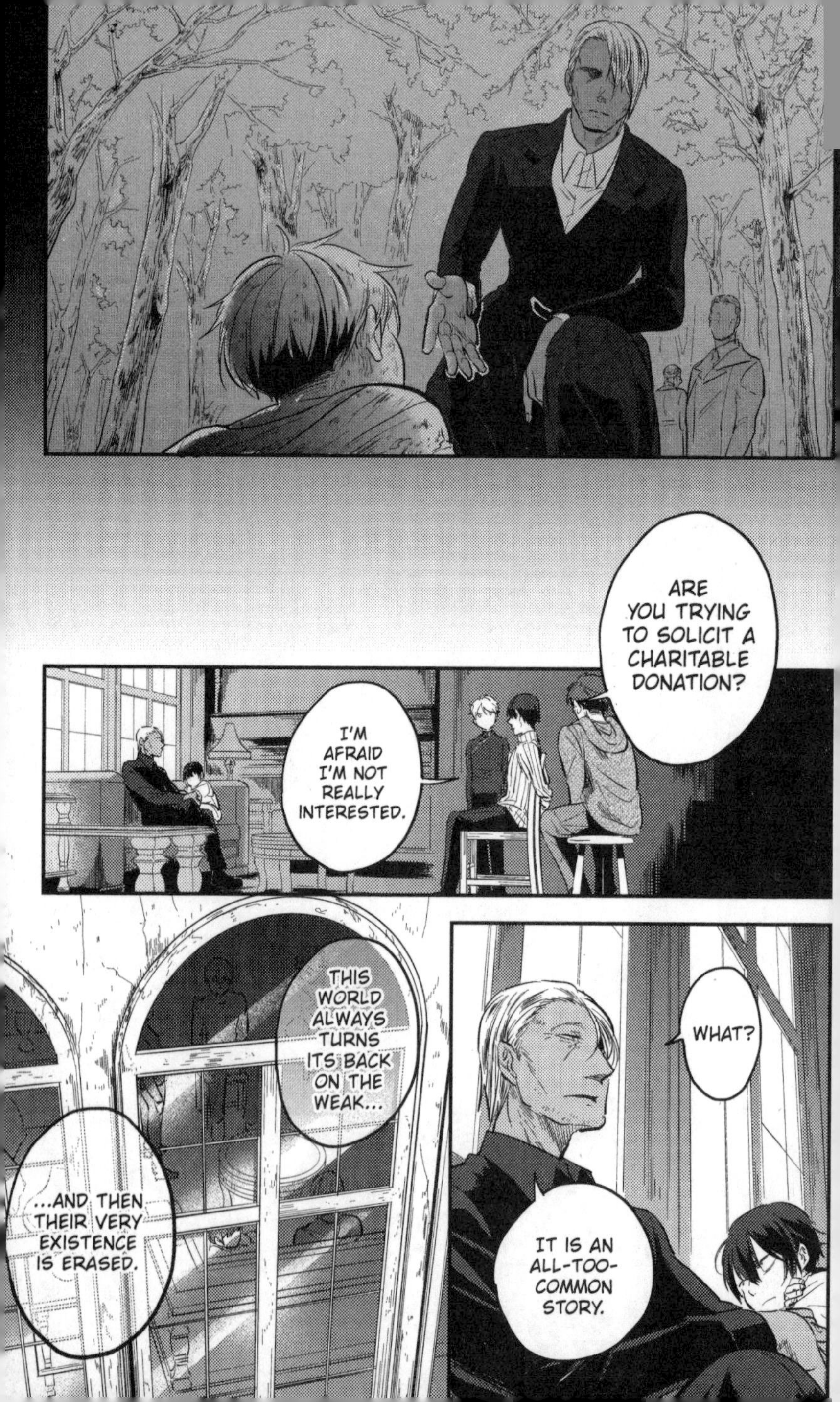
ARE YOU TRYING TO SOLICIT A CHARITABLE DONATION?
I'M AFRAID I'M NOT REALLY INTERESTED.
WHAT?
IT IS AN ALL-TOO-COMMON STORY.
THIS WORLD ALWAYS TURNS ITS BACK ON THE WEAK...
...AND THEN THEIR VERY EXISTENCE IS ERASED.

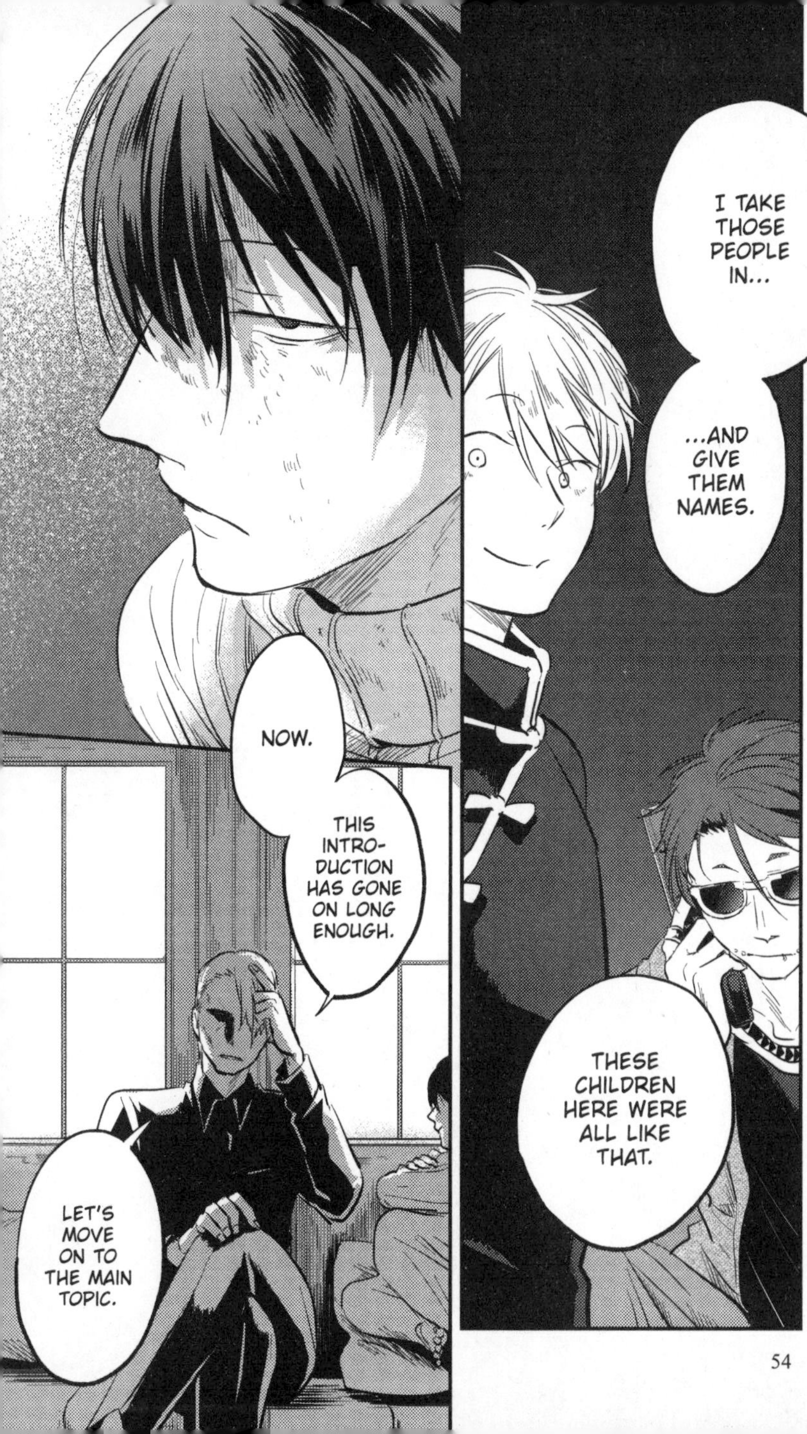
I TAKE THOSE PEOPLE IN...
...AND GIVE THEM NAMES.
THESE CHILDREN HERE WERE ALL LIKE THAT.
NOW.
THIS INTRO-DUCTION HAS GONE ON LONG ENOUGH.
LET'S MOVE ON TO THE MAIN TOPIC.

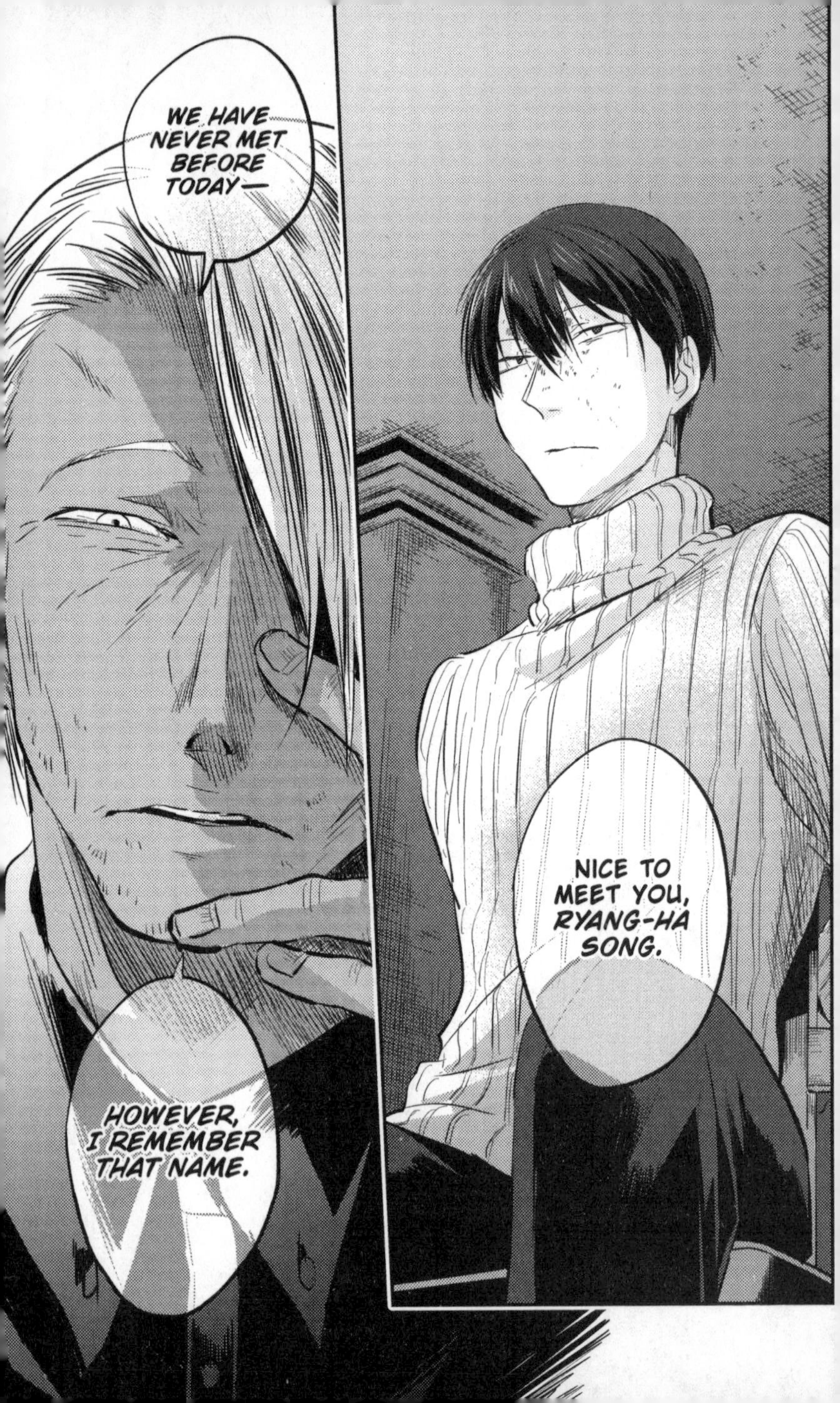
NICE TO MEET YOU, RYANG-HA SONG.
WE HAVE NEVER MET BEFORE TODAY—
HOWEVER, I REMEMBER THAT NAME.

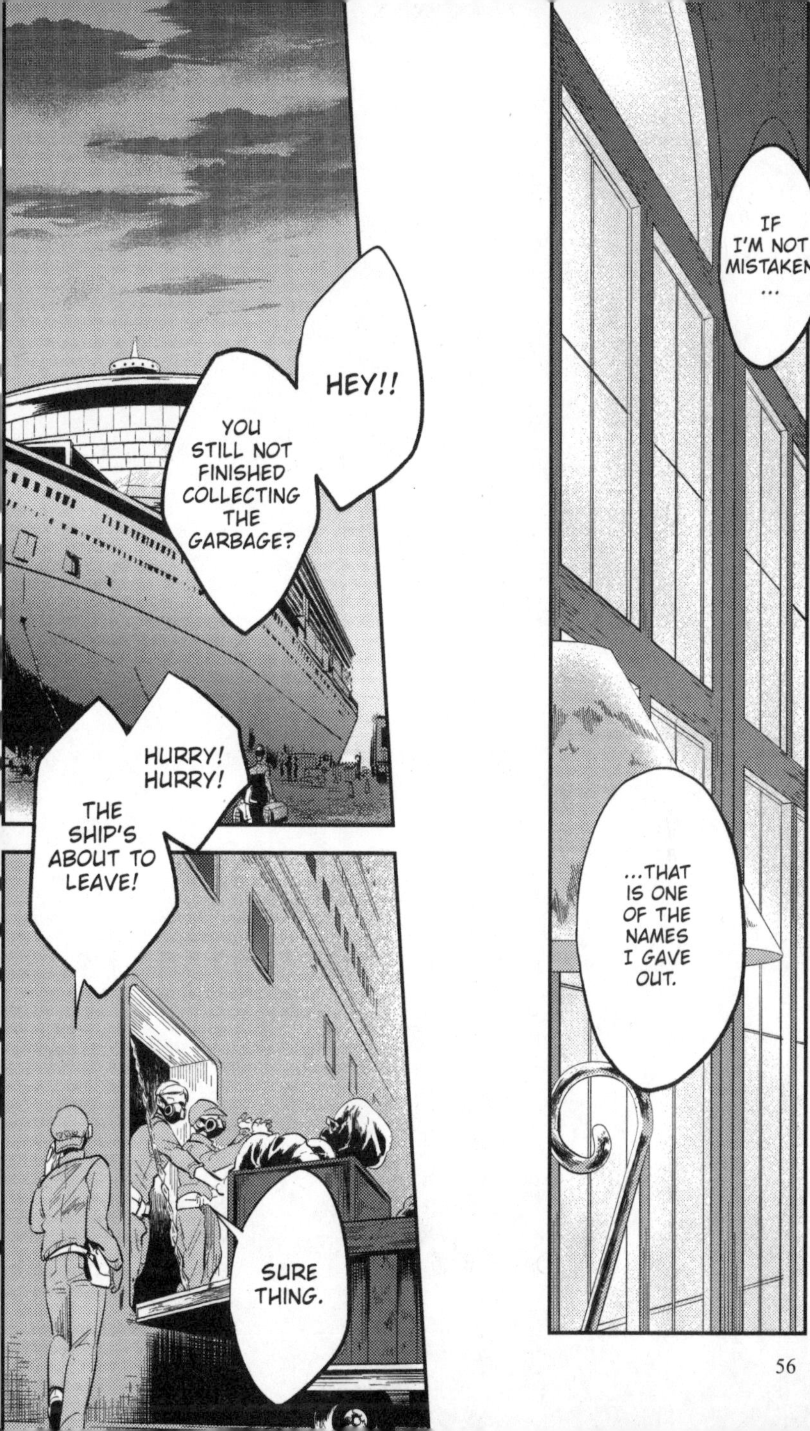
IF I'M NOT MISTAKEN ...
...THAT IS ONE OF THE NAMES I GAVE OUT.
HEY!!
YOU STILL NOT FINISHED COLLECTING THE GARBAGE?
HURRY! HURRY!
THE SHIP'S ABOUT TO LEAVE!
SURE THING.

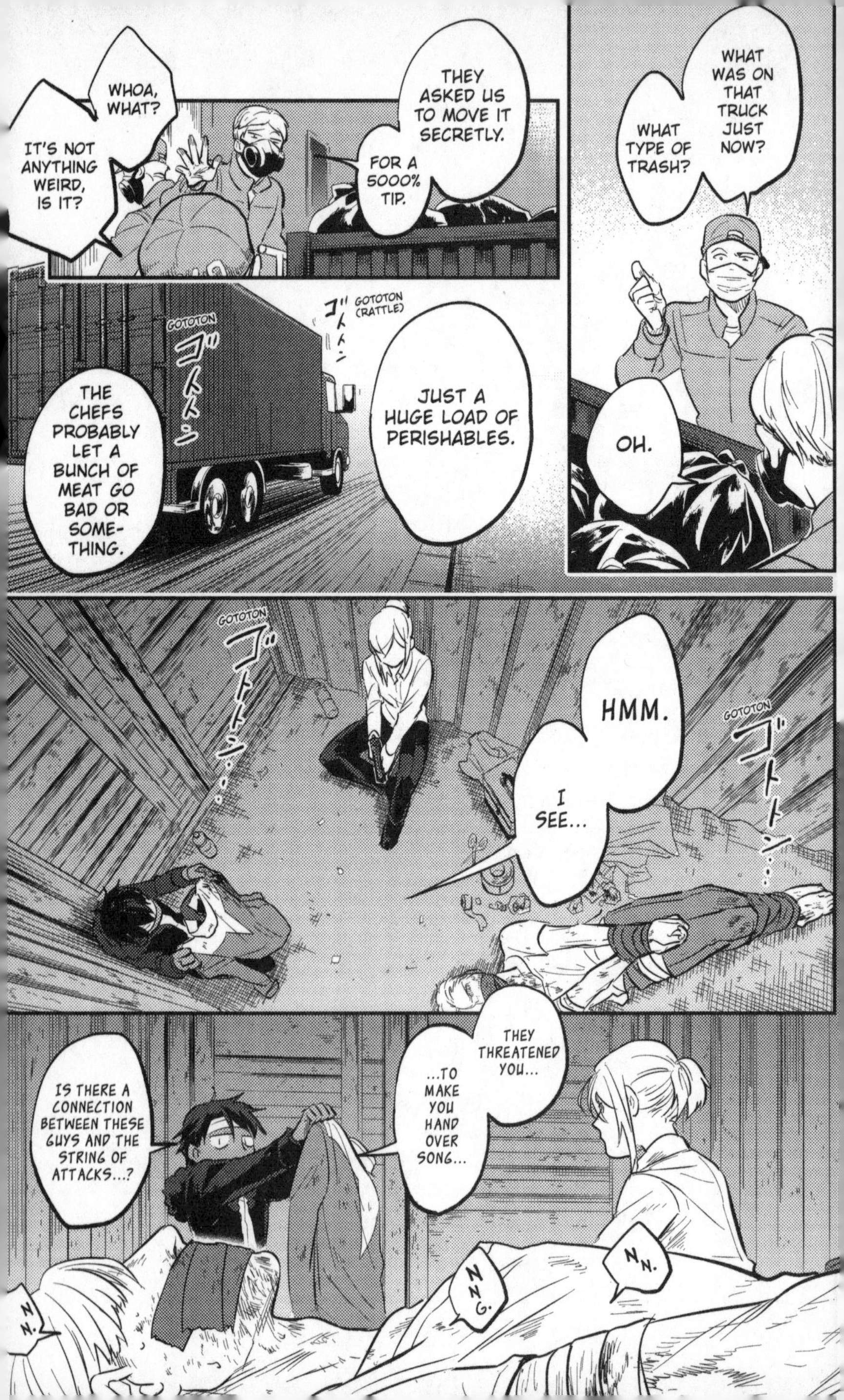
WHAT WAS ON THAT TRUCK JUST NOW?
WHAT TYPE OF TRASH?
OH.
THEY ASKED US TO MOVE IT SECRETLY.
FOR A 5000% TIP.
WHOA, WHAT?
IT'S NOT ANYTHING WEIRD, IS IT?
GOTOTON (RATTLE)
ゴトトン
JUST A HUGE LOAD OF PERISHABLES.
GOTOTON
ゴトトン
THE CHEFS PROBABLY LET A BUNCH OF MEAT GO BAD OR SOME-THING.
GOTOTON
ゴトトン…
HMM.
I SEE…
GOTOTON
ゴトトン…
THEY THREATENED YOU…
…TO MAKE YOU HAND OVER SONG…
NN.
NNG.
IS THERE A CONNECTION BETWEEN THESE GUYS AND THE STRING OF ATTACKS…?
NN.

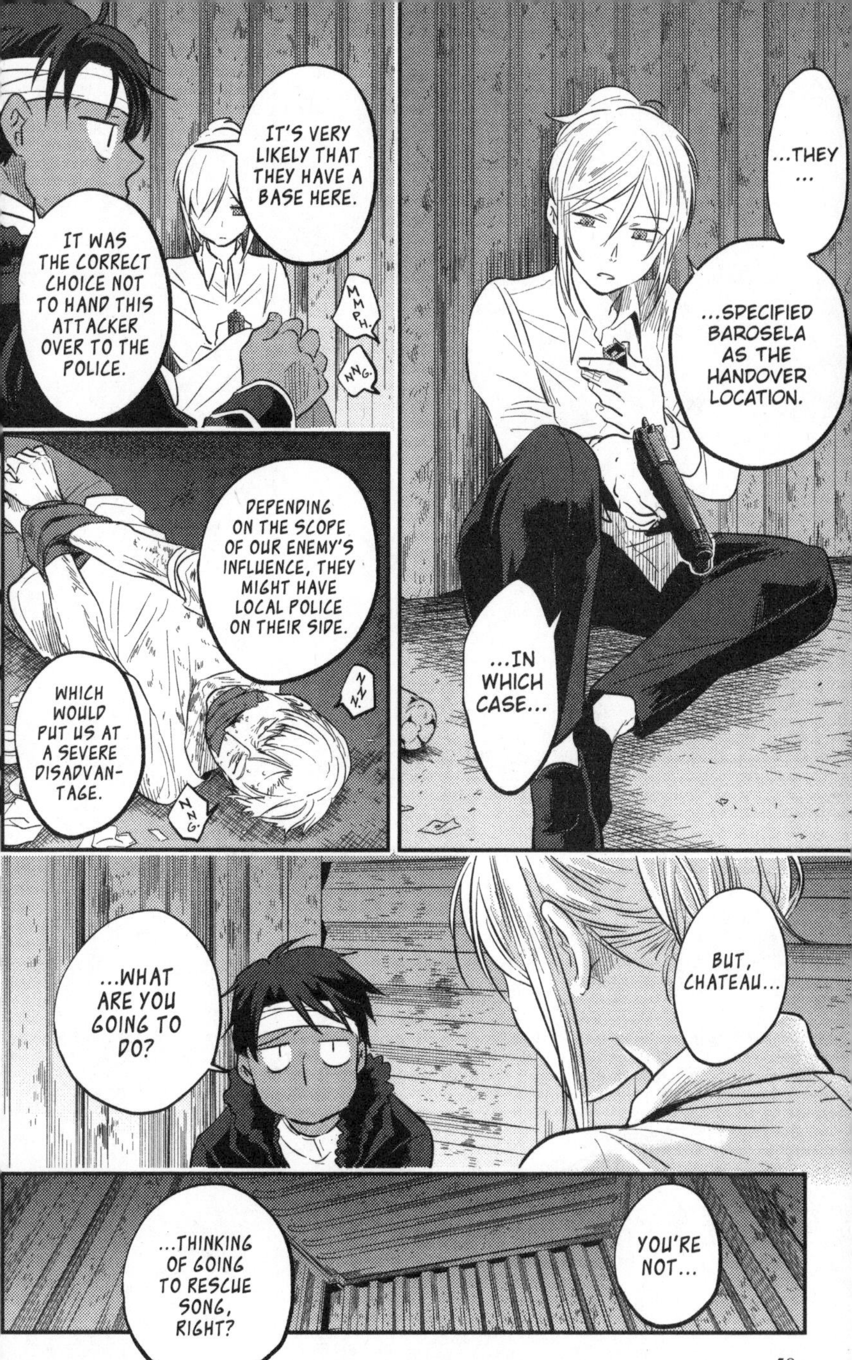
...THEY ...
...SPECIFIED BAROSELA AS THE HANDOVER LOCATION.
...IN WHICH CASE...
IT'S VERY LIKELY THAT THEY HAVE A BASE HERE.
IT WAS THE CORRECT CHOICE NOT TO HAND THIS ATTACKER OVER TO THE POLICE.
MMPH.
NNG.
DEPENDING ON THE SCOPE OF OUR ENEMY'S INFLUENCE, THEY MIGHT HAVE LOCAL POLICE ON THEIR SIDE.
NNN.
WHICH WOULD PUT US AT A SEVERE DISADVAN-TAGE.
NNG.
BUT, CHATEAU...
...WHAT ARE YOU GOING TO DO?
YOU'RE NOT...
...THINKING OF GOING TO RESCUE SONG, RIGHT?

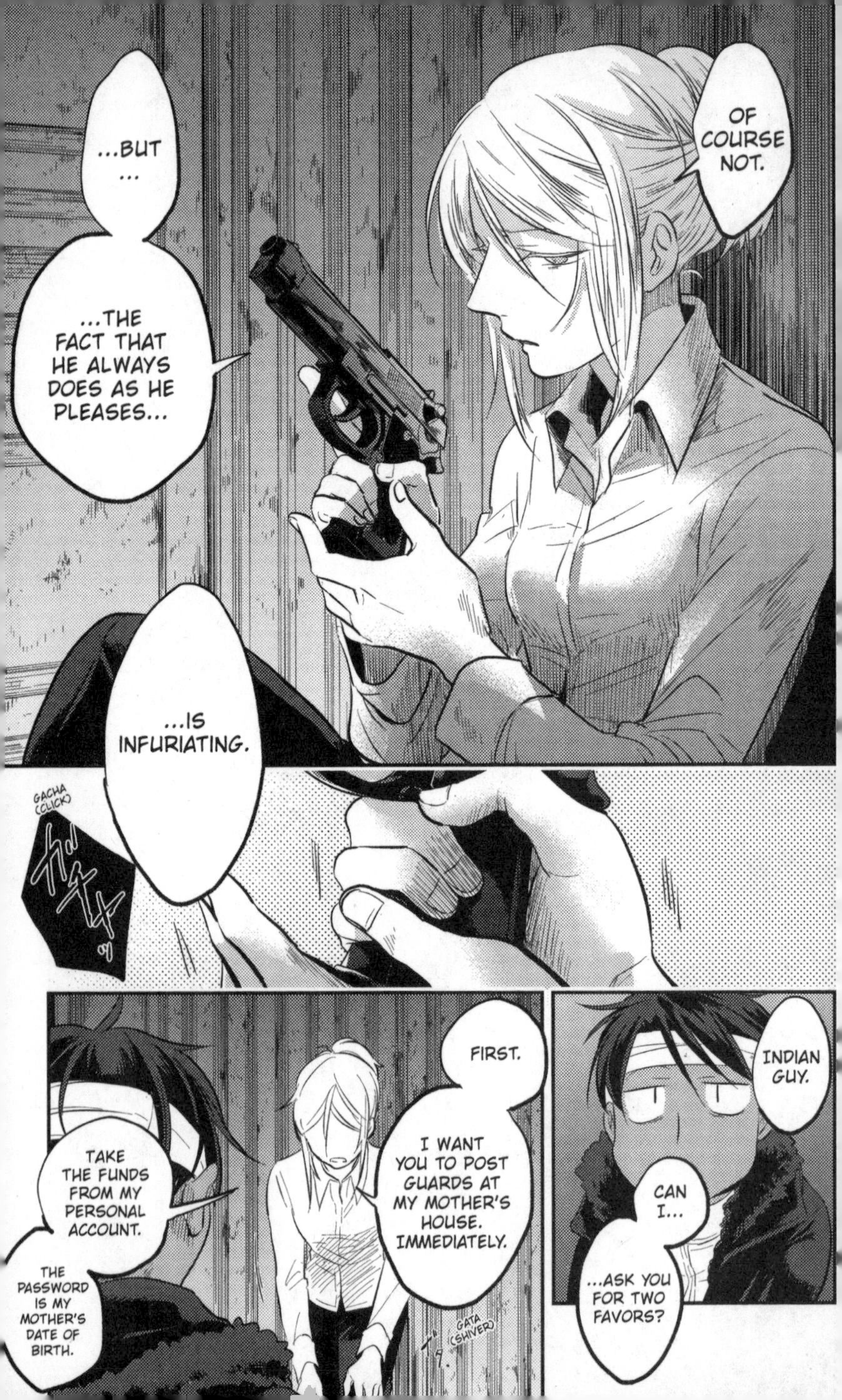
OF COURSE NOT.
...BUT ...
...THE FACT THAT HE ALWAYS DOES AS HE PLEASES...
...IS INFURIATING.
GACHA (CLICK)
INDIAN GUY.
CAN I...
...ASK YOU FOR TWO FAVORS?
FIRST.
I WANT YOU TO POST GUARDS AT MY MOTHER'S HOUSE. IMMEDIATELY.
TAKE THE FUNDS FROM MY PERSONAL ACCOUNT.
THE PASSWORD IS MY MOTHER'S DATE OF BIRTH.
GATA (SHIVER)

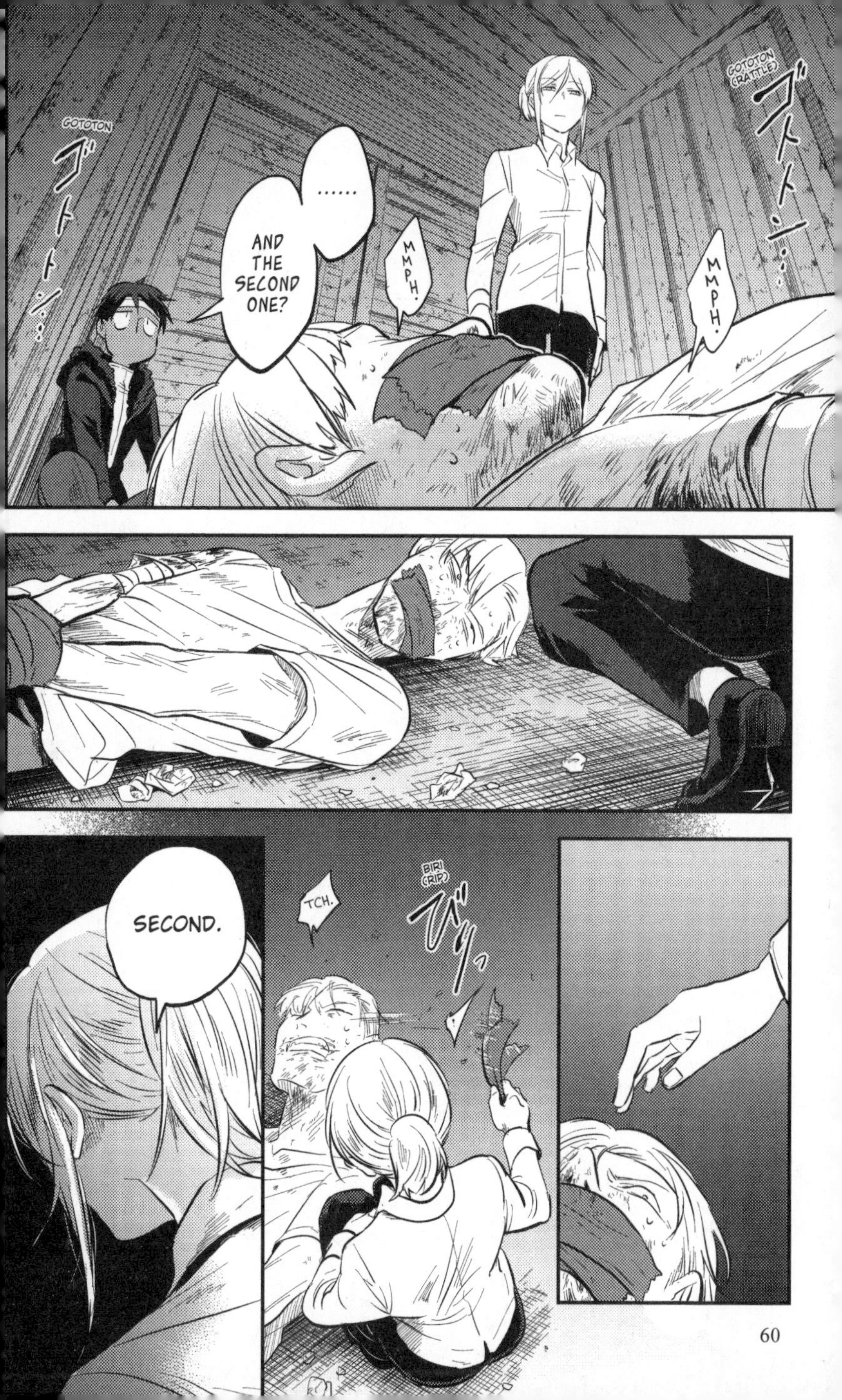
GOTOTON (RATTLE)
ゴトトン…
MMPH!
MMPH!
......
AND THE SECOND ONE?
GOTOTON
ゴトトン…
BIRI (RIP)
びりっ
TCH.
SECOND.

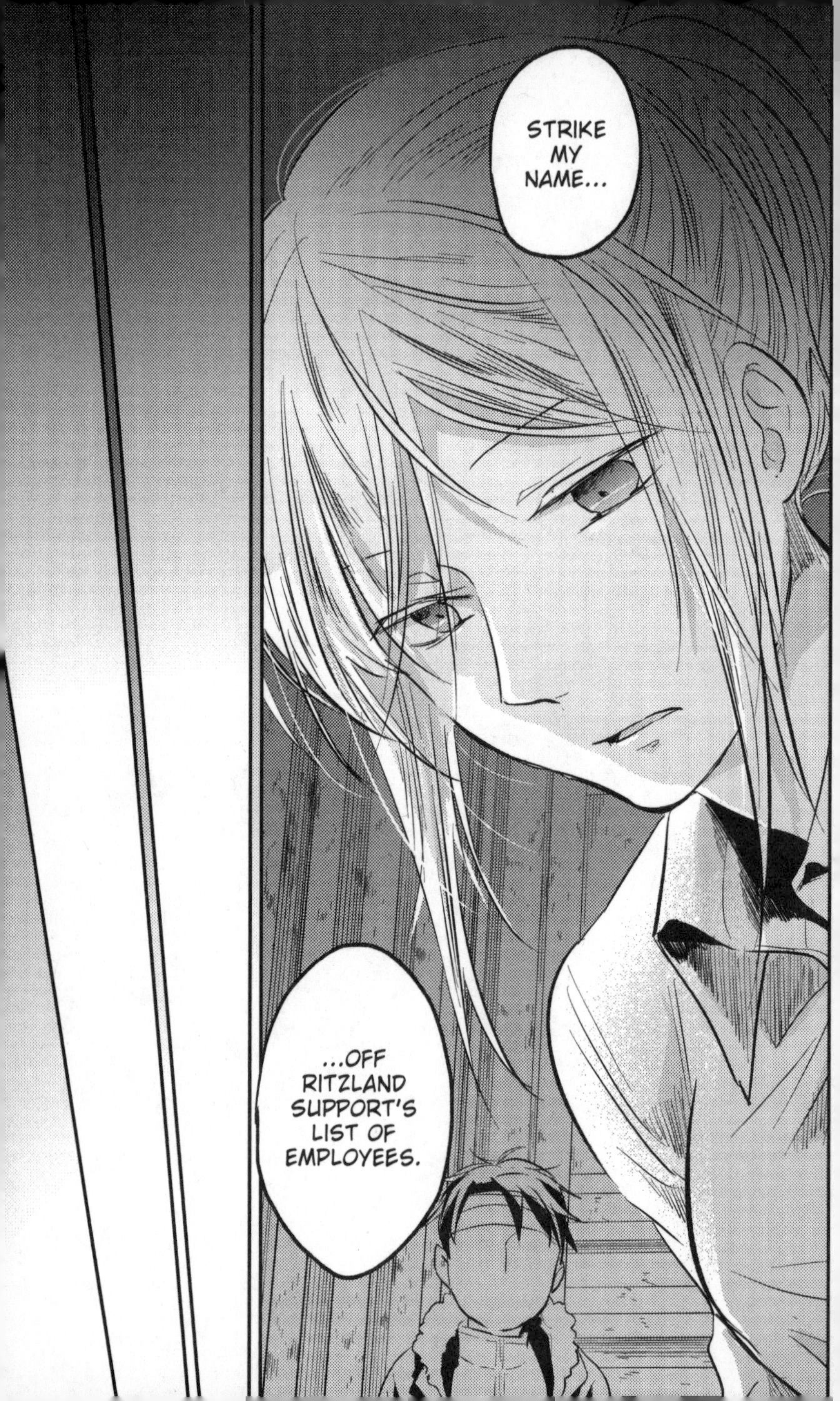
STRIKE MY NAME...
...OFF RITZLAND SUPPORT'S LIST OF EMPLOYEES.

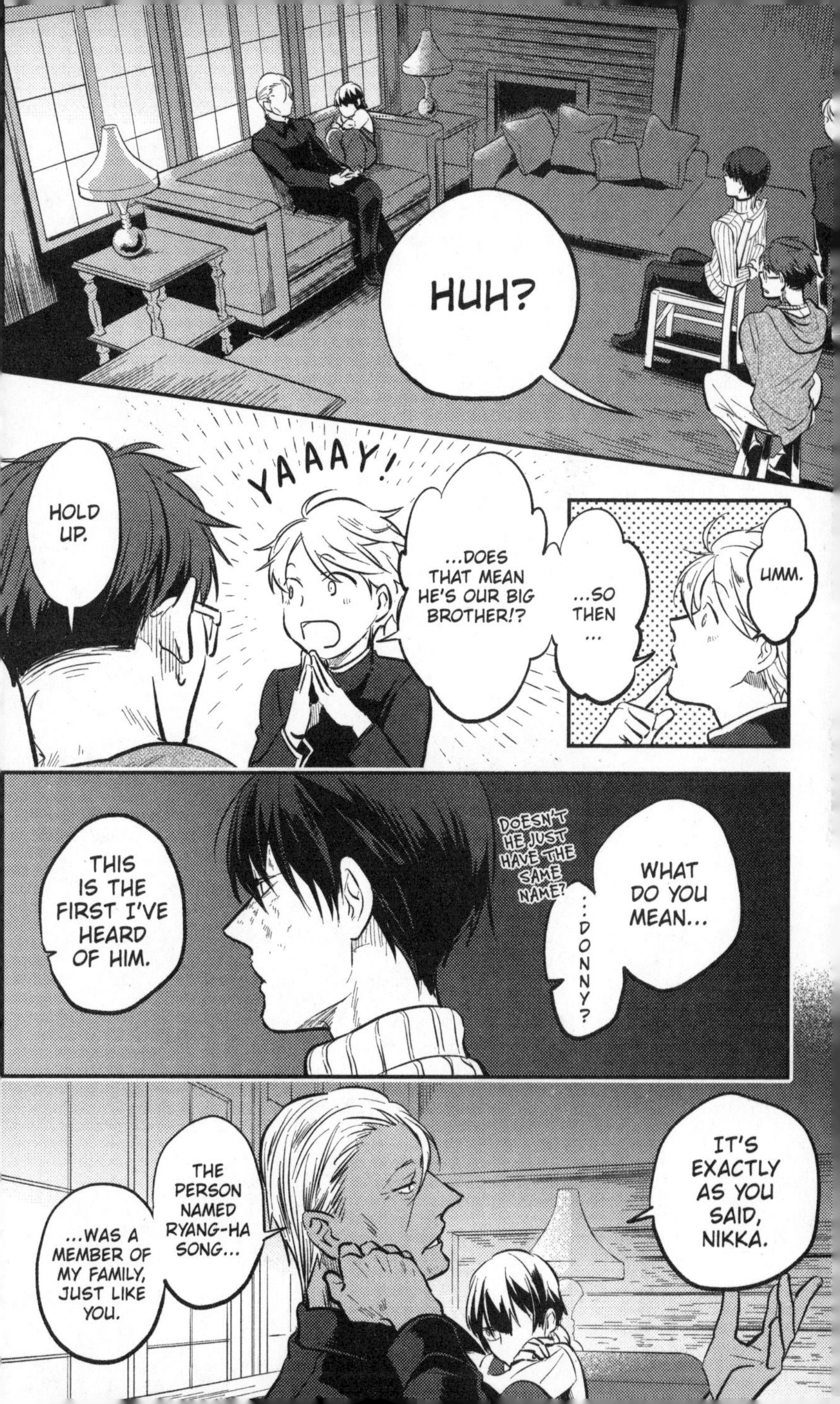
HUH?
UMM.
...SO THEN ...
...DOES THAT MEAN HE'S OUR BIG BROTHER!?
YAAAY!
HOLD UP.
WHAT DO YOU MEAN...
...DONNY?
DOESN'T HE JUST HAVE THE SAME NAME?
THIS IS THE FIRST I'VE HEARD OF HIM.
IT'S EXACTLY AS YOU SAID, NIKKA.
THE PERSON NAMED RYANG-HA SONG...
...WAS A MEMBER OF MY FAMILY, JUST LIKE YOU.

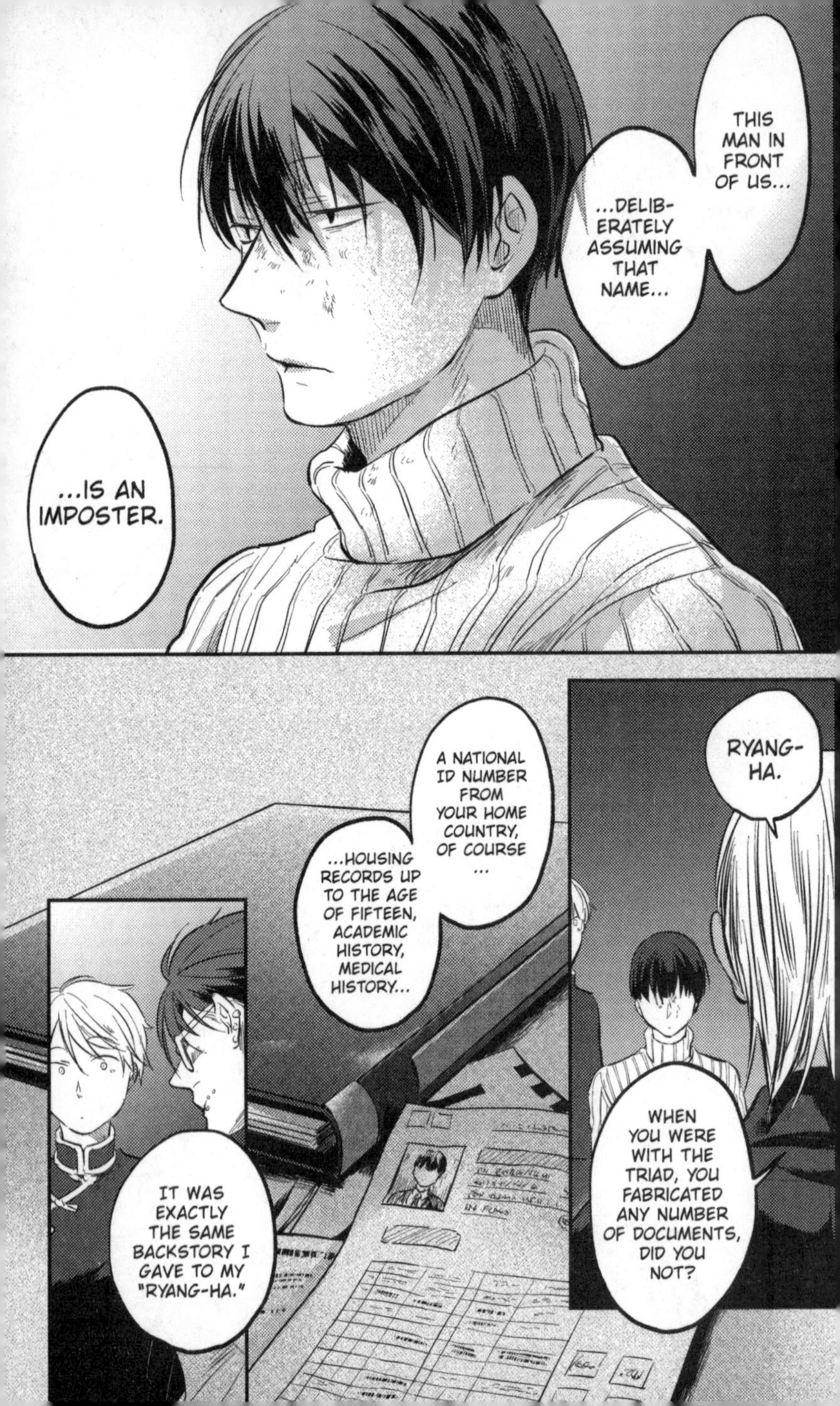
THIS MAN IN FRONT OF US...
...DELIB-ERATELY ASSUMING THAT NAME...
...IS AN IMPOSTER.
RYANG-HA.
WHEN YOU WERE WITH THE TRIAD, YOU FABRICATED ANY NUMBER OF DOCUMENTS, DID YOU NOT?
A NATIONAL ID NUMBER FROM YOUR HOME COUNTRY, OF COURSE...
...HOUSING RECORDS UP TO THE AGE OF FIFTEEN, ACADEMIC HISTORY, MEDICAL HISTORY...
IT WAS EXACTLY THE SAME BACKSTORY I GAVE TO MY "RYANG-HA."

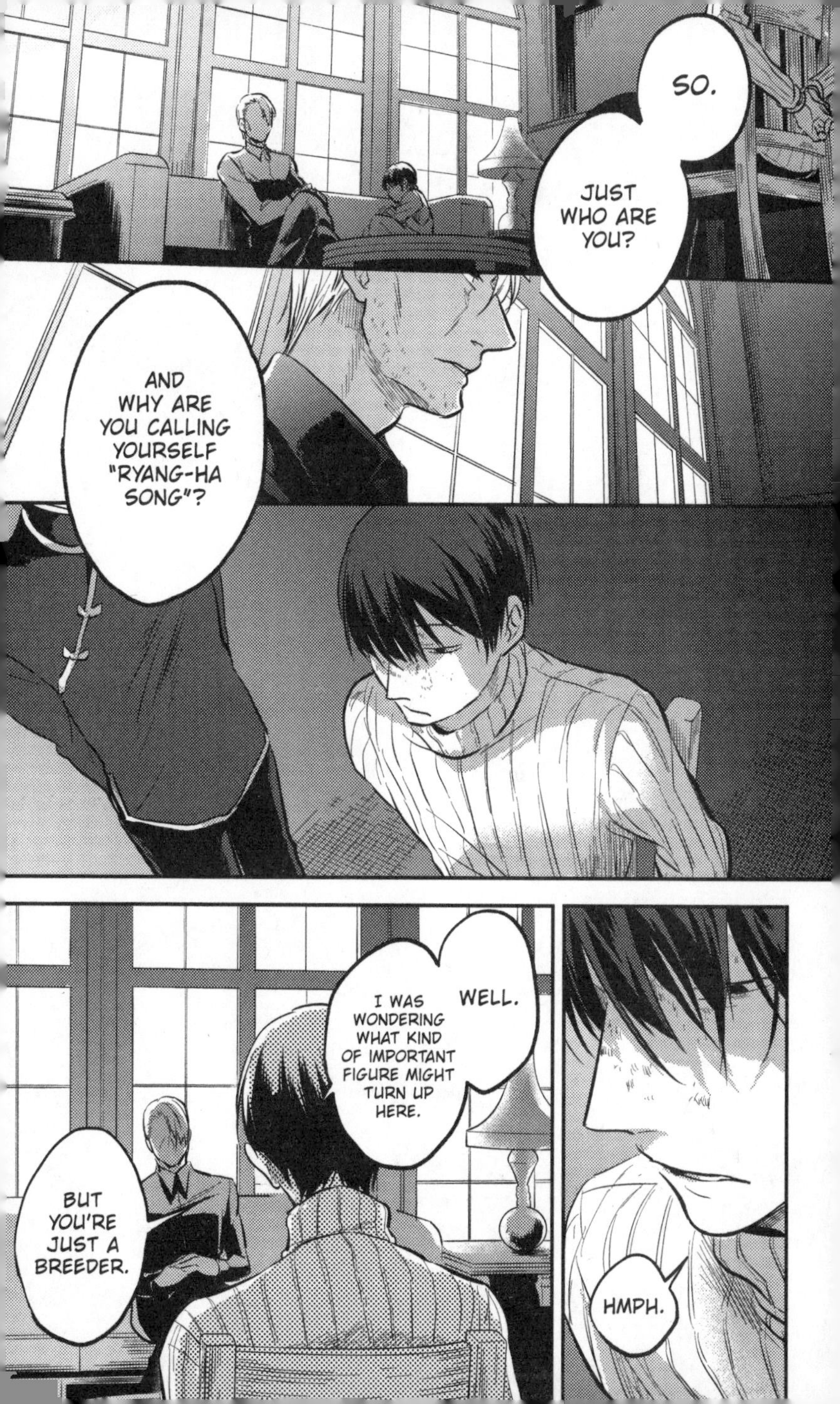
SO.
JUST WHO ARE YOU?
AND WHY ARE YOU CALLING YOURSELF "RYANG-HA SONG"?
HMPH.
WELL.
I WAS WONDERING WHAT KIND OF IMPORTANT FIGURE MIGHT TURN UP HERE.
BUT YOU'RE JUST A BREEDER.

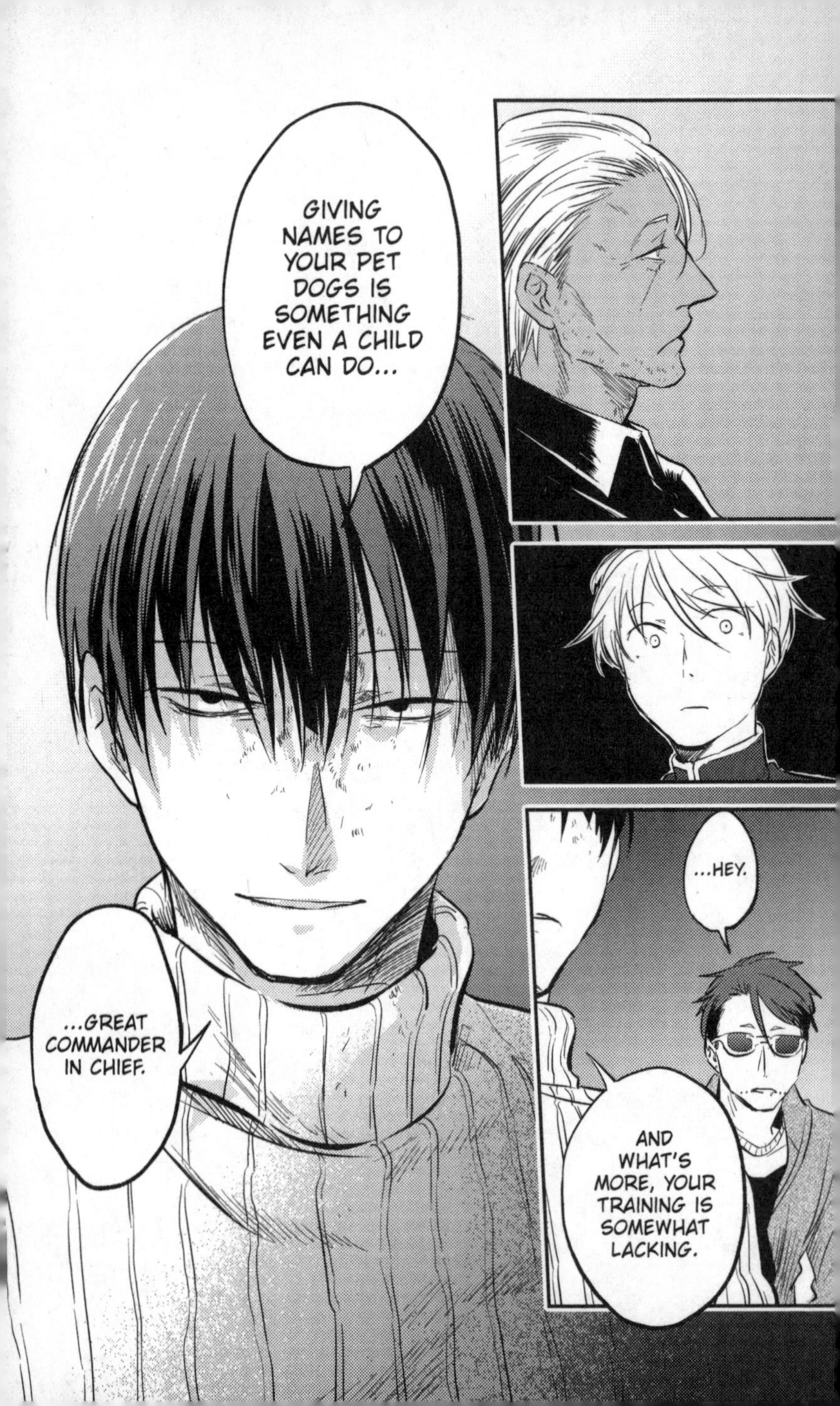
GIVING NAMES TO YOUR PET DOGS IS SOMETHING EVEN A CHILD CAN DO...
...GREAT COMMANDER IN CHIEF.
...HEY.
AND WHAT'S MORE, YOUR TRAINING IS SOMEWHAT LACKING.

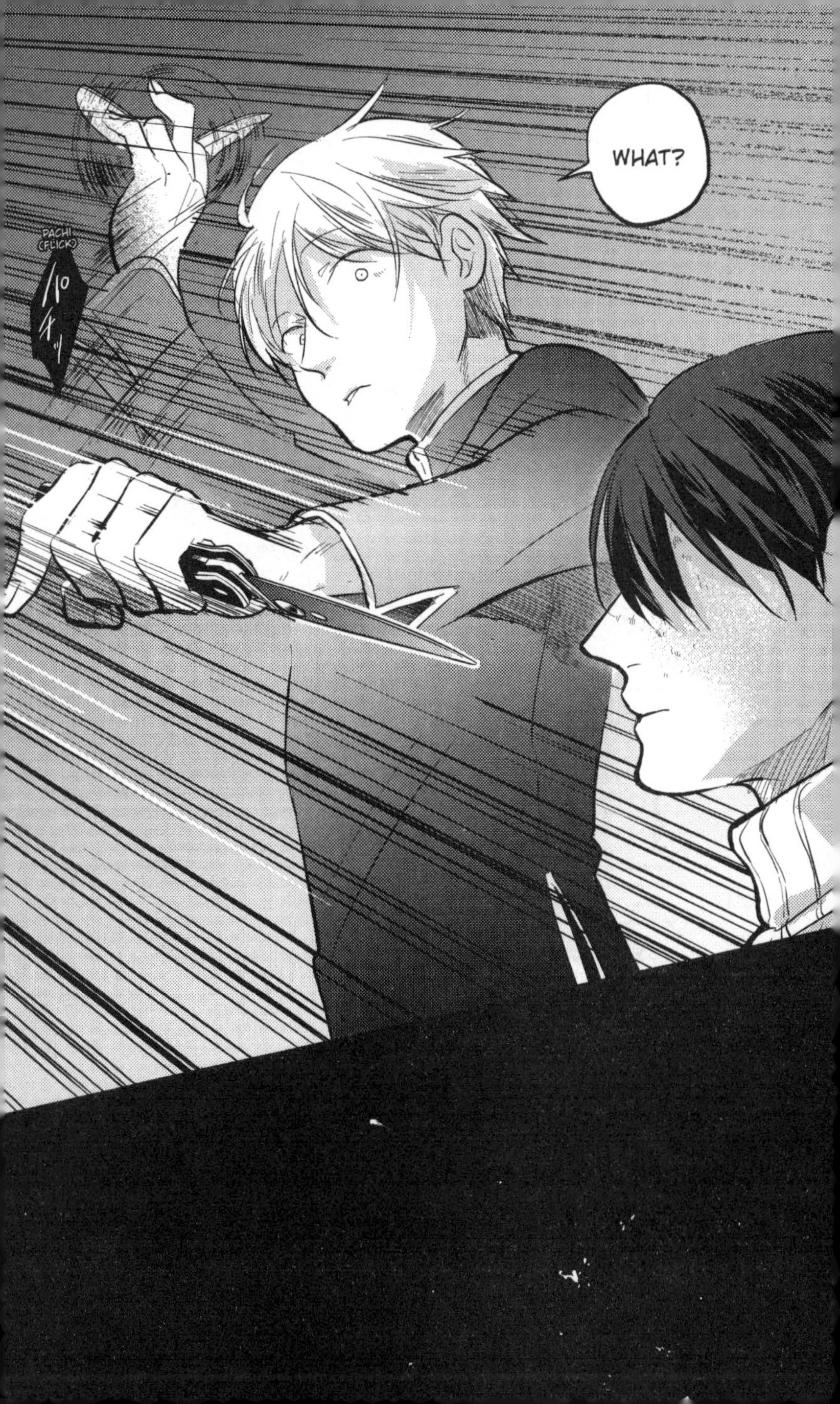
WHAT?
PACHI (FLICK)
パチッ

FILE 25: FIND

IT'S KIND OF AMAZING HOW HIGH AN OPINION NIKKA HAS OF RYANG-HA, LOL. JINON IS NOT THE TYPE TO SHOW MUCH INTEREST IN OTHER PEOPLE, BUT NIKKA SEEMS NOSY, DOESN'T HE?

INCIDENTALLY, 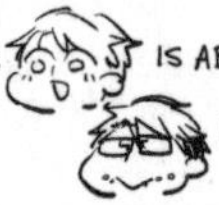 IS ABOUT EIGHTEEN, IS IN HIS EARLY-TO-MID-TWENTIES.

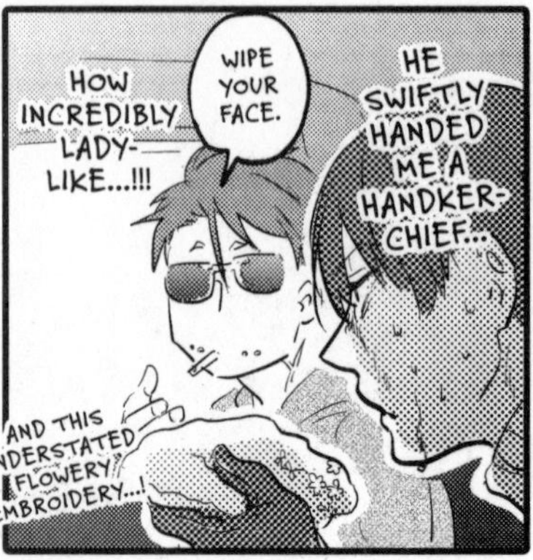
HE SWIFTLY HANDED ME A HANDKER-CHIEF...
WIPE YOUR FACE.
HOW INCREDIBLY LADY-LIKE...!!!
AND THIS UNDERSTATED FLOWERY EMBROIDERY...!

PREPARING SOME SHARDS OF GLASS FOR THE NEXT COVER

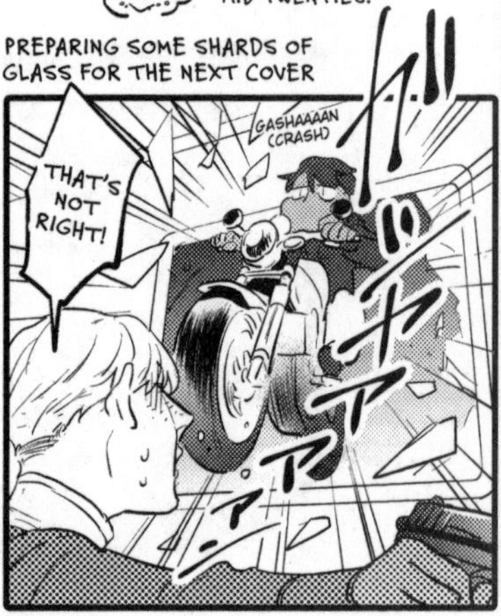
GASHAAAAN (CRASH)
THAT'S NOT RIGHT!
THIS GUY

FILE 26: CONFUSION

IF YOU NEED SOME GLASS BROKEN, INDIAN GUY IS THE MAN FOR THE JOB. (NOTE: SEE INSIDE THE COVER OF VOLUME 2.) SO THIS CHAPTER HAD INDIAN GUY AND CHATEAU'S FIRST (?) TEAM-UP, LOL. BUT THEN THERE'S THIS FORGETTABLE ENEMY CHARACTER—EVEN I FORGET IF HE'S CALLED SAM OR TOM—AND HE CONTINUES TO BE THOROUGHLY UNREMARKABLE...LOL.

FILE 27: IMPOSTER

I FEEL LIKE THIS CHAPTER UNINTENTIONALLY ENDED UP WITH A HUGE AMOUNT OF EXPOSITION IN IT. REREADING IT, I WISH I HAD MANAGED TO SUMMARIZE EVERYTHING A LITTLE BETTER...
ALSO, RYANG-HA GETS EXTREMELY SULLEN WHEN CHATEAU ISN'T NEAR HIM...LOL.

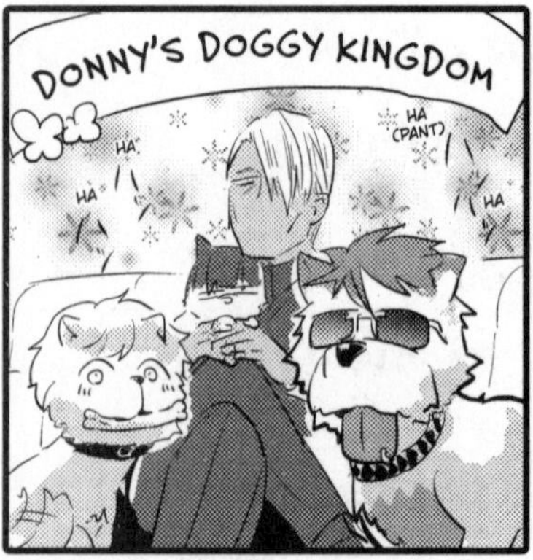
DONNY'S DOGGY KINGDOM
HA (PANT)
HA
HA
HA

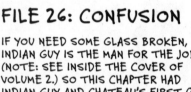

AND NOW, A COMPLETE RIP-OFF
OF A (PAST) REGULAR SEGMENT
FROM *COMIC GENE!*

THIS VOLUME'S
SPECIAL GUEST IS

EURIPEDES RITZLAND!!

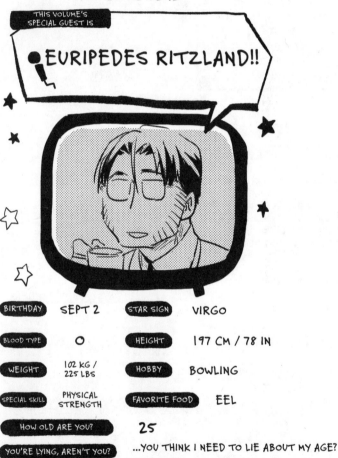

BIRTHDAY	SEPT 2	STAR SIGN	VIRGO
BLOOD TYPE	O	HEIGHT	197 CM / 78 IN
WEIGHT	102 KG / 225 LBS	HOBBY	BOWLING
SPECIAL SKILL	PHYSICAL STRENGTH	FAVORITE FOOD	EEL

HOW OLD ARE YOU? 25

YOU'RE LYING, AREN'T YOU? ...YOU THINK I NEED TO LIE ABOUT MY AGE?

FRANKLY, DON'T YOU LOOK OLD? ISN'T THAT A BIT TOO FRANK?

BY THE WAY, BOSS, YOUR WIFE CALLED ME A LITTLE WHILE AGO

I KNEW IT WAS YOU!!!

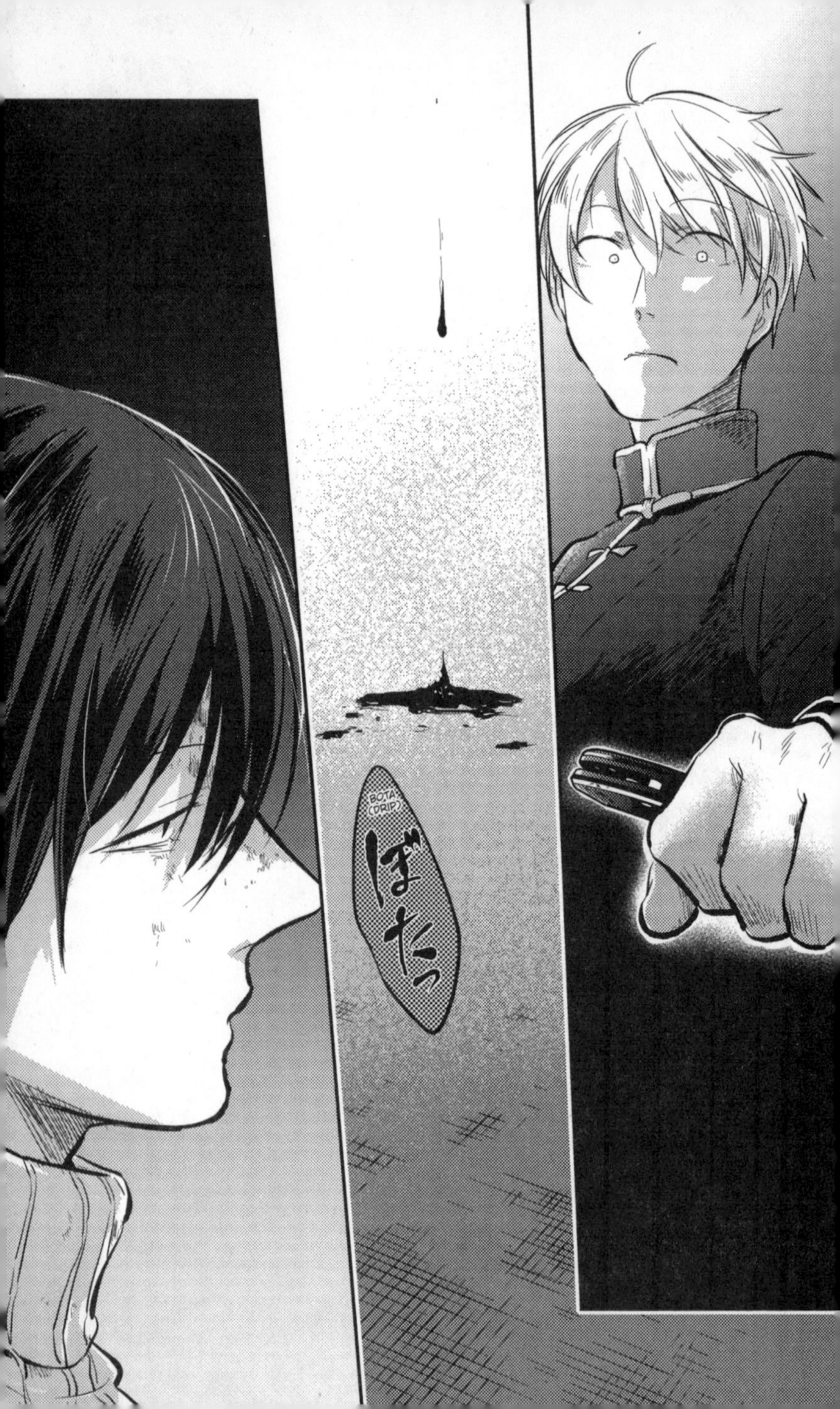
BOTA (DRIP)
ぼたっ

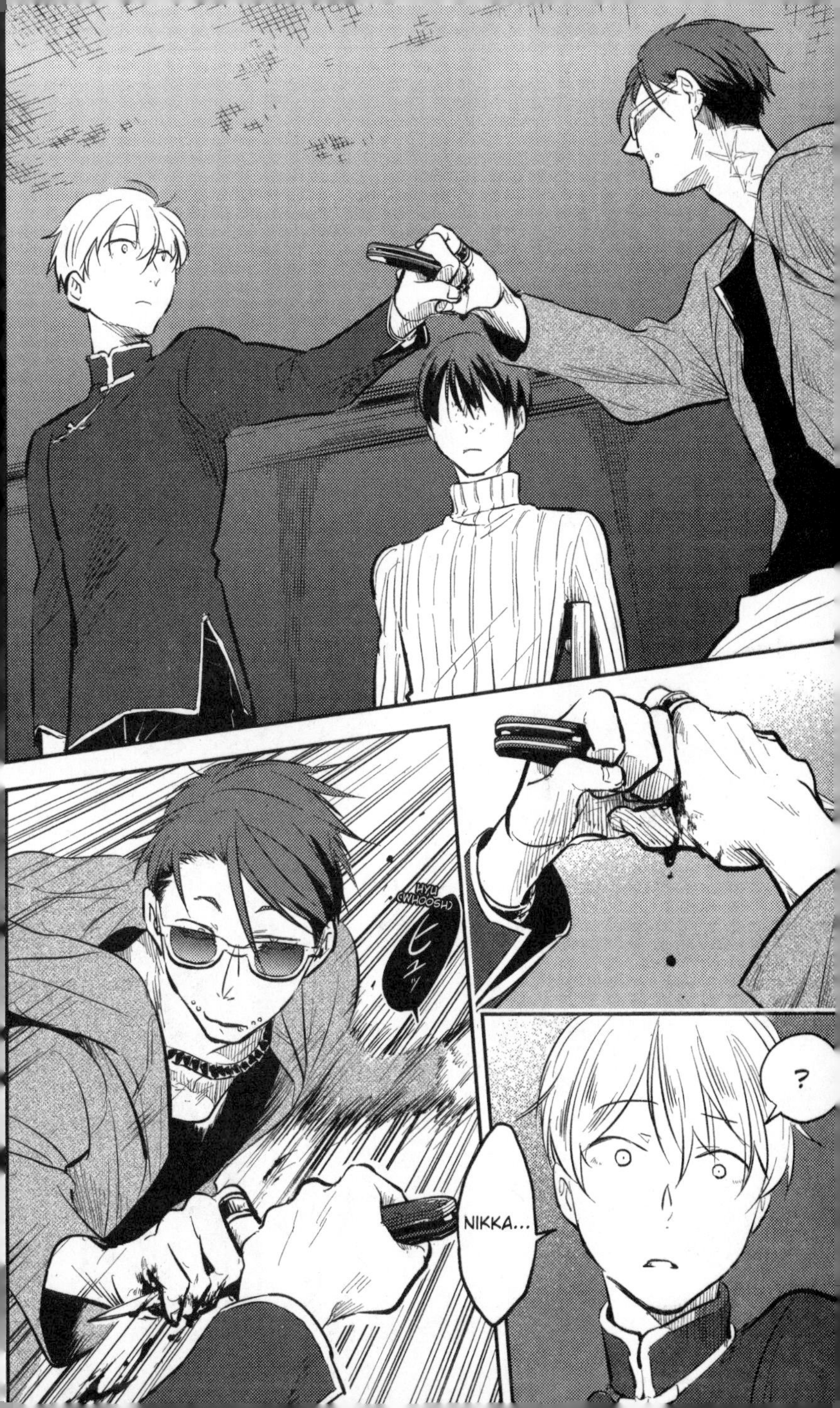
HYU (WHOOSH)
ヒュッ
?
NIKKA...

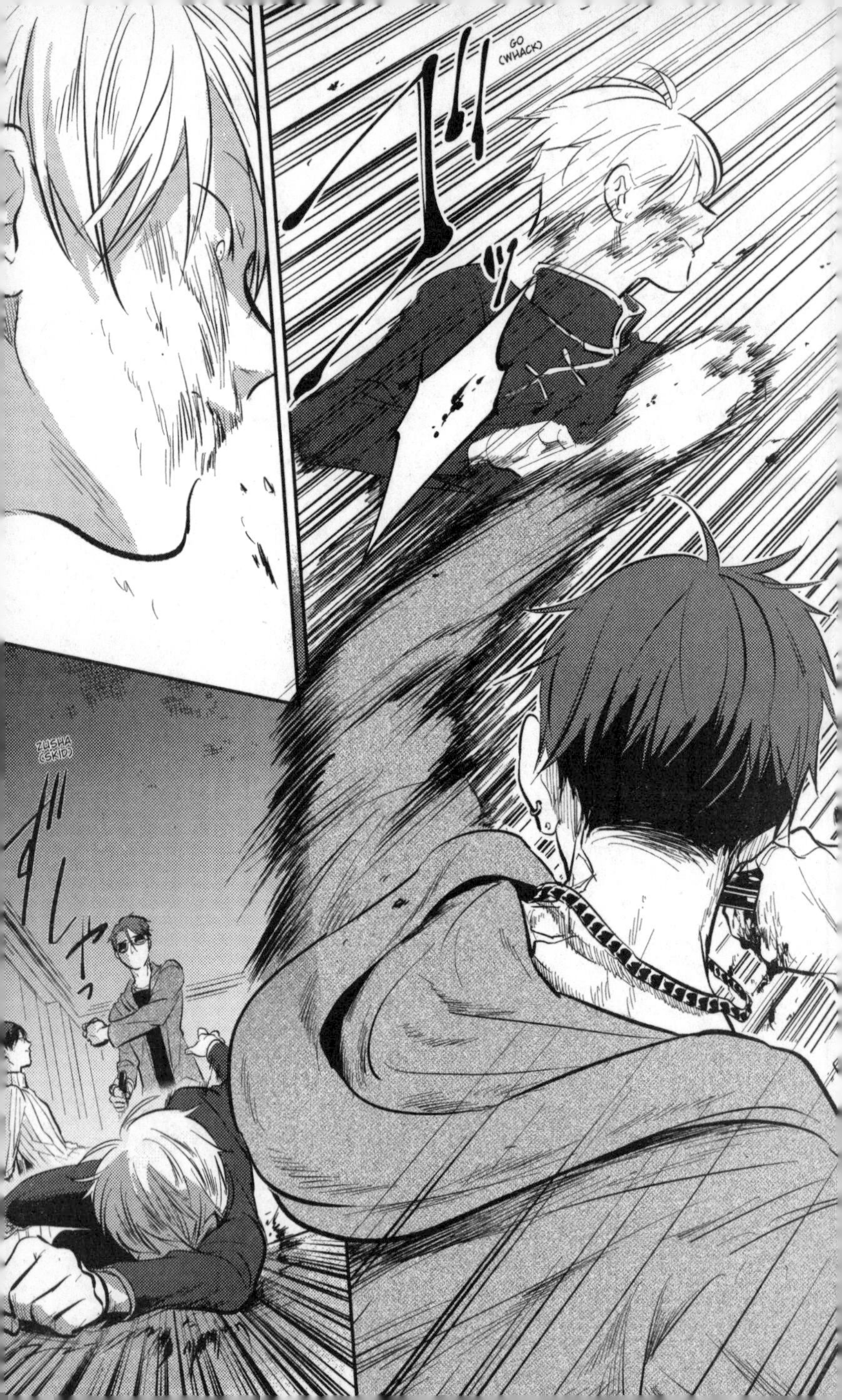
GO
(WHACK)
ZUSHA
(SKID)

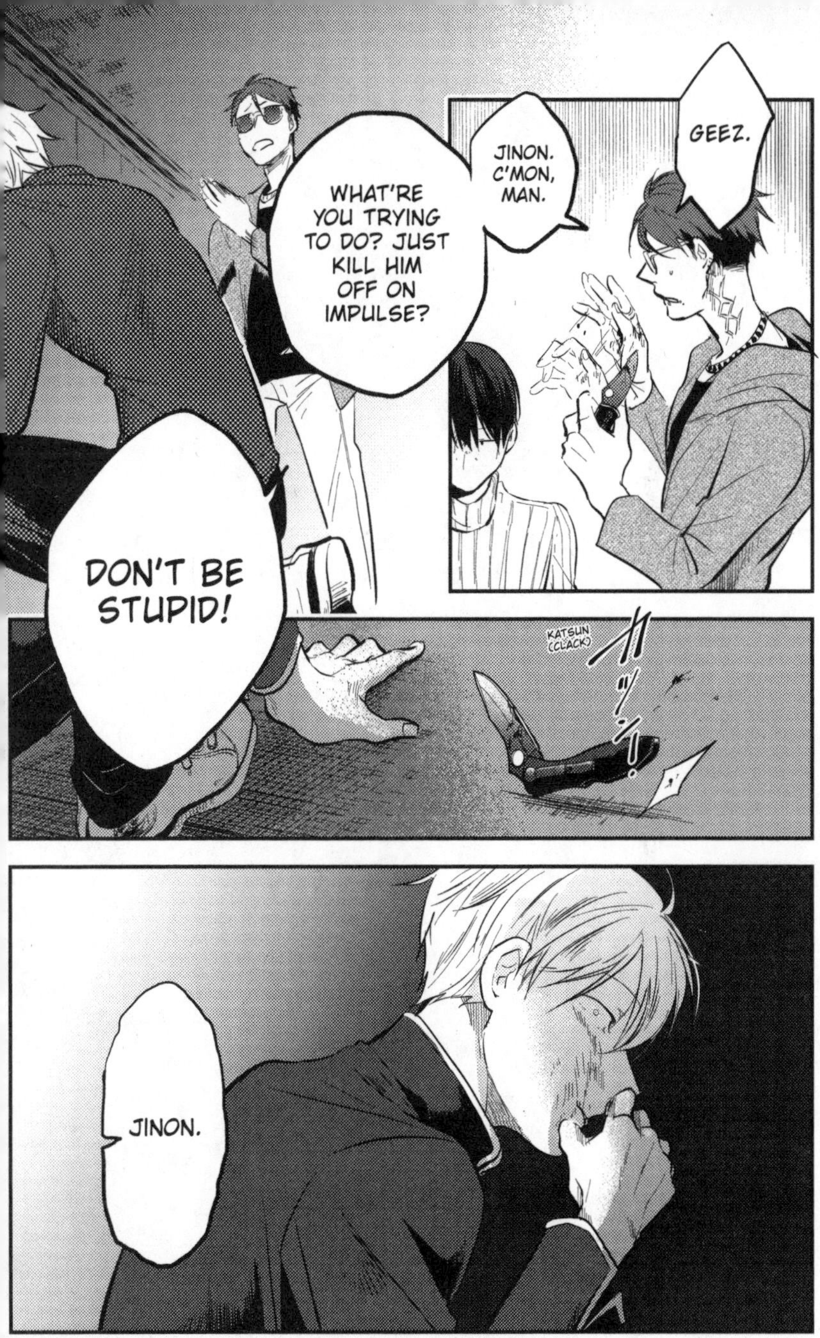
GEEZ.
JINON. C'MON, MAN.
WHAT'RE YOU TRYING TO DO? JUST KILL HIM OFF ON IMPULSE?
DON'T BE STUPID!
KATSUN (CLACK)
JINON.

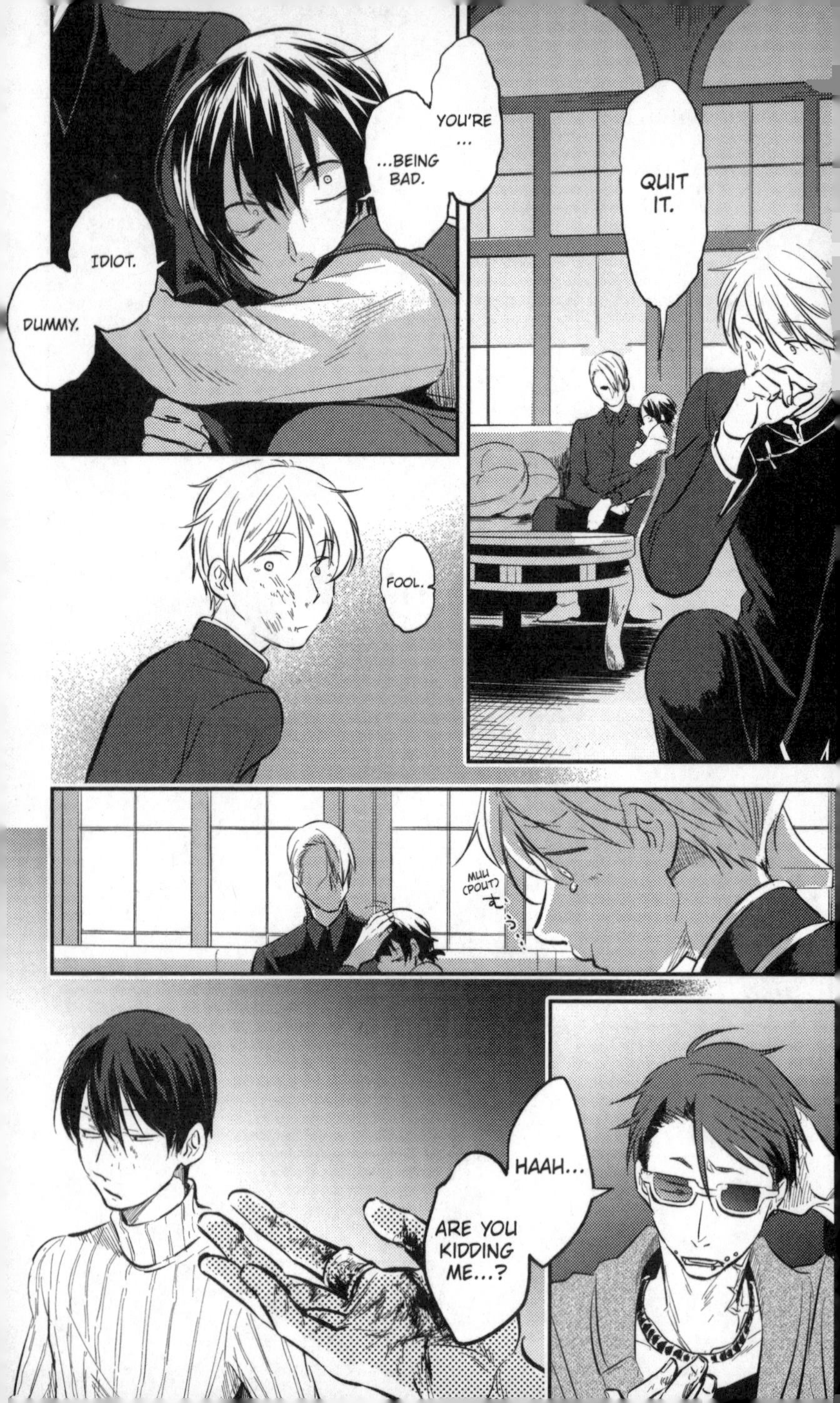
QUIT IT.
YOU'RE ...
...BEING BAD.
IDIOT.
DUMMY.
FOOL.
MUU (POUT)
む
HAAH...
ARE YOU KIDDING ME...?

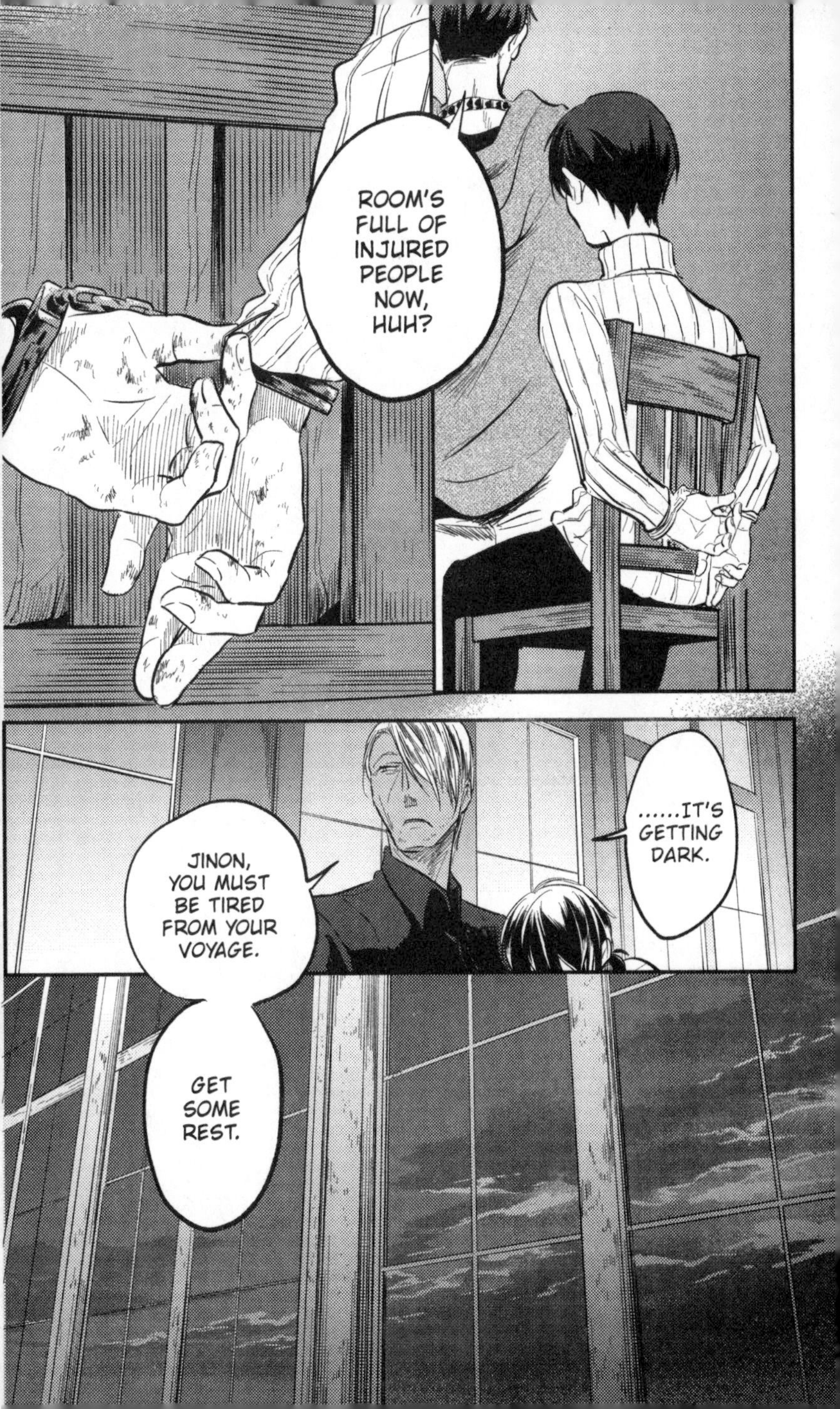
ROOM'S FULL OF INJURED PEOPLE NOW, HUH?
......IT'S GETTING DARK.
JINON, YOU MUST BE TIRED FROM YOUR VOYAGE.
GET SOME REST.

FILE 28 A WAR TRIGGER

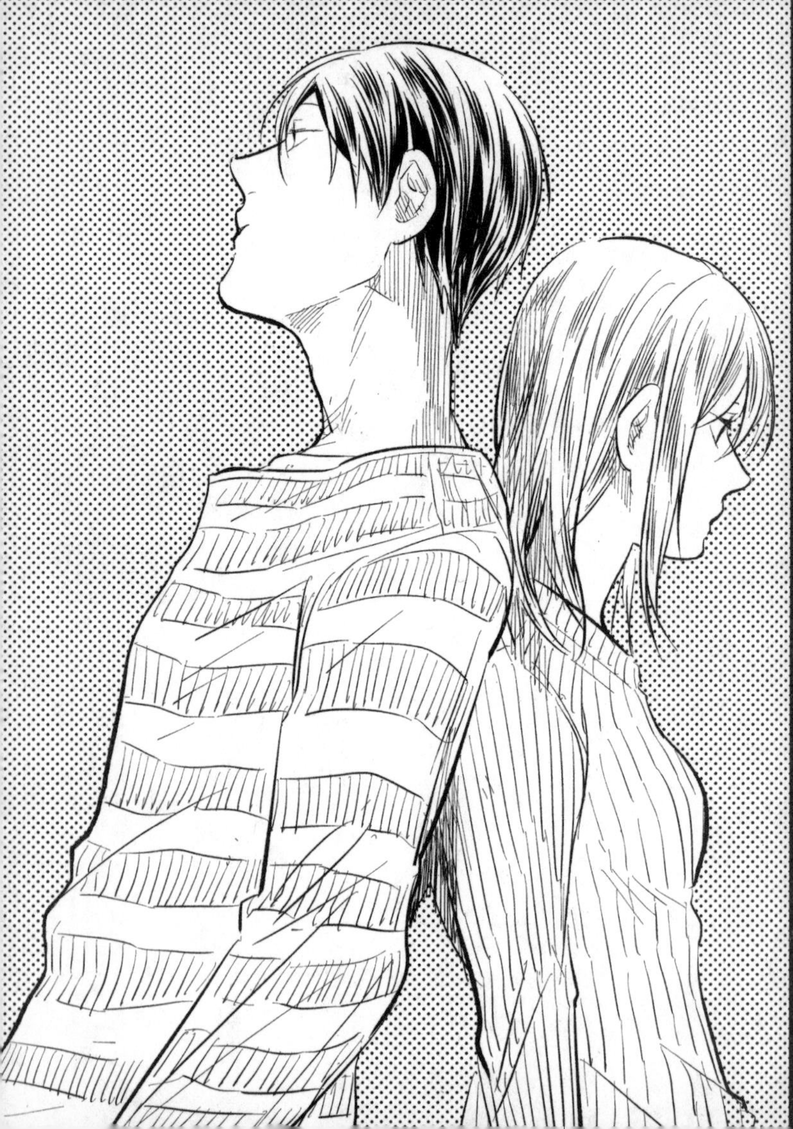

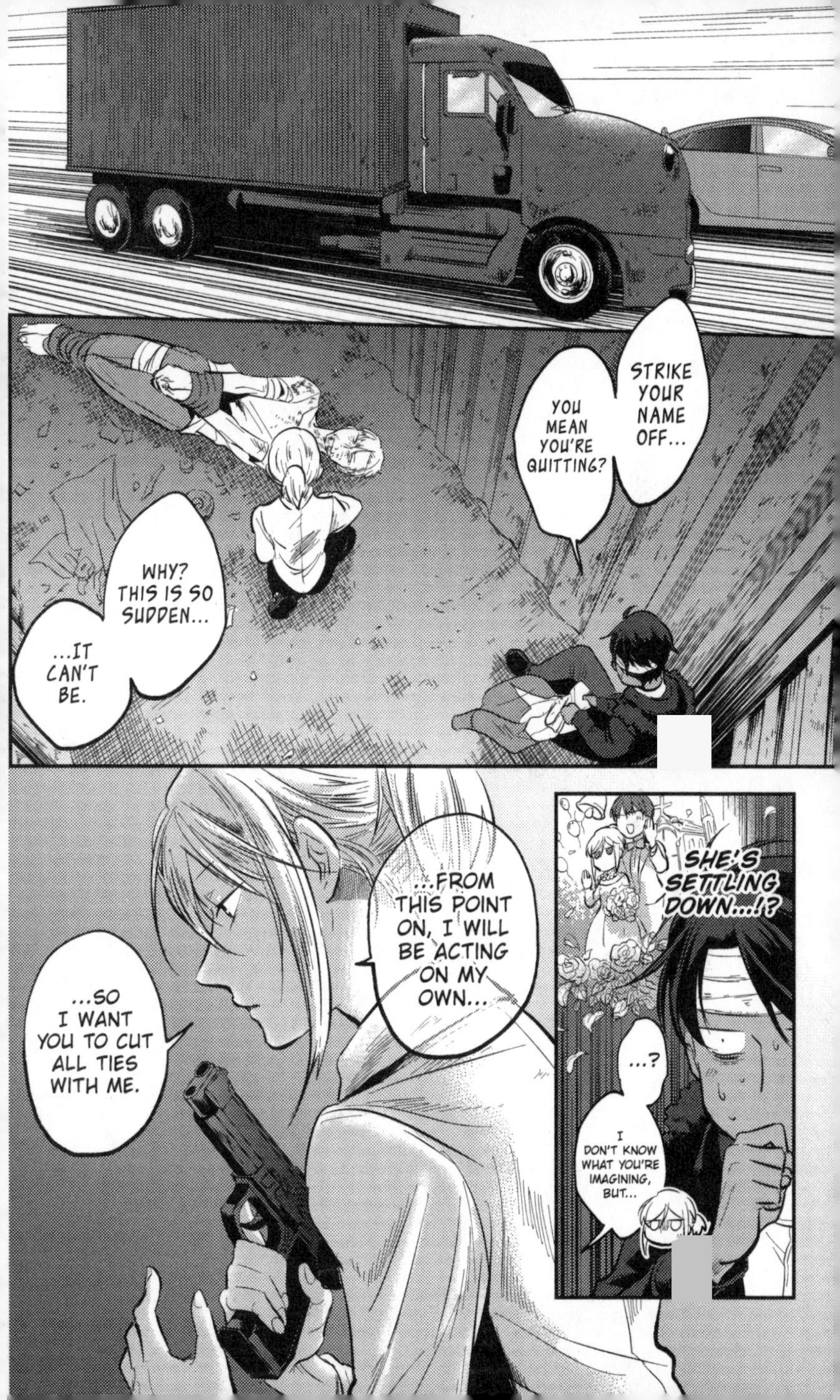
STRIKE YOUR NAME OFF...
YOU MEAN YOU'RE QUITTING?
WHY? THIS IS SO SUDDEN...
...IT CAN'T BE.
SHE'S SETTLING DOWN...!?
...?
I DON'T KNOW WHAT YOU'RE IMAGINING, BUT...
...FROM THIS POINT ON, I WILL BE ACTING ON MY OWN...
...SO I WANT YOU TO CUT ALL TIES WITH ME.

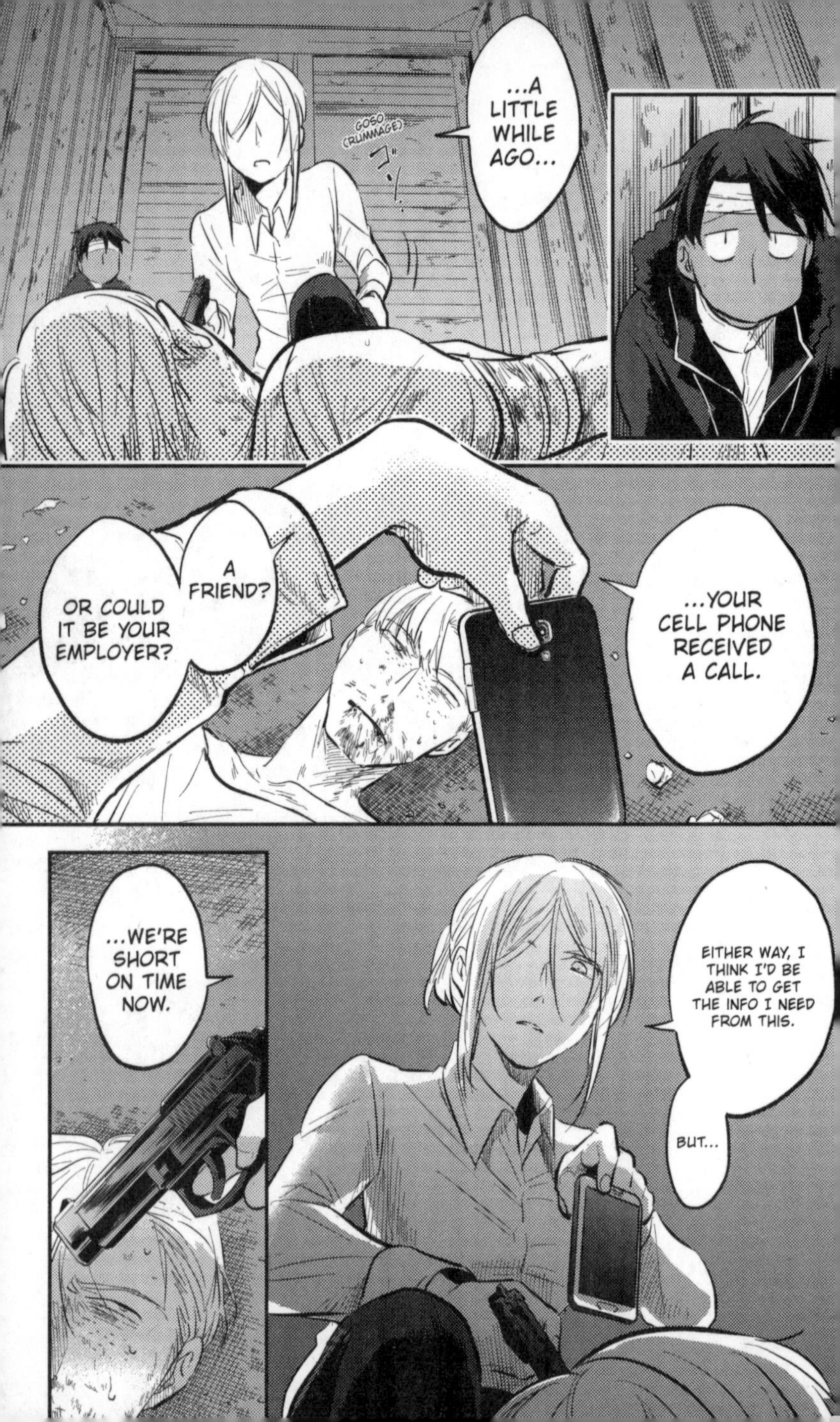
...A LITTLE WHILE AGO...
GOSO (RUMMAGE)
...YOUR CELL PHONE RECEIVED A CALL.
A FRIEND?
OR COULD IT BE YOUR EMPLOYER?
EITHER WAY, I THINK I'D BE ABLE TO GET THE INFO I NEED FROM THIS.
BUT...
...WE'RE SHORT ON TIME NOW.

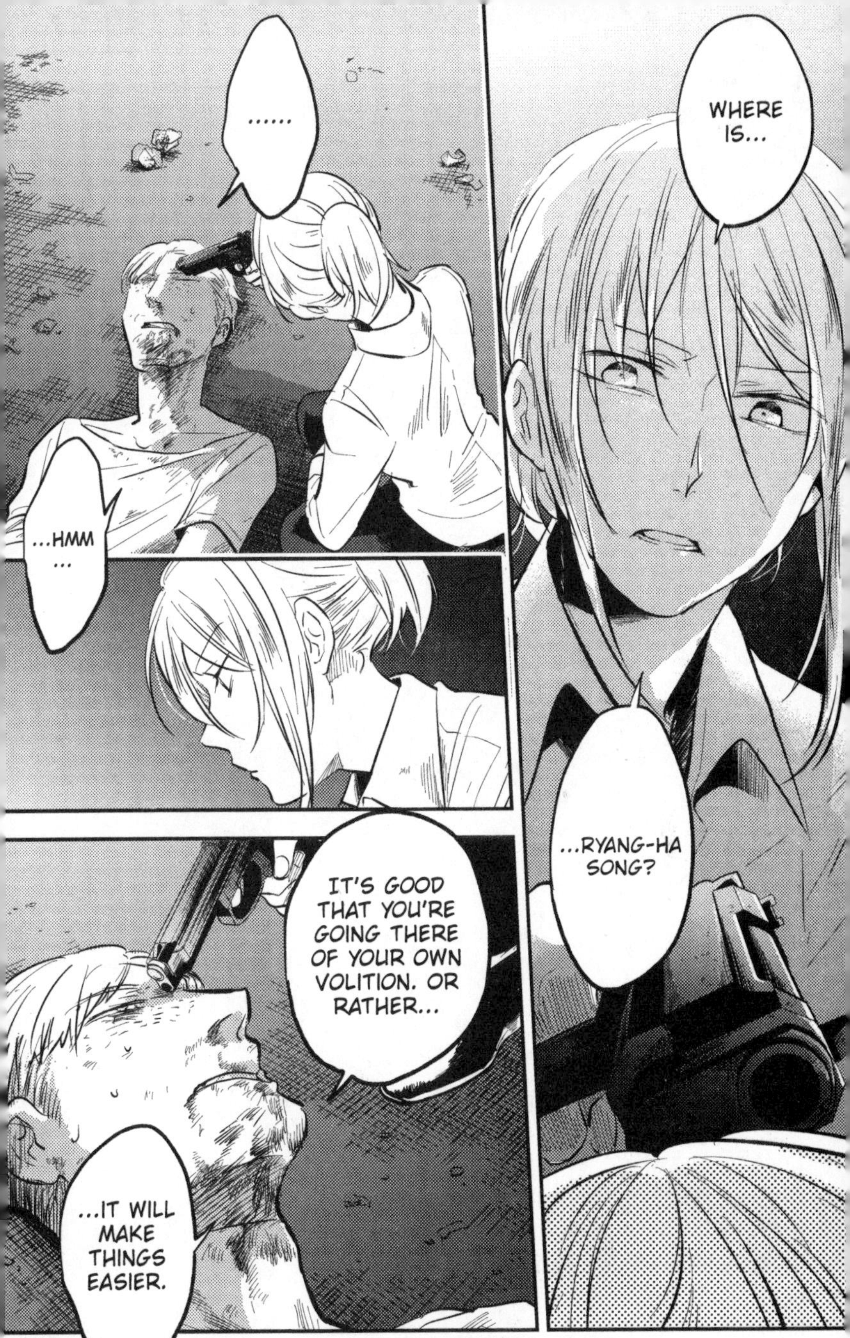
WHERE IS...
...RYANG-HA SONG?
......
...HMM ...
IT'S GOOD THAT YOU'RE GOING THERE OF YOUR OWN VOLITION. OR RATHER...
...IT WILL MAKE THINGS EASIER.

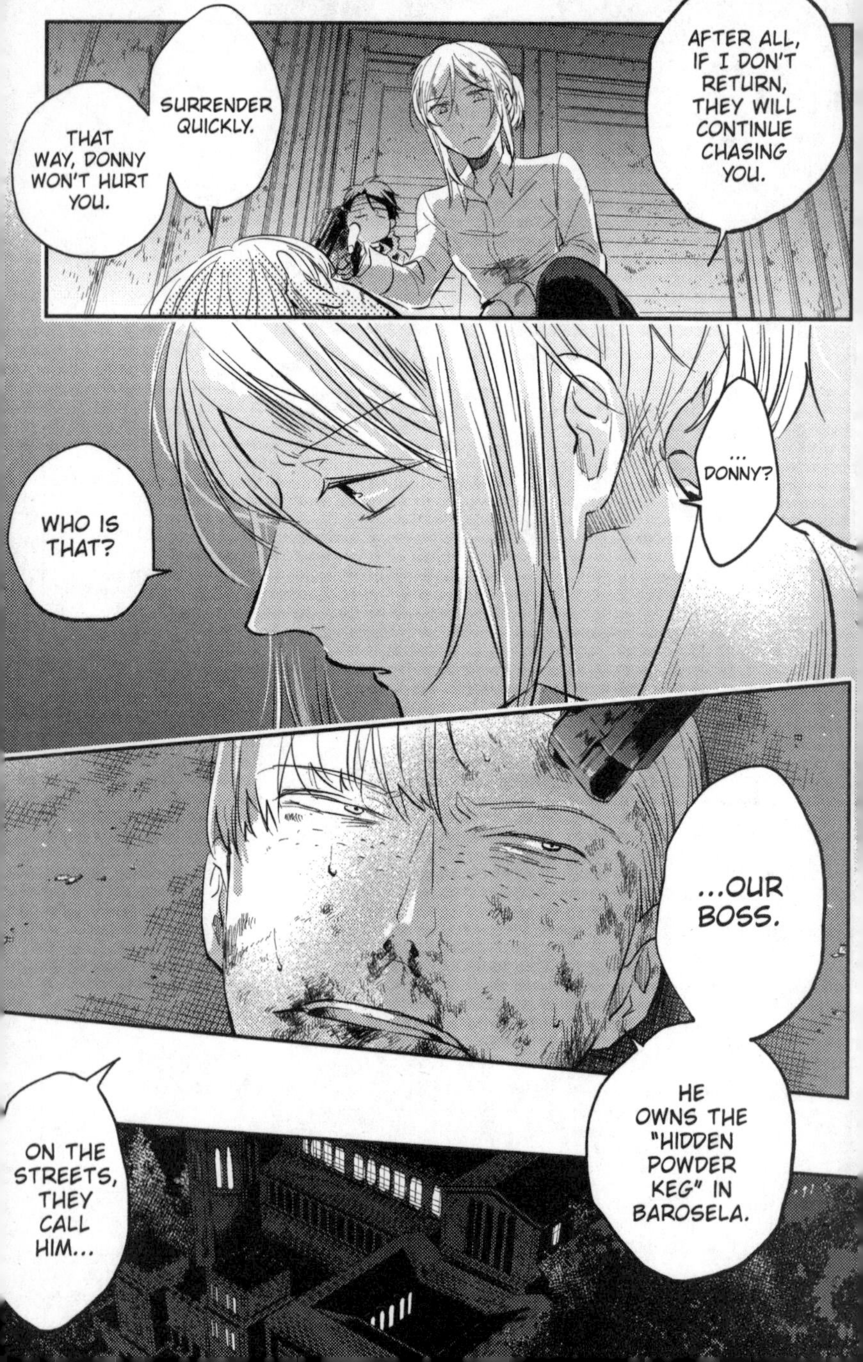
AFTER ALL, IF I DON'T RETURN, THEY WILL CONTINUE CHASING YOU.
SURRENDER QUICKLY.
THAT WAY, DONNY WON'T HURT YOU.
... DONNY?
WHO IS THAT?
...OUR BOSS.
HE OWNS THE "HIDDEN POWDER KEG" IN BAROSELA.
ON THE STREETS, THEY CALL HIM...

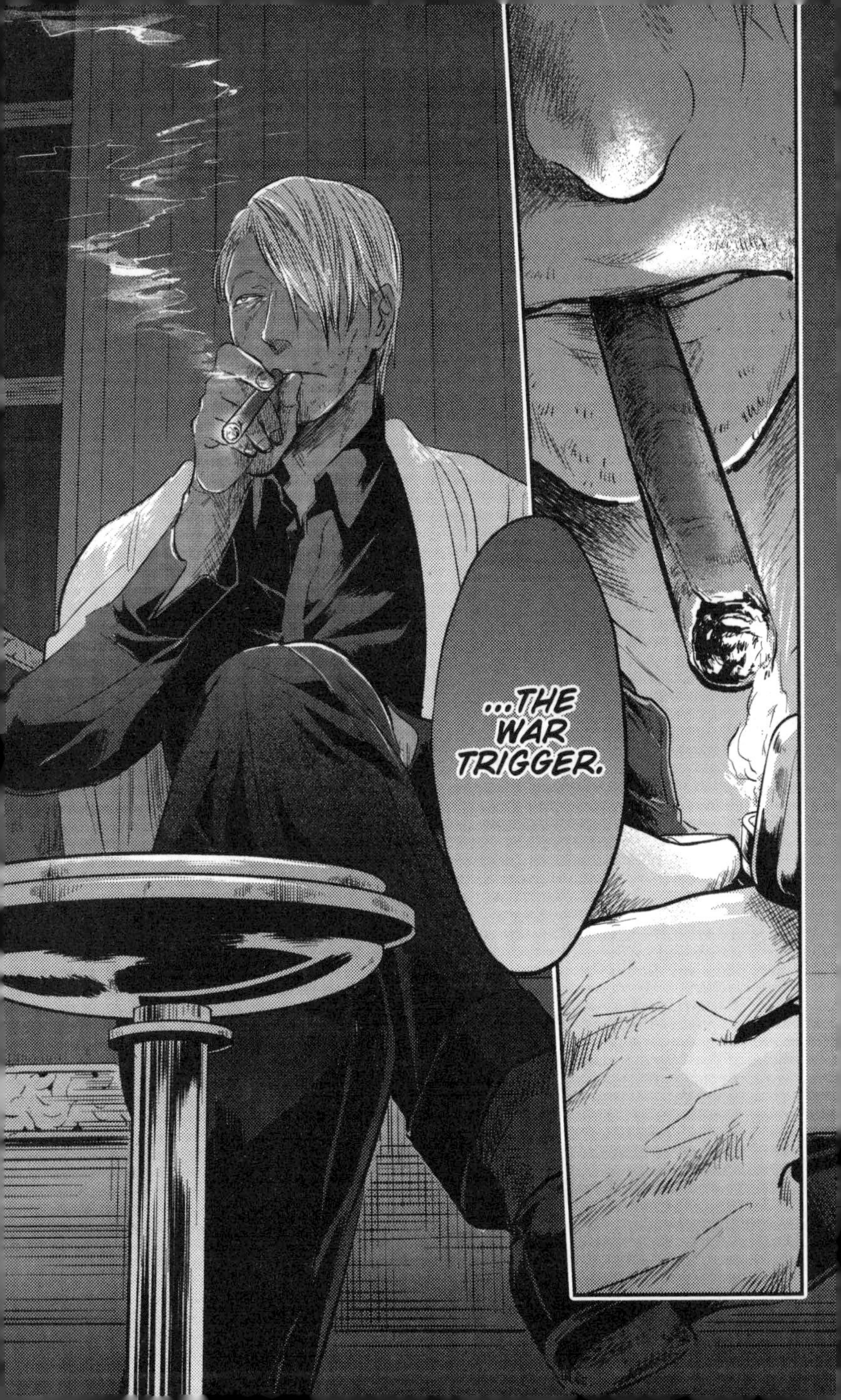
...THE WAR TRIGGER.

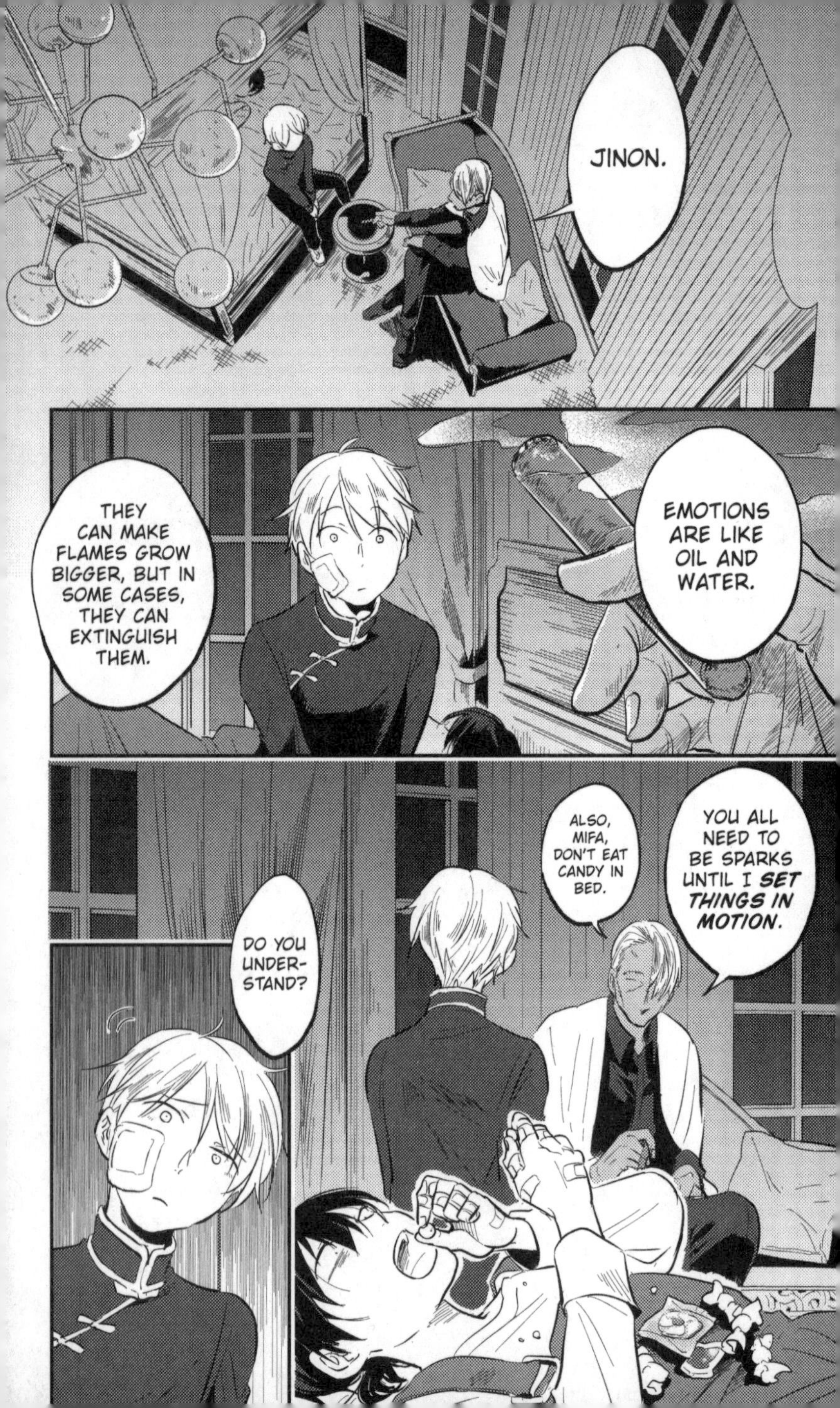
JINON.
EMOTIONS ARE LIKE OIL AND WATER.
THEY CAN MAKE FLAMES GROW BIGGER, BUT IN SOME CASES, THEY CAN EXTINGUISH THEM.
YOU ALL NEED TO BE SPARKS UNTIL I *SET THINGS IN MOTION*.
ALSO, MIFA, DON'T EAT CANDY IN BED.
DO YOU UNDER-STAND?

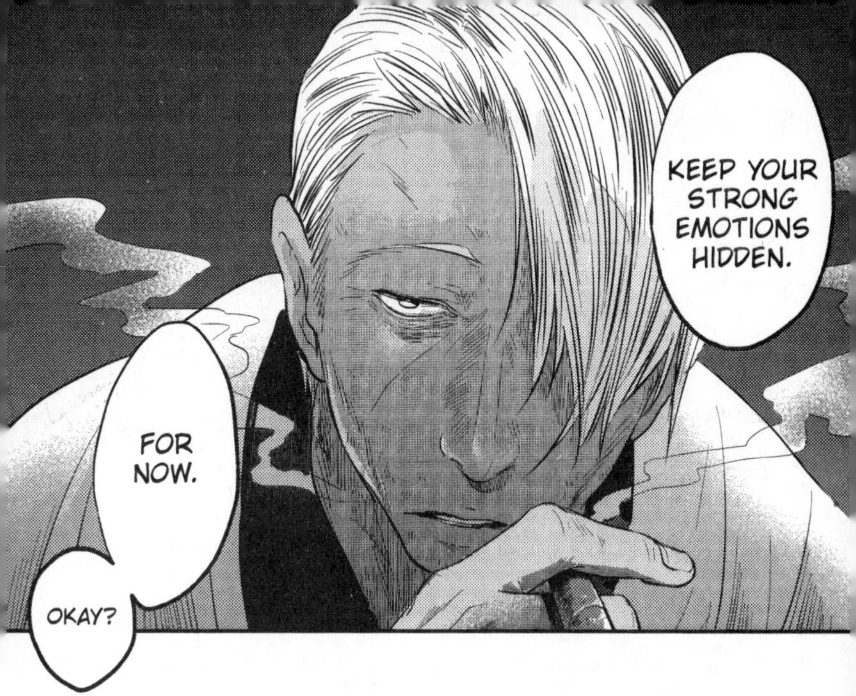
KEEP YOUR STRONG EMOTIONS HIDDEN.
FOR NOW.
OKAY?

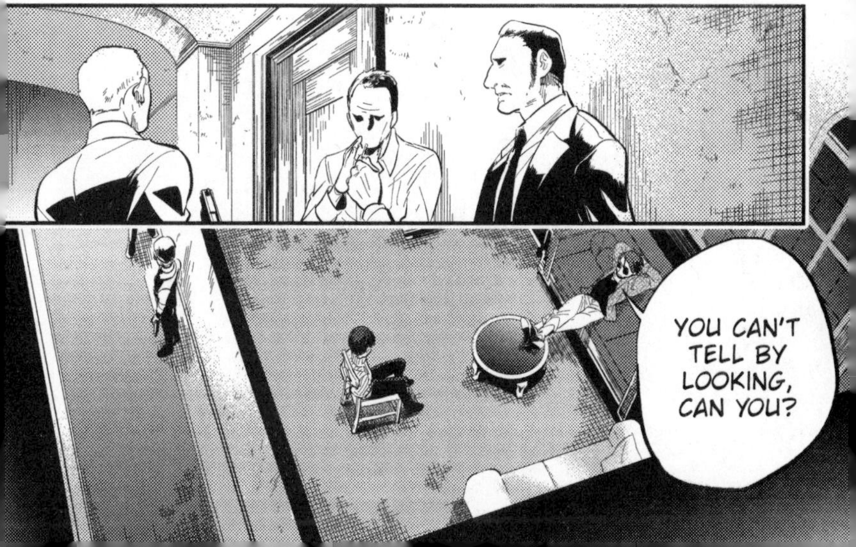
YOU CAN'T TELL BY LOOKING, CAN YOU?

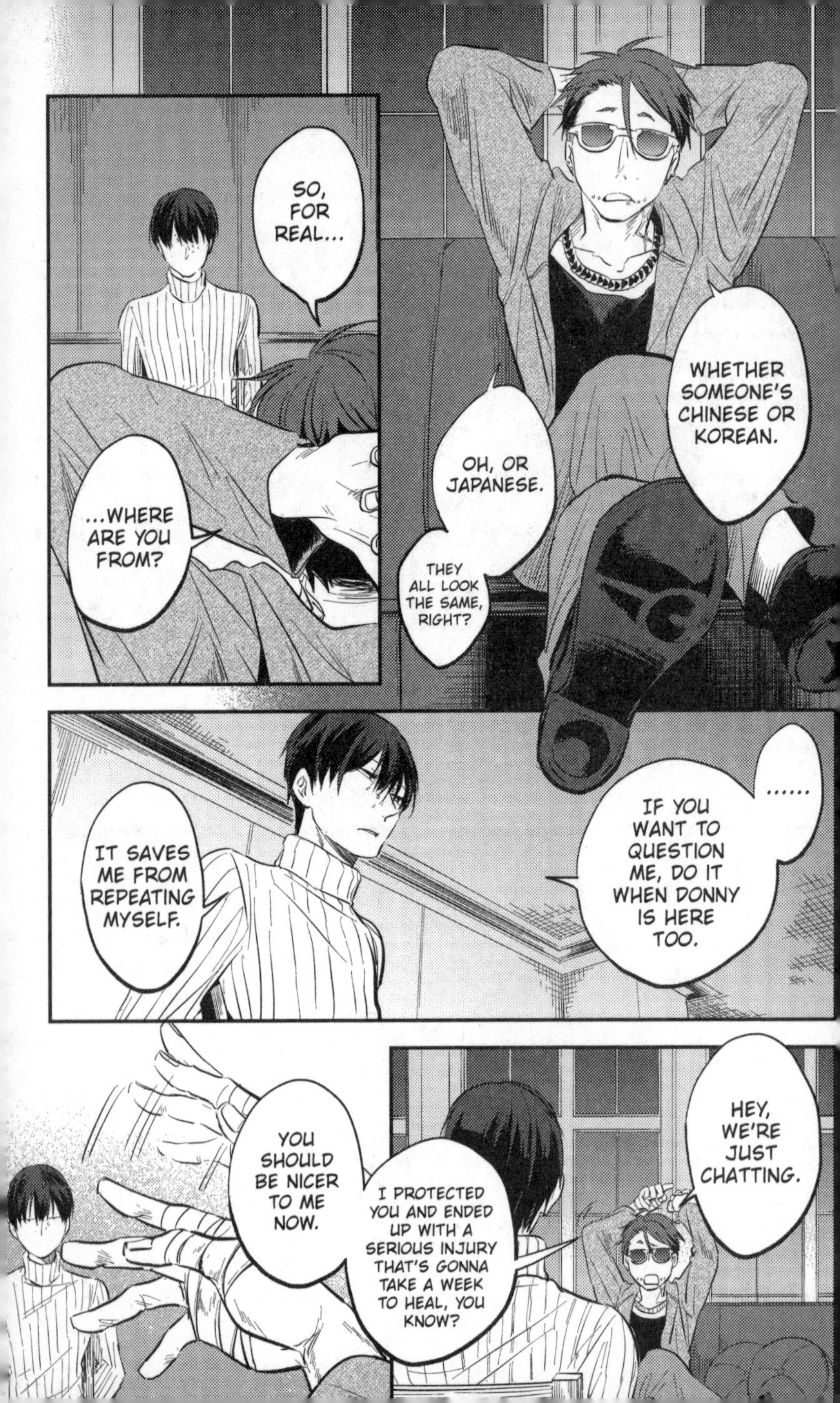
WHETHER SOMEONE'S CHINESE OR KOREAN.
OH, OR JAPANESE.
THEY ALL LOOK THE SAME, RIGHT?
SO, FOR REAL...
...WHERE ARE YOU FROM?
......
IF YOU WANT TO QUESTION ME, DO IT WHEN DONNY IS HERE TOO.
IT SAVES ME FROM REPEATING MYSELF.
HEY, WE'RE JUST CHATTING.
I PROTECTED YOU AND ENDED UP WITH A SERIOUS INJURY THAT'S GONNA TAKE A WEEK TO HEAL, YOU KNOW?
YOU SHOULD BE NICER TO ME NOW.

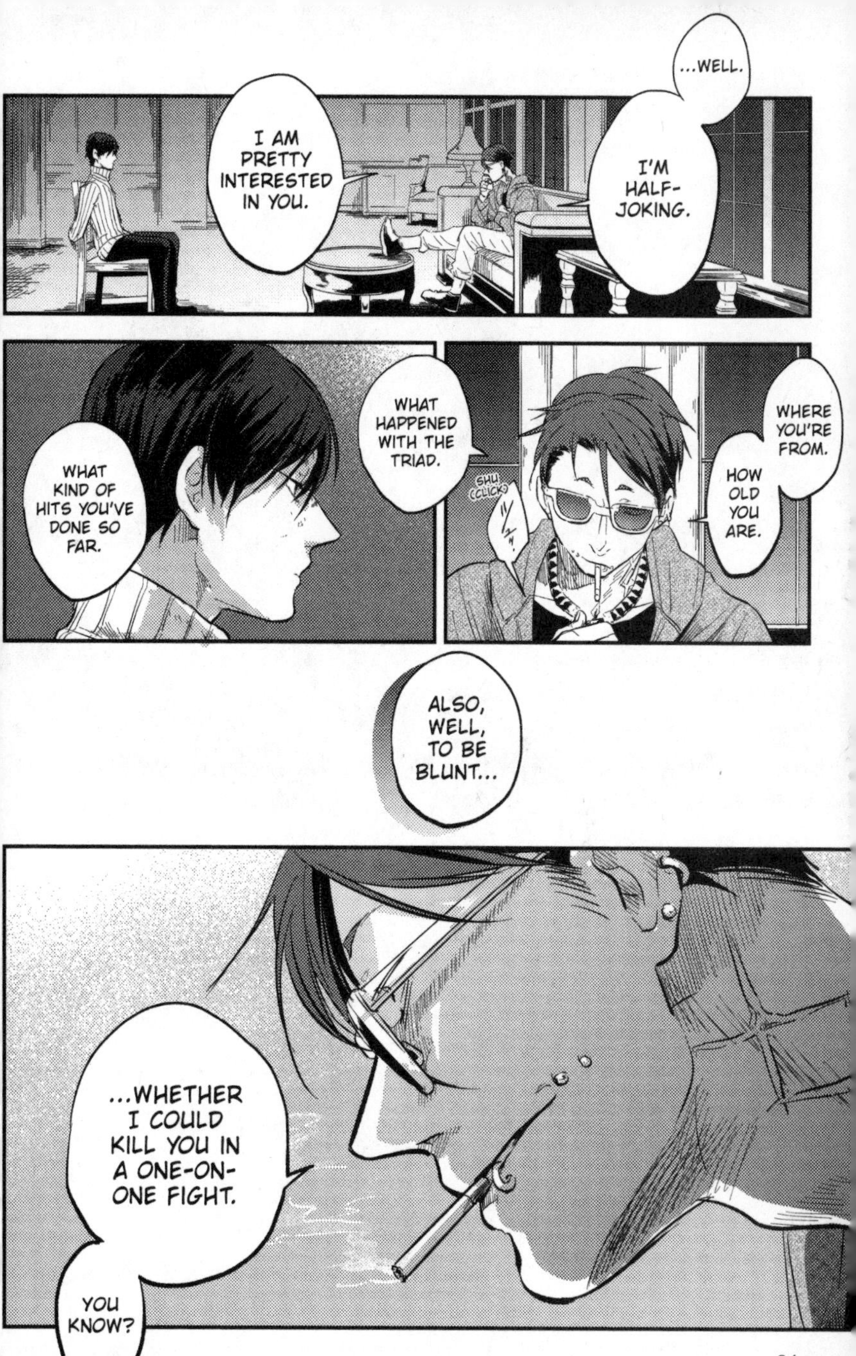
...WELL.
I'M HALF-JOKING.
I AM PRETTY INTERESTED IN YOU.
WHERE YOU'RE FROM.
HOW OLD YOU ARE.
SHU (CLICK)
WHAT HAPPENED WITH THE TRIAD.
WHAT KIND OF HITS YOU'VE DONE SO FAR.
ALSO, WELL, TO BE BLUNT...
...WHETHER I COULD KILL YOU IN A ONE-ON-ONE FIGHT.
YOU KNOW?

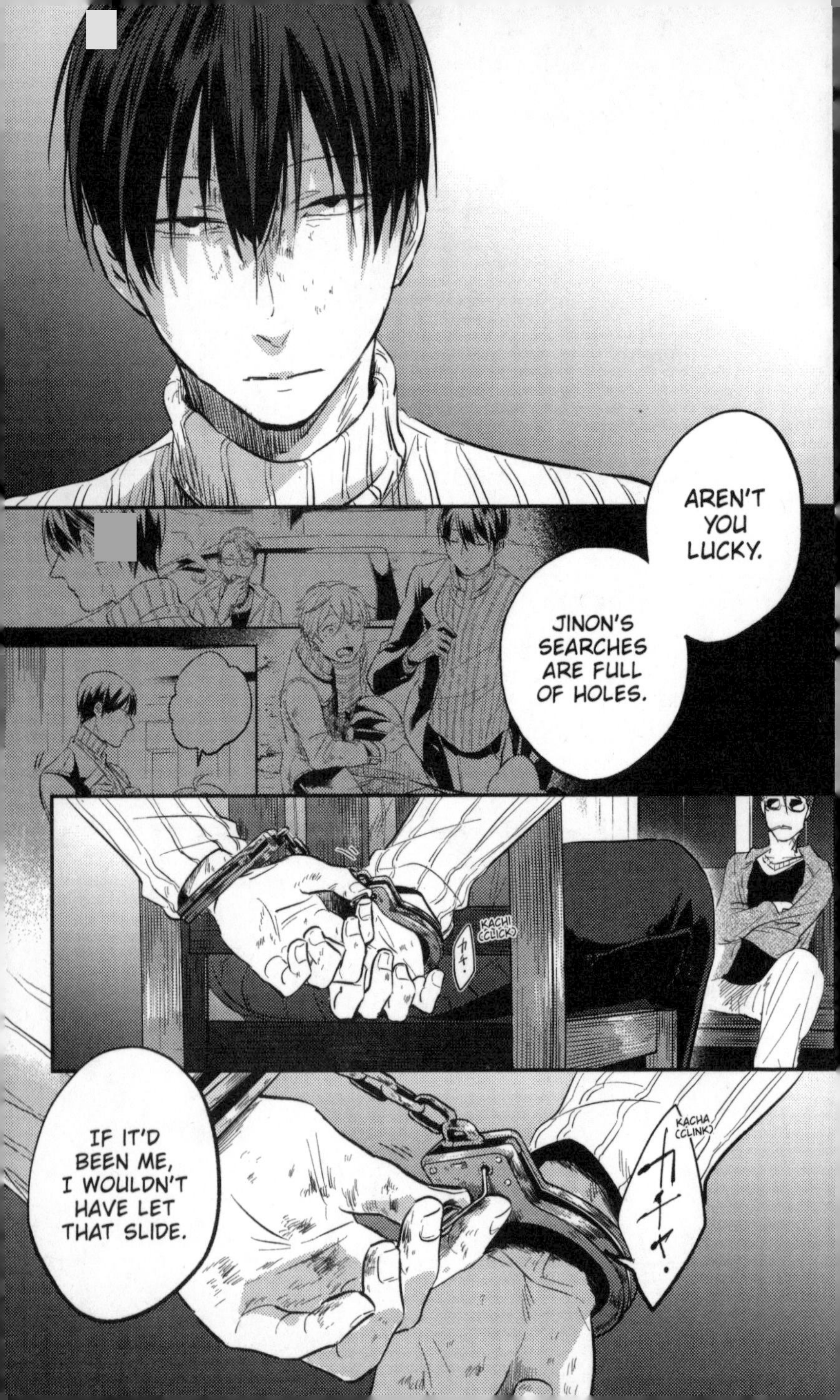

AREN'T YOU LUCKY.
JINON'S SEARCHES ARE FULL OF HOLES.
KACHI (CLICK)
KACHA (CLINK)
IF IT'D BEEN ME, I WOULDN'T HAVE LET THAT SLIDE.

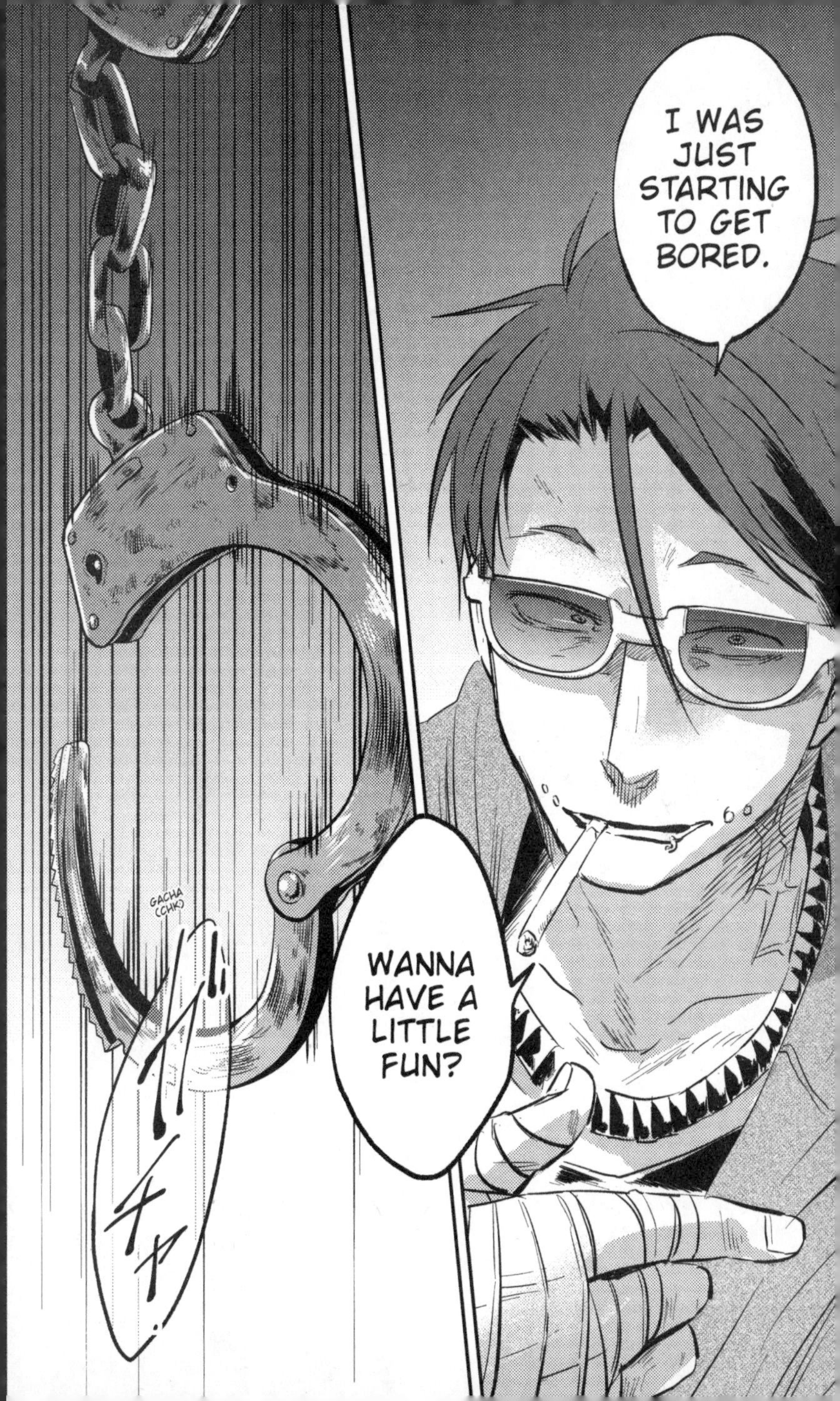
I WAS JUST STARTING TO GET BORED.
WANNA HAVE A LITTLE FUN?
GACHA (CHK)

GENE HISTORY

IN THIS SEGMENT, WE LEARN THE HISTORY OF ARTISTS WHOSE WORK IS PRINTED IN *COMIC GENE*♪
MAYBE WE'LL FIND OUT ABOUT THE HARDSHIPS OR SURPRISING ASPECTS OF WHAT GOES INTO BECOMING A MANGA ARTIST!?

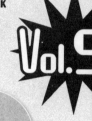

Vol.9

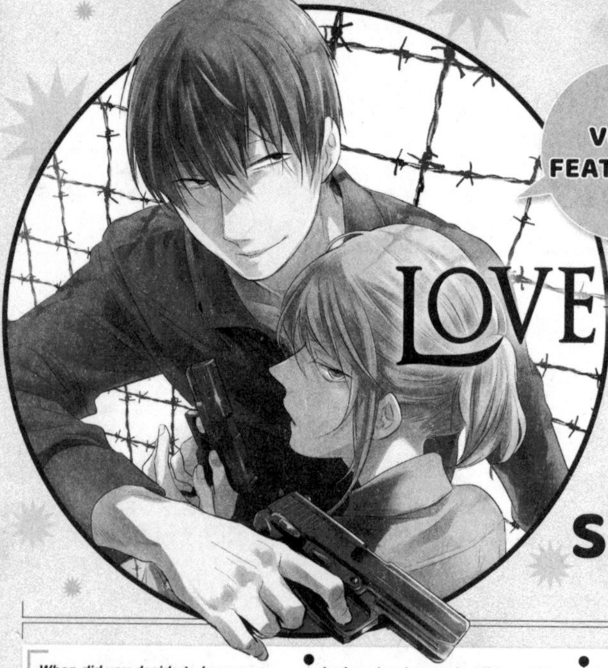

VOL.9 FEATURES...

LOVE OF KILL

FE-SENSEI

When did you decide to become a manga artist? What made you set your heart on being a manga artist?

I feel like I dreamed of being a manga artist when I was in elementary school. But I'm not sure you could say I had set my heart on it...Although I did have aspirations, beyond a certain age I gave up on them, or rather I didn't think I could make it as a manga artist. I earnestly enjoyed drawing, so while working for a company, I used to create something like a manga online as a hobby.

When did you make your first submission?

I have never submitted anything for a manga prize.

How did you make your debut?

I was uploading bits and pieces of a manga called *I Just Wanna Read a Short Comic About a Couple of Killers* to Pixiv for fun when I was asked if I would like to publish it as a series. They contacted me through social media, so I was suspicious, thinking it might be a prank, and called the Kadokawa support center. That is a good memory now, lol.

How did you feel when your debut work was published?

I felt more embarrassed than happy. I couldn't look directly at the issue of *Comic Gene* that my manga was printed in and left it as an offering on the Buddhist altar for several days.

Are there any differences between how you pictured being a manga artist and the reality of the job?

I thought that editors would be much scarier, so I was surprised when they turned out to be quite nice, lol.

What do you like about working as a manga artist?

Drawing pictures and manga was already a hobby of mine in itself, but knowing that something I drew could be a source of enjoyment for someone else and that this counts as a job makes me feel very happy and fulfilled.

What is your favorite step of the manga-making process?

I am only able to excitedly draw out storyboards on rare occasions, but those are my favorite moments. On the other hand, I am not so fond of inking. Having to somehow clean up all the sloppy lines that I glossed over during the sketching stage is painful...

How did you feel about* Love of Kill *being adapted into a drama CD?

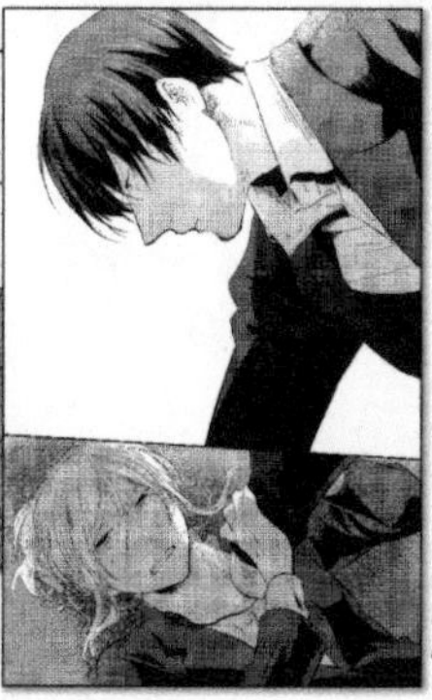

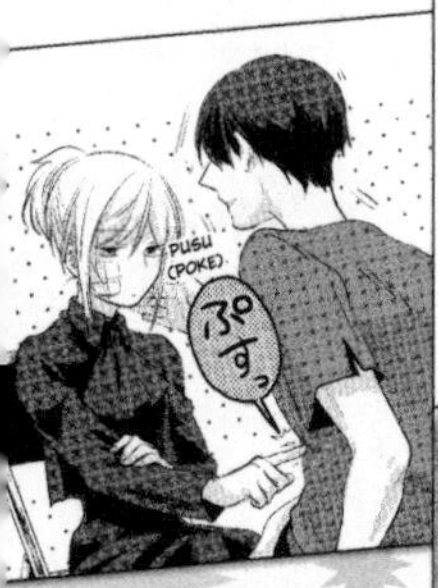
PUSU (POKE)
ぷすっ

SOMETIMES HOSTILE, SOMETIMES FRIENDLY...RYANG-HA AND CHATEAU KEEP AN IMPECCABLE DISTANCE IN THEIR RELATIONSHIP.

When I first heard about it from my editor, I felt quite doubtful...Would they really launch a project like that for my manga? Once voice actors were finalized and drafts were handed over to a scriptwriter and it all started to feel real, I was honestly extremely happy. When I think about all the different people who were involved in the recording and production aspects of making the CD adaptation, I am filled with gratitude.

One of the charms of Love of Kill is its wide variety of characters, but do you have a particular favorite?

Naturally, I have a fondness for the two main characters. Because this manga started off, so to speak, with just these two characters, Ryang-Ha and Chateau. In addition, I suppose I like a lot of the relationships between the characters, such as the boss and Indian Guy's interactions, and Hou and Seung-Woo's mentor-mentee relationship.

Even as the serious developments in the story increase, Indian Guy is there to provide comfort. Please tell us about how he came to be.

I hadn't planned to make him a regular character. He came about because, right when I was thinking that there should be a supporting character working at the company, I heard from someone that people from India are supposedly very good at data processing. I never imagined that the manga would be serialized, and he would be given a voice actor, all while he still had the name Indian Guy...

What book genres do you generally read?

A lot of manga, but I occasionally read fiction and light novels as well. I also like looking at photobooks of foreign cities and interior design books. Recently, in the name of gathering reference material, I started buying men's fashion magazines, but they haven't had any effect at all on my work...lol.

Are there any works that have influenced you, or artists you think of as role models?

When I first started drawing, I feel like I was influenced by the members of CLAMP. I came to love manga

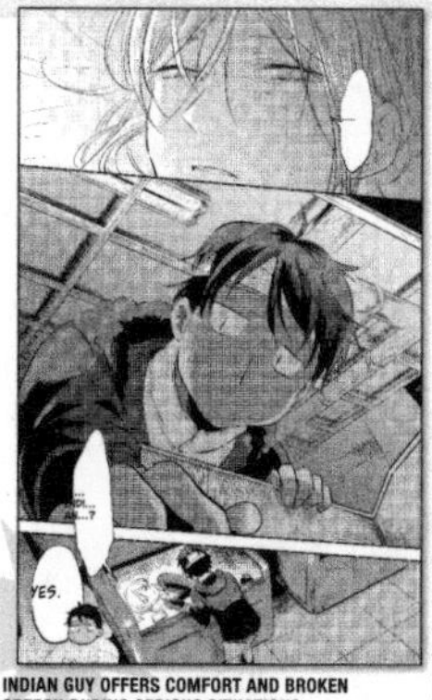
YES.

INDIAN GUY OFFERS COMFORT AND BROKEN SPEECH DURING SERIOUS SITUATIONS.

because of Yoshihiro Togashi-sensei's *Hunter x Hunter*. It has many cruel plot twists that thrill me every time. *Love of Kill* itself was hugely influenced by Keitaro Takahashi-sensei's *Destro 246*. I have far too many other favorite titles and artists and couldn't possibly list them all. As for role models...this feels presumptuous to say, but I deeply believe that all the manga artists who remain active as creators for ten years, or even tens of years, are truly amazing.

What has been the toughest thing so far as a manga artist?

When a collected volume goes on sale, my workload practically doubles, so I'm run ragged every time...One time, when we were putting out the Animate special edition, on top of the work for the collected volume, I had to draw an entire bonus story for the special booklet. I then perceived various truths, thinking to myself, "I don't think I can do this anymore..." I caused my editor a great deal of trouble on that occasion...

What has made you happiest so far as a manga artist?

Receiving letters, the collected volumes taking shape, being given the chance to do lead color pages and covers...There are so many things that I can't decide on a number one. I am also very happy that there are people who create derivative works, including fan art and fan fiction, based on *Love of Kill*. I look at them all the time.

Is there anything you would like to say to the readers of Gene?

Love of Kill has been coming out for over two years now, and I am truly grateful that you have stuck with me this long. I want to keep working hard on this manga for a little while longer, and I hope I can make you proud. Thank you!

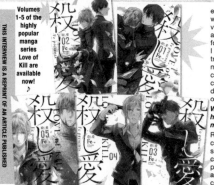

THIS INTERVIEW IS A REPRINT OF AN ARTICLE PUBLISHED IN THE MARCH 2018 ISSUE OF *MONTHLY COMIC GENE*.

Volumes 1-5 of the highly popular manga series Love of Kill are available now! ♪

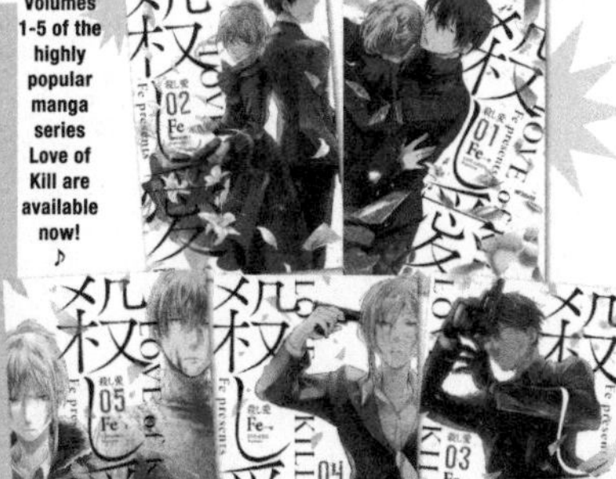

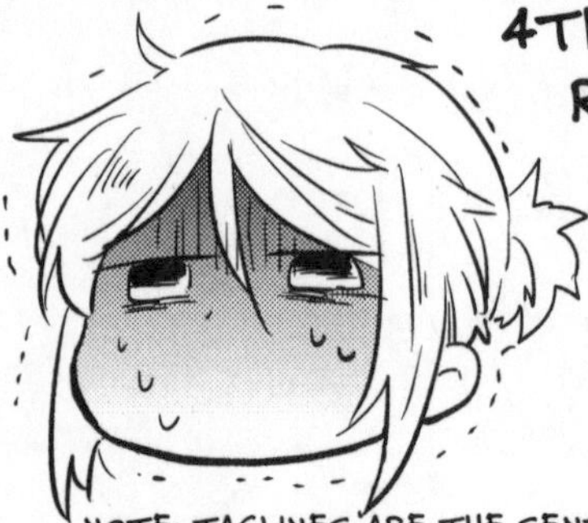

4TH TAGLINE RANKING

A REGULAR SEGMENT!

HOW PALE DO THEY MAKE CHATEAU'S FACE TURN?

NOTE: TAGLINES ARE THE SENTENCES INCLUDED ON TITLE PAGES AND SUCH WHEN A MANGA IS PUBLISHED IN A MAGAZINE. MY EDITOR, WHO ALWAYS COMES UP WITH THESE TAGLINES, TOLD ME, "RECENTLY, I'VE GOTTEN INTO A RUT WITH WRITING TAGLINES." PLEASE KEEP GOING!!!!!

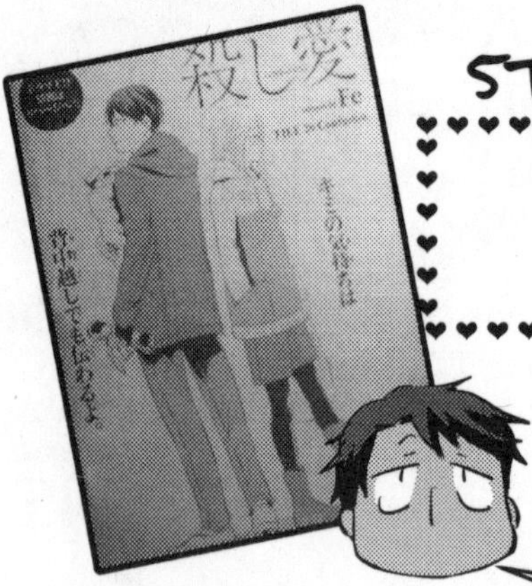

5TH

EVEN BACK-TO-BACK, YOUR FEELINGS GET THROUGH TO ME.
(CHAPTER 26, TITLE PAGE)

PALLOR LEVEL: 1

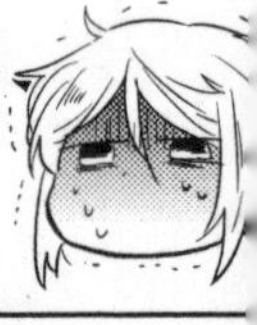

IT SEEMS YOU'RE COMMUNICATING WITH HIM, CHATEAU. HE MUST BE PSYCHIC.

4TH

HOWEVER MUCH IT DIRTIES MY HANDS, I WILL PROTECT MY ONE, SINGLE FOUNDATION.

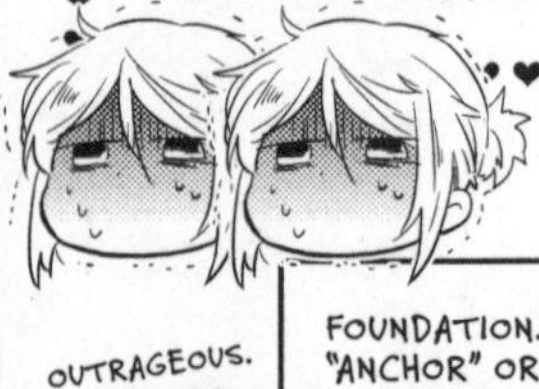

PALLOR LEVEL: 2

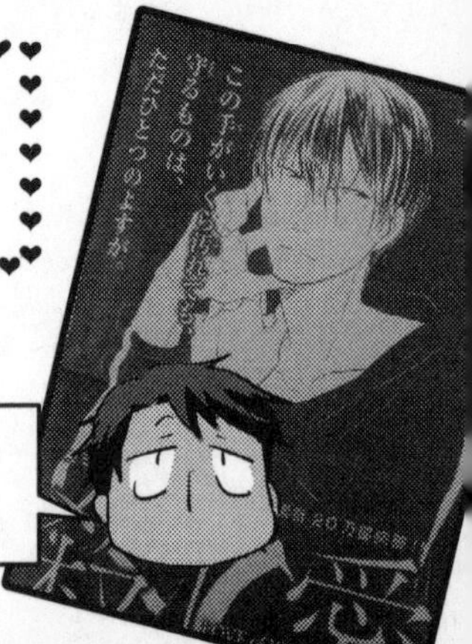

FOUNDATION...APPARENTLY, HERE IT MEANS "ANCHOR" OR "PERSON TO RELY ON." WOW, SONG IS A PRETTY DEEP PERSON...

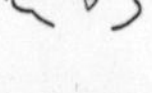

OUTRAGEOUS.

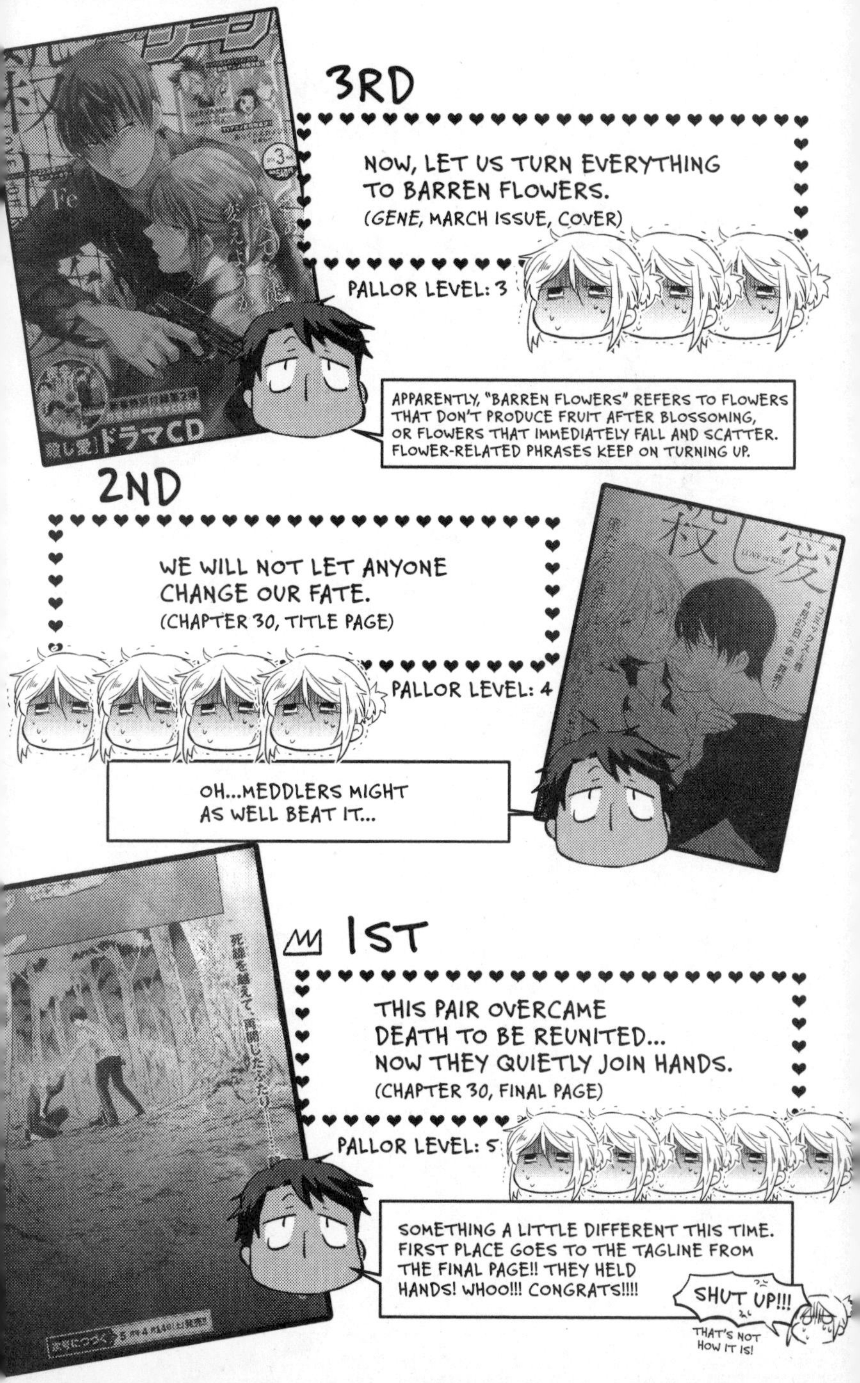
3RD
NOW, LET US TURN EVERYTHING TO BARREN FLOWERS.
(GENE, MARCH ISSUE, COVER)
PALLOR LEVEL: 3
APPARENTLY, "BARREN FLOWERS" REFERS TO FLOWERS THAT DON'T PRODUCE FRUIT AFTER BLOSSOMING, OR FLOWERS THAT IMMEDIATELY FALL AND SCATTER. FLOWER-RELATED PHRASES KEEP ON TURNING UP.
2ND
WE WILL NOT LET ANYONE CHANGE OUR FATE.
(CHAPTER 30, TITLE PAGE)
PALLOR LEVEL: 4
OH...MEDDLERS MIGHT AS WELL BEAT IT...
1ST
THIS PAIR OVERCAME DEATH TO BE REUNITED... NOW THEY QUIETLY JOIN HANDS.
(CHAPTER 30, FINAL PAGE)
PALLOR LEVEL: 5
SOMETHING A LITTLE DIFFERENT THIS TIME. FIRST PLACE GOES TO THE TAGLINE FROM THE FINAL PAGE!! THEY HELD HANDS! WHOO!!! CONGRATS!!!!
SHUT UP!!!
THAT'S NOT HOW IT IS!

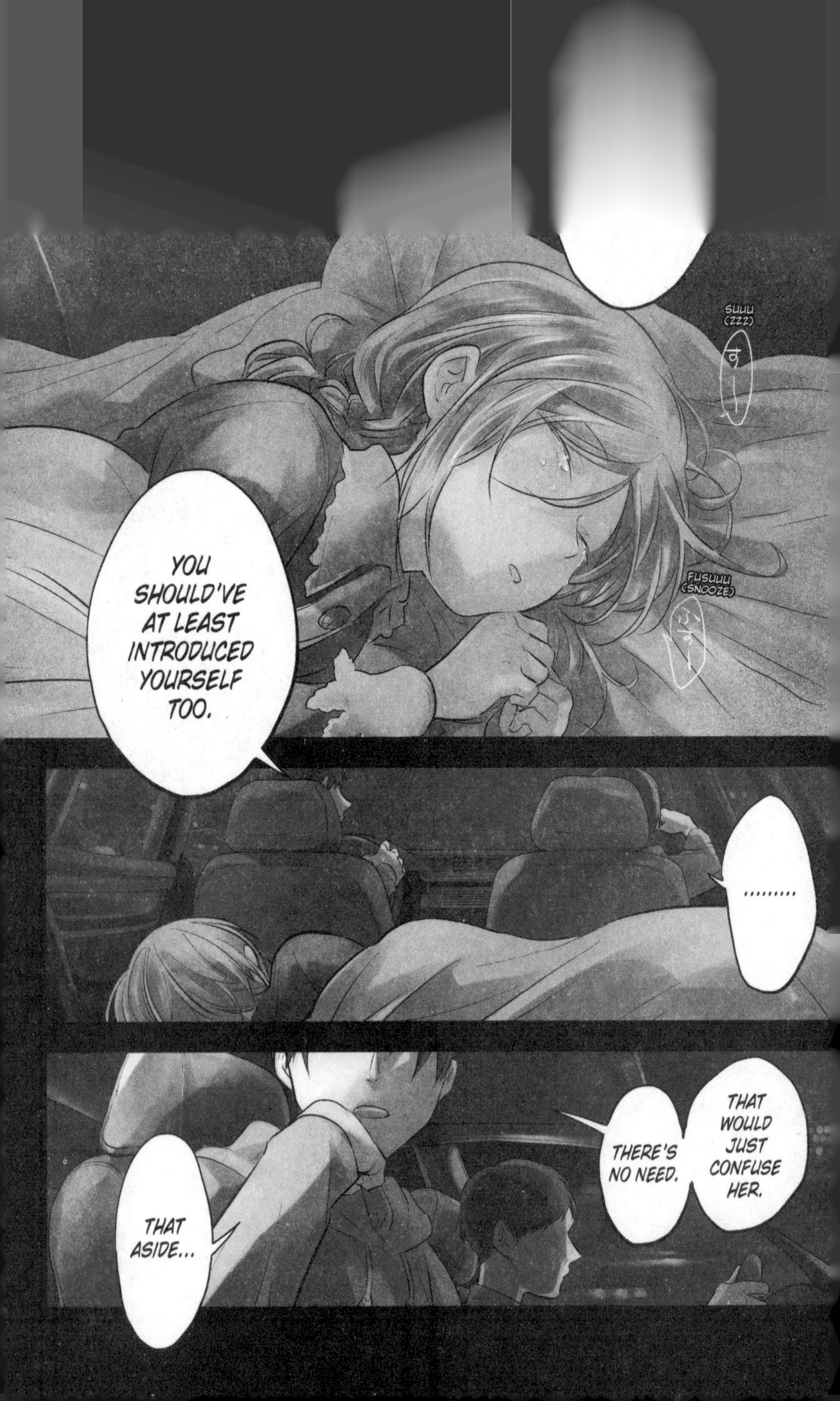
SUUU (ZZZ)
FUSUUU (SNOOZE)
YOU SHOULD'VE AT LEAST INTRODUCED YOURSELF TOO.
....
THAT WOULD JUST CONFUSE HER.
THERE'S NO NEED.
THAT ASIDE...

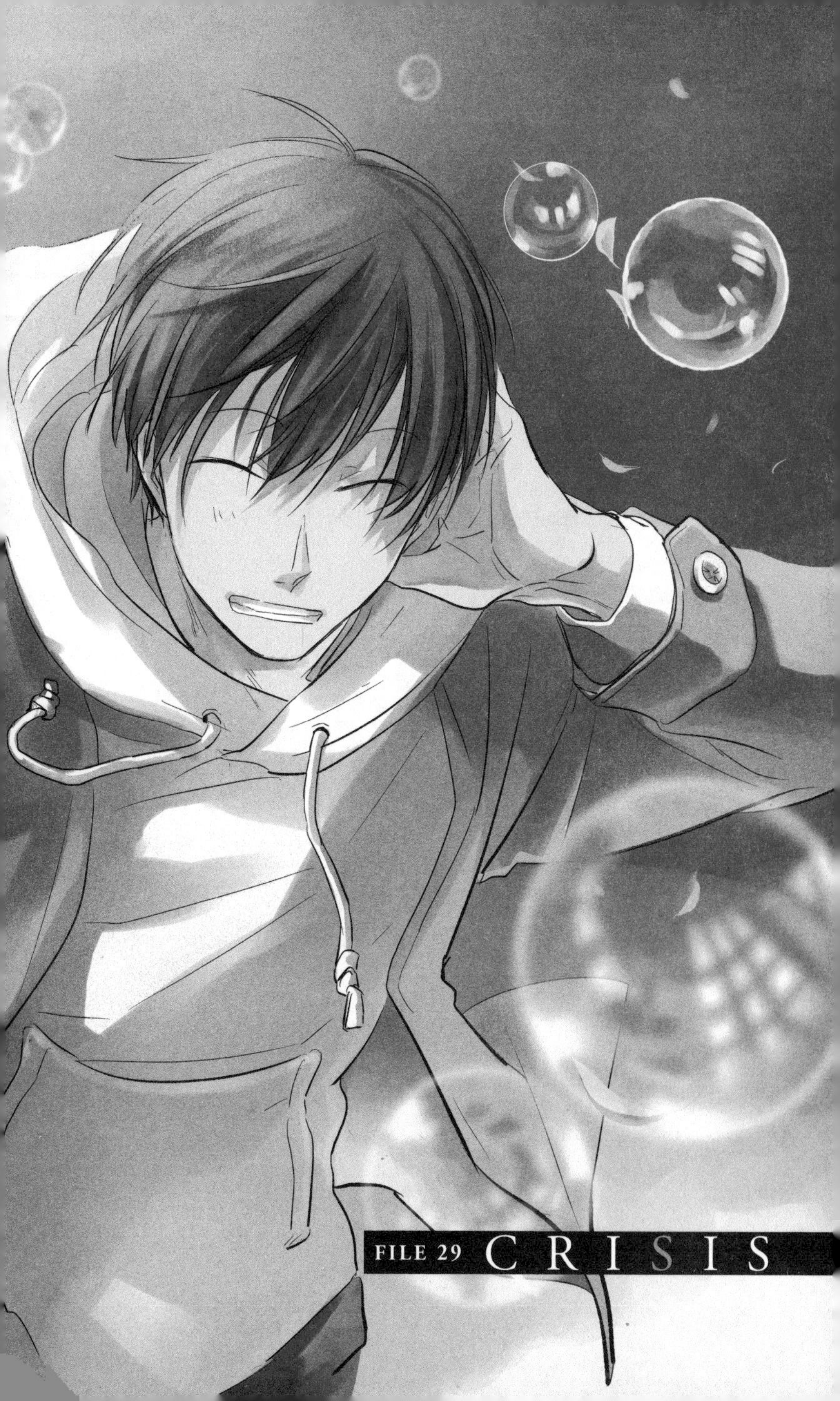
FILE 29 CRISIS

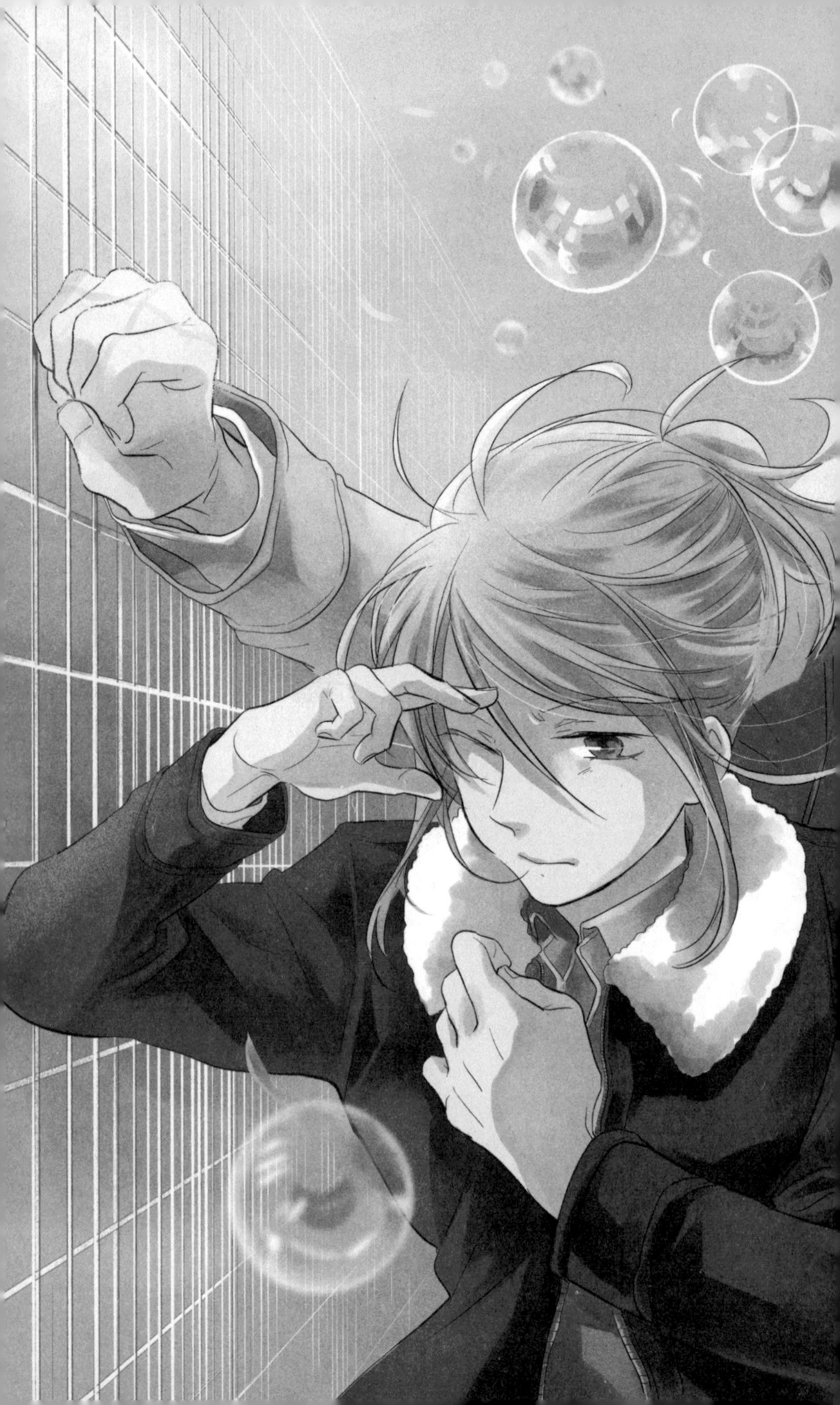

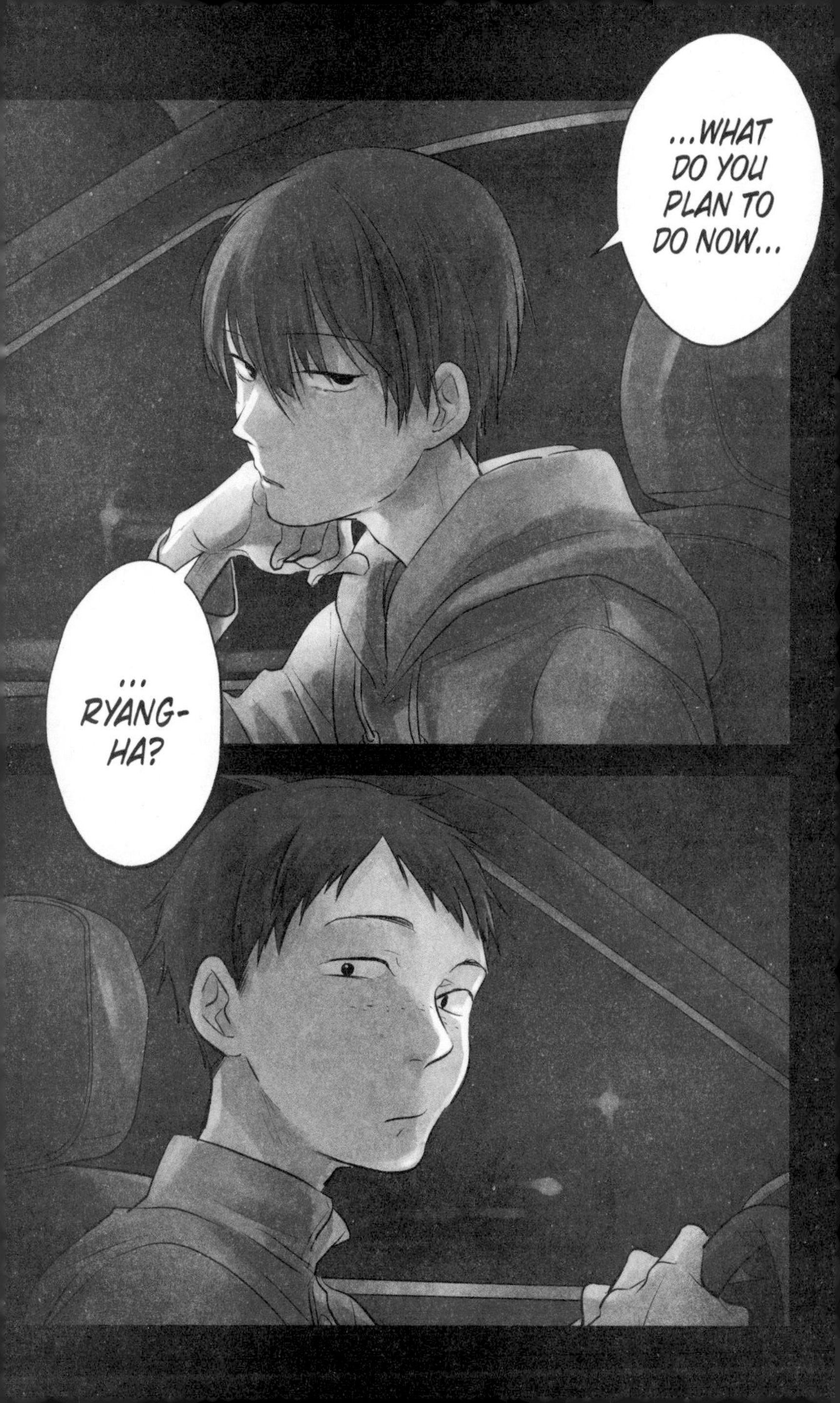
...WHAT DO YOU PLAN TO DO NOW...
... RYANG-HA?

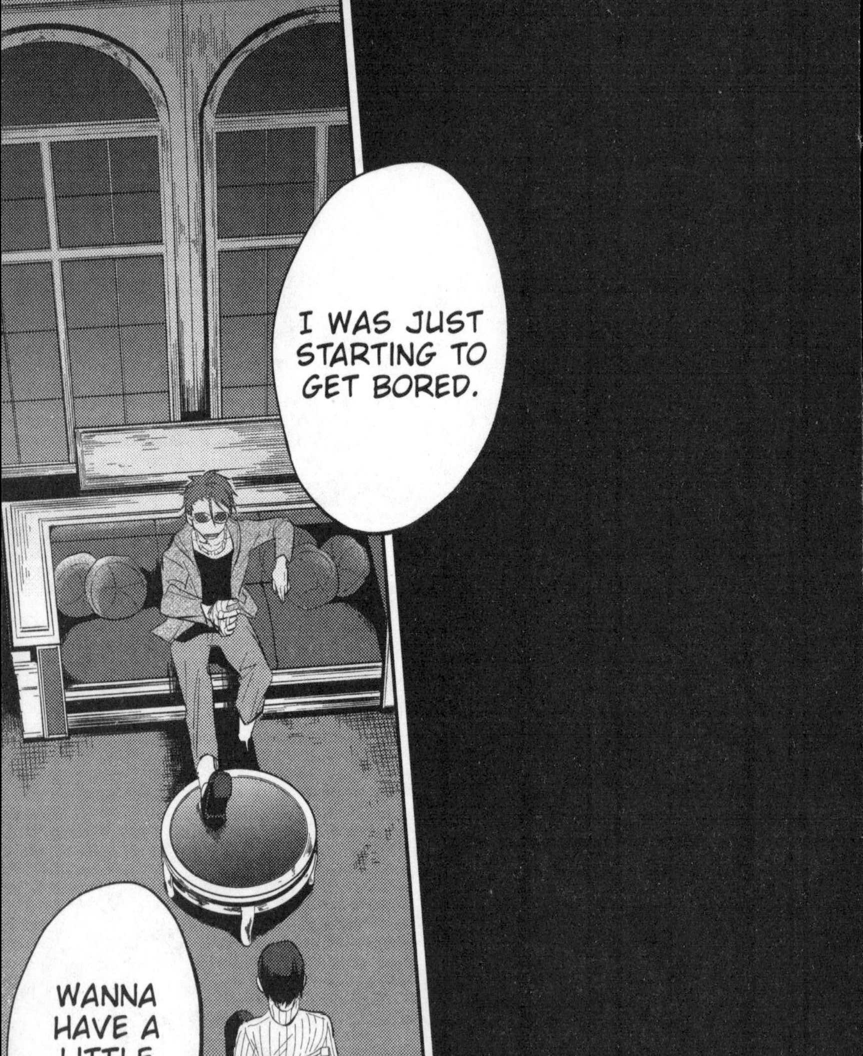
I WAS JUST STARTING TO GET BORED.
WANNA HAVE A LITTLE FUN?

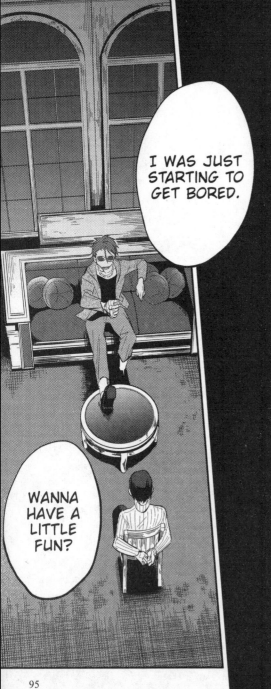

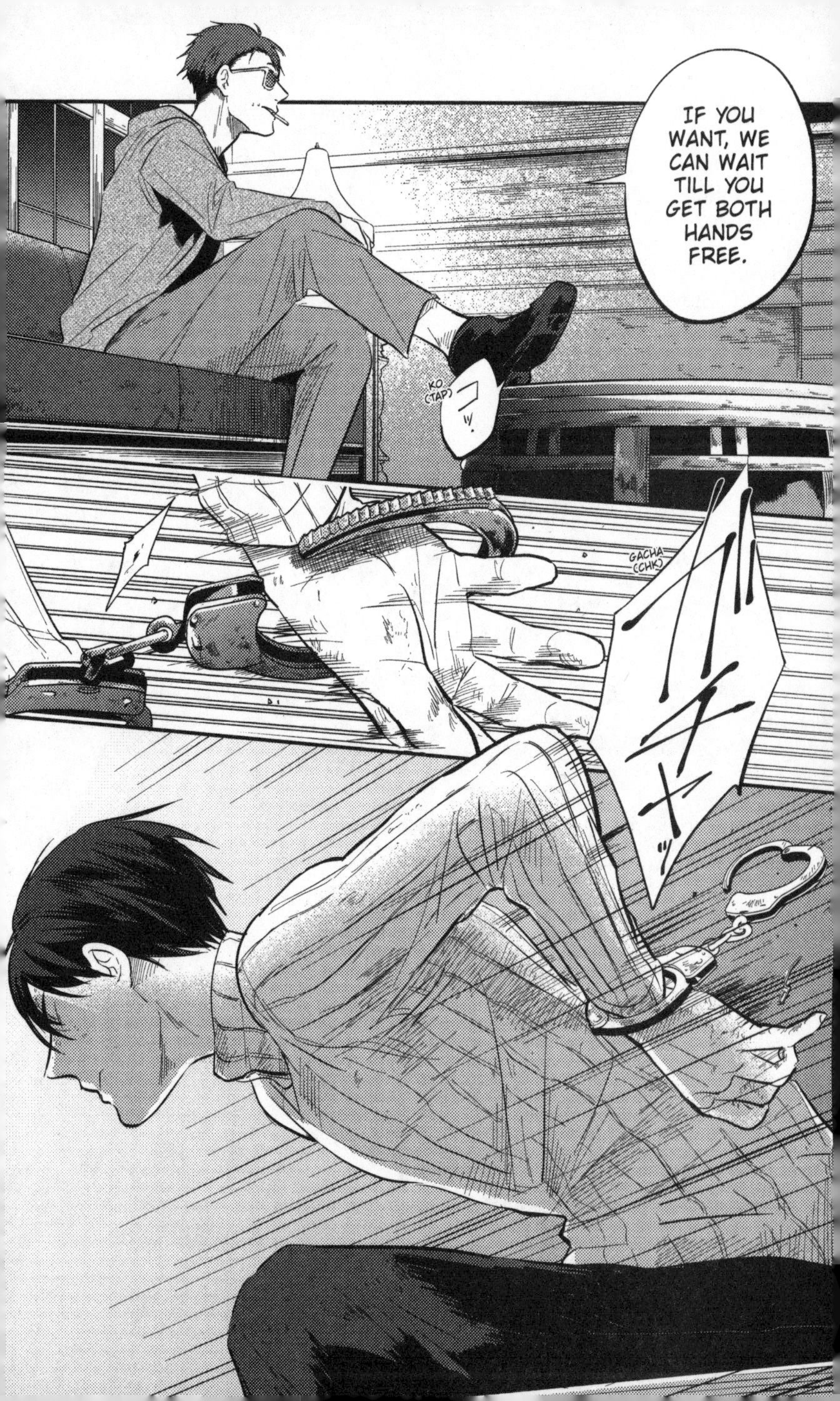
IF YOU WANT, WE CAN WAIT TILL YOU GET BOTH HANDS FREE.
KO (TAP)
GACHA (CHK)

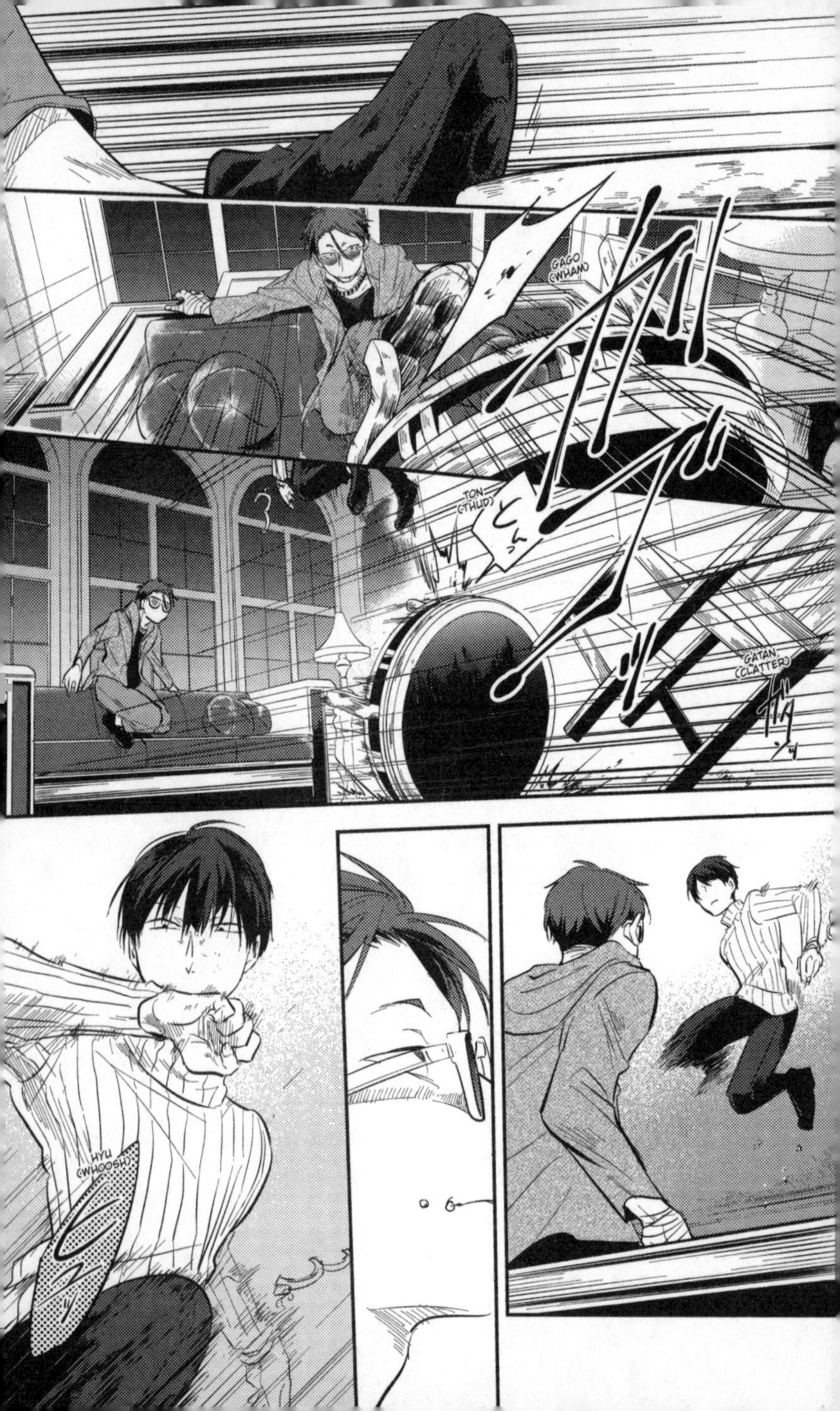
GAGO (WHAM)
TON (THUD)
GATAN (CLATTER)
HYU (WHOOSH)

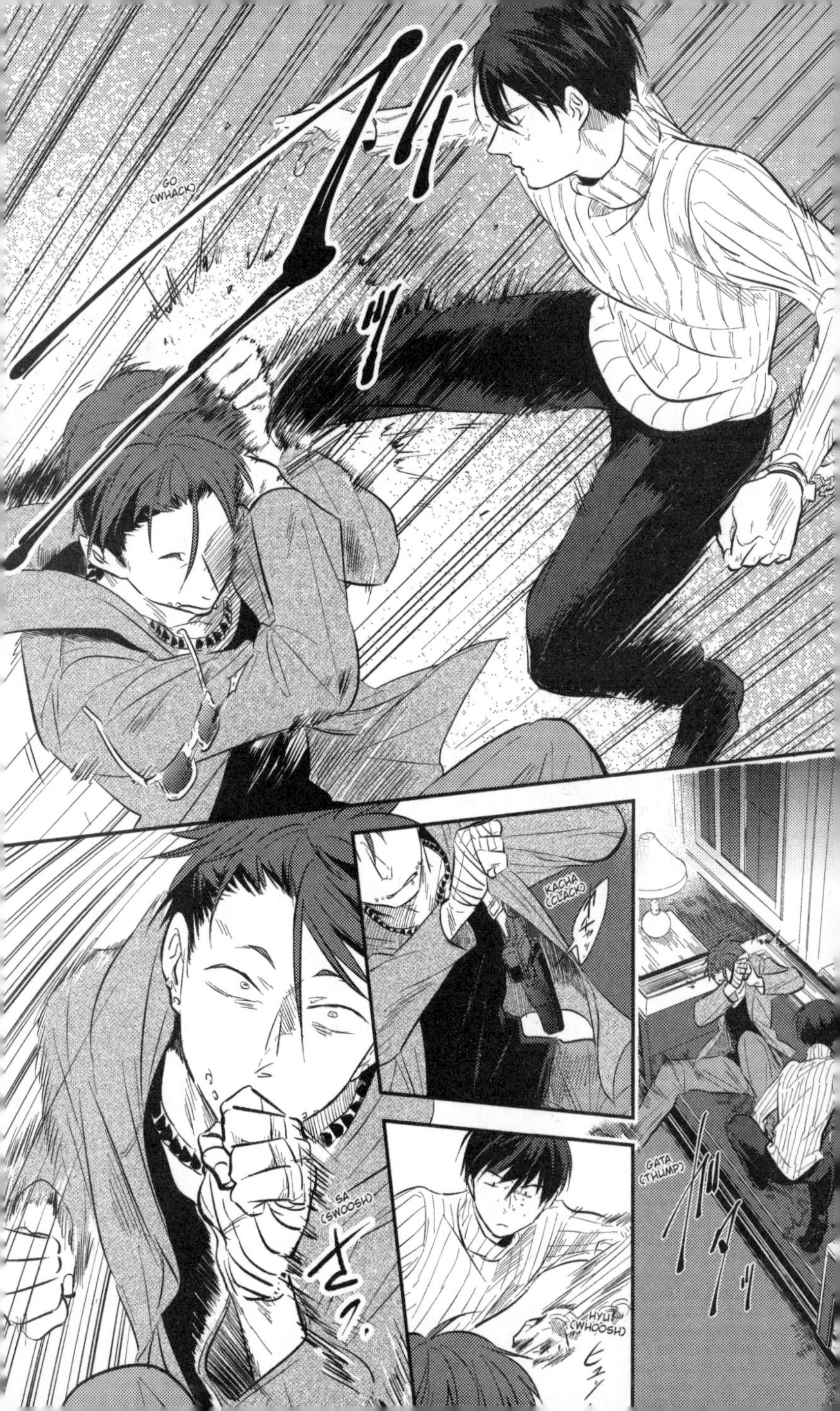
GO (WHACK)
GATA (THUMP)
KACHA (CLACK)
HYUI (WHOOSH)
SA (SWOOSH)

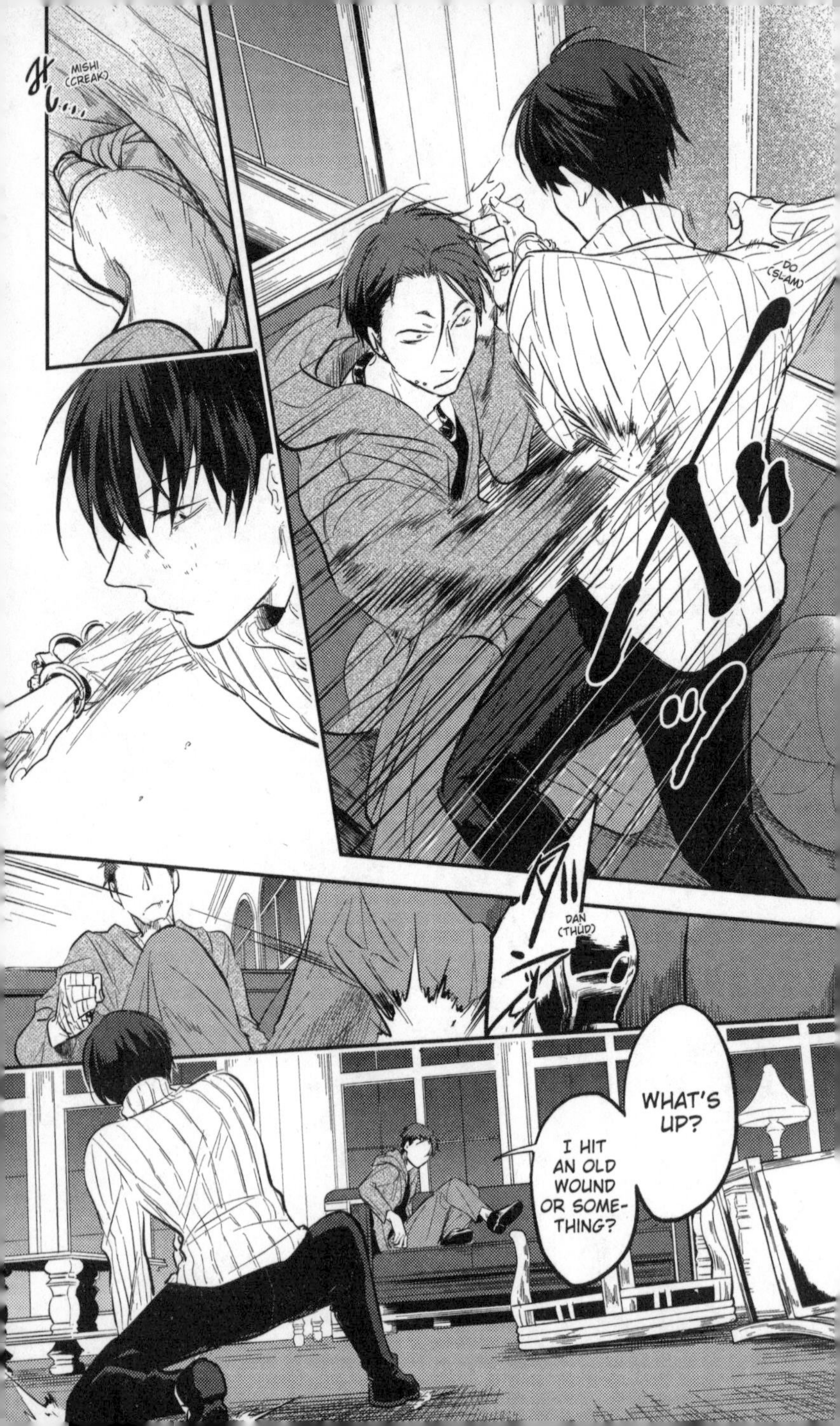
DO (SLAM)
MISHI (CREAK)
DAN (THUD)
WHAT'S UP?
I HIT AN OLD WOUND OR SOMETHING?

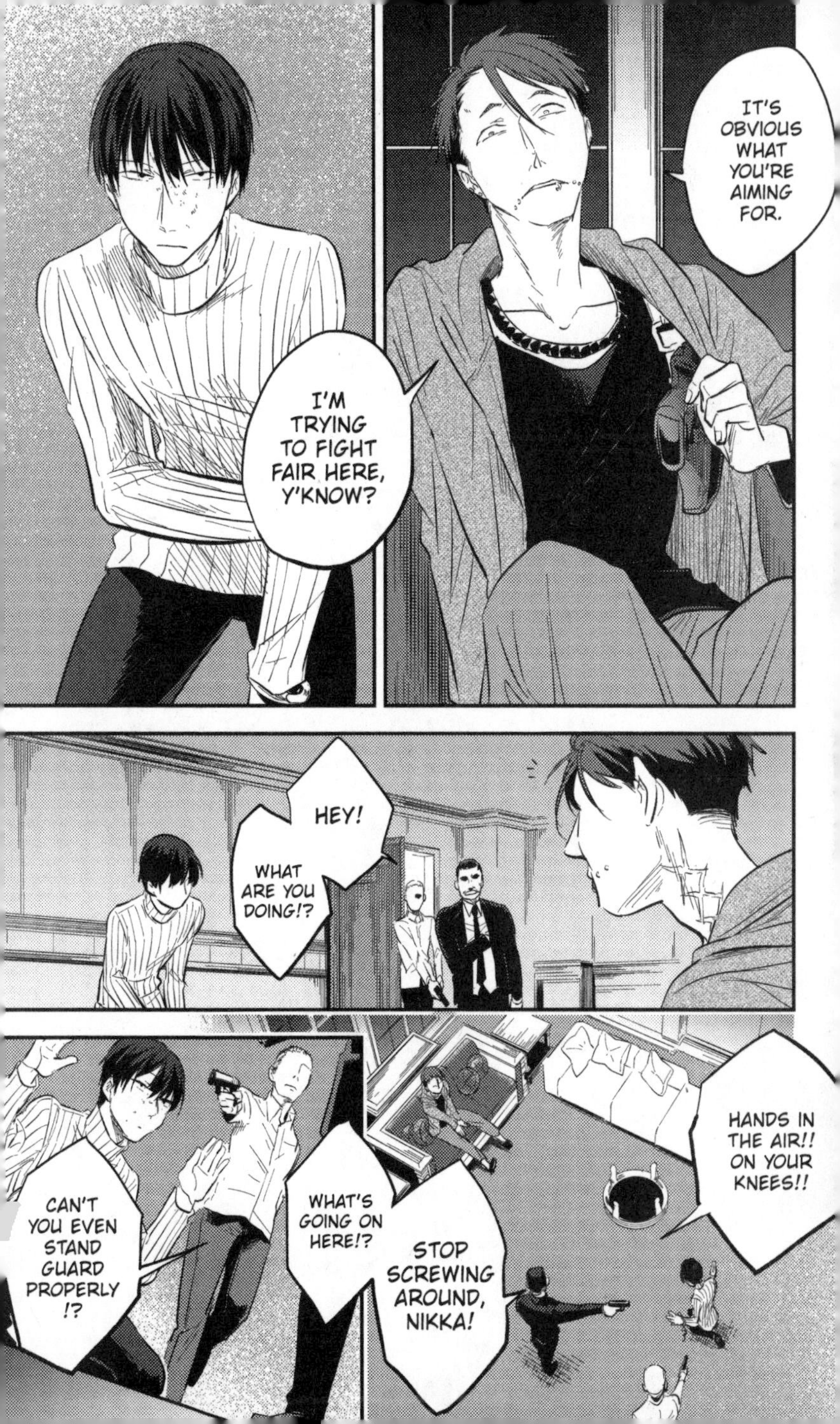
IT'S OBVIOUS WHAT YOU'RE AIMING FOR.
I'M TRYING TO FIGHT FAIR HERE, Y'KNOW?
HEY!
WHAT ARE YOU DOING!?
HANDS IN THE AIR!! ON YOUR KNEES!!
STOP SCREWING AROUND, NIKKA!
WHAT'S GOING ON HERE!?
CAN'T YOU EVEN STAND GUARD PROPERLY!?

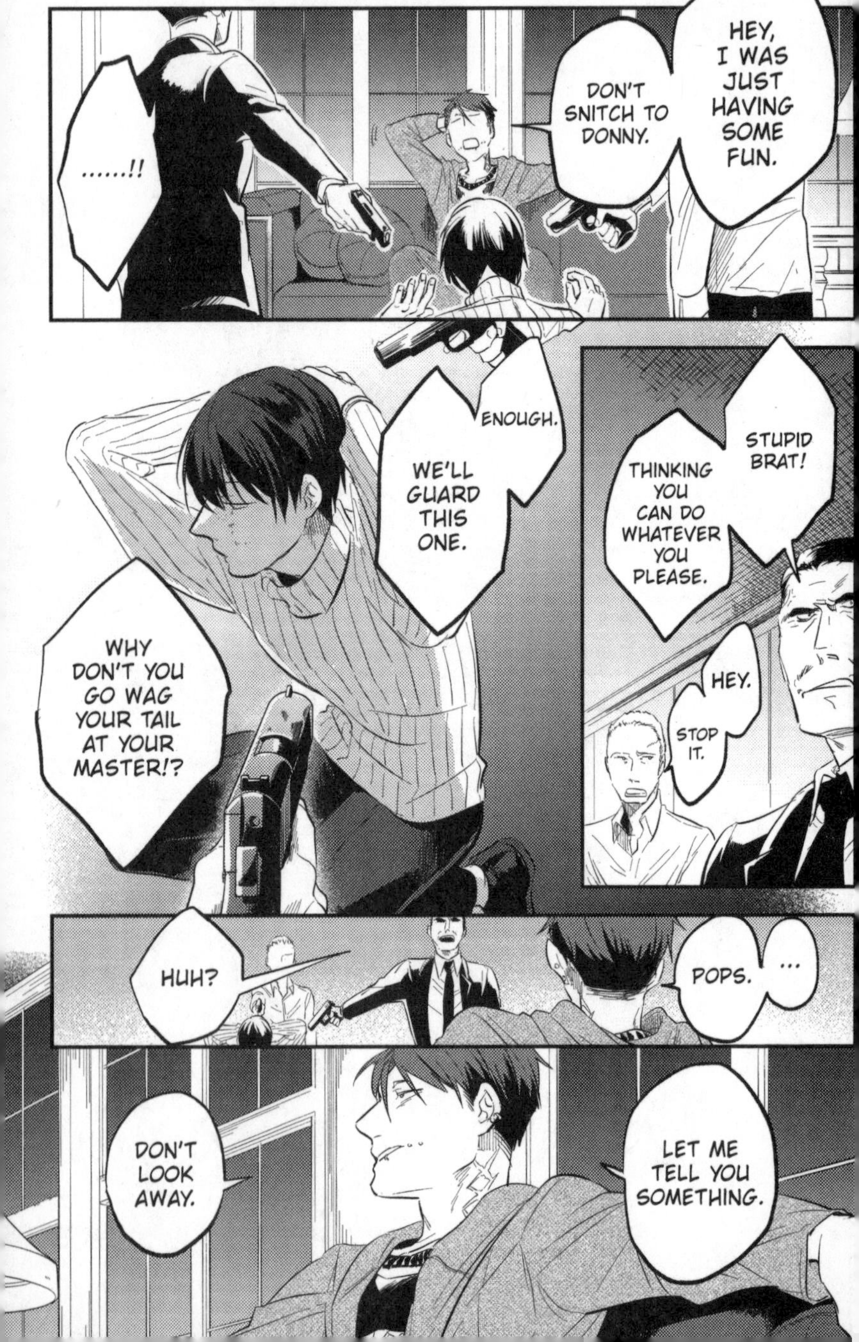
HEY, I WAS JUST HAVING SOME FUN.
DON'T SNITCH TO DONNY.
......!!
STUPID BRAT!
THINKING YOU CAN DO WHATEVER YOU PLEASE.
HEY.
STOP IT.
ENOUGH.
WE'LL GUARD THIS ONE.
WHY DON'T YOU GO WAG YOUR TAIL AT YOUR MASTER!?
...
POPS.
HUH?
LET ME TELL YOU SOMETHING.
DON'T LOOK AWAY.

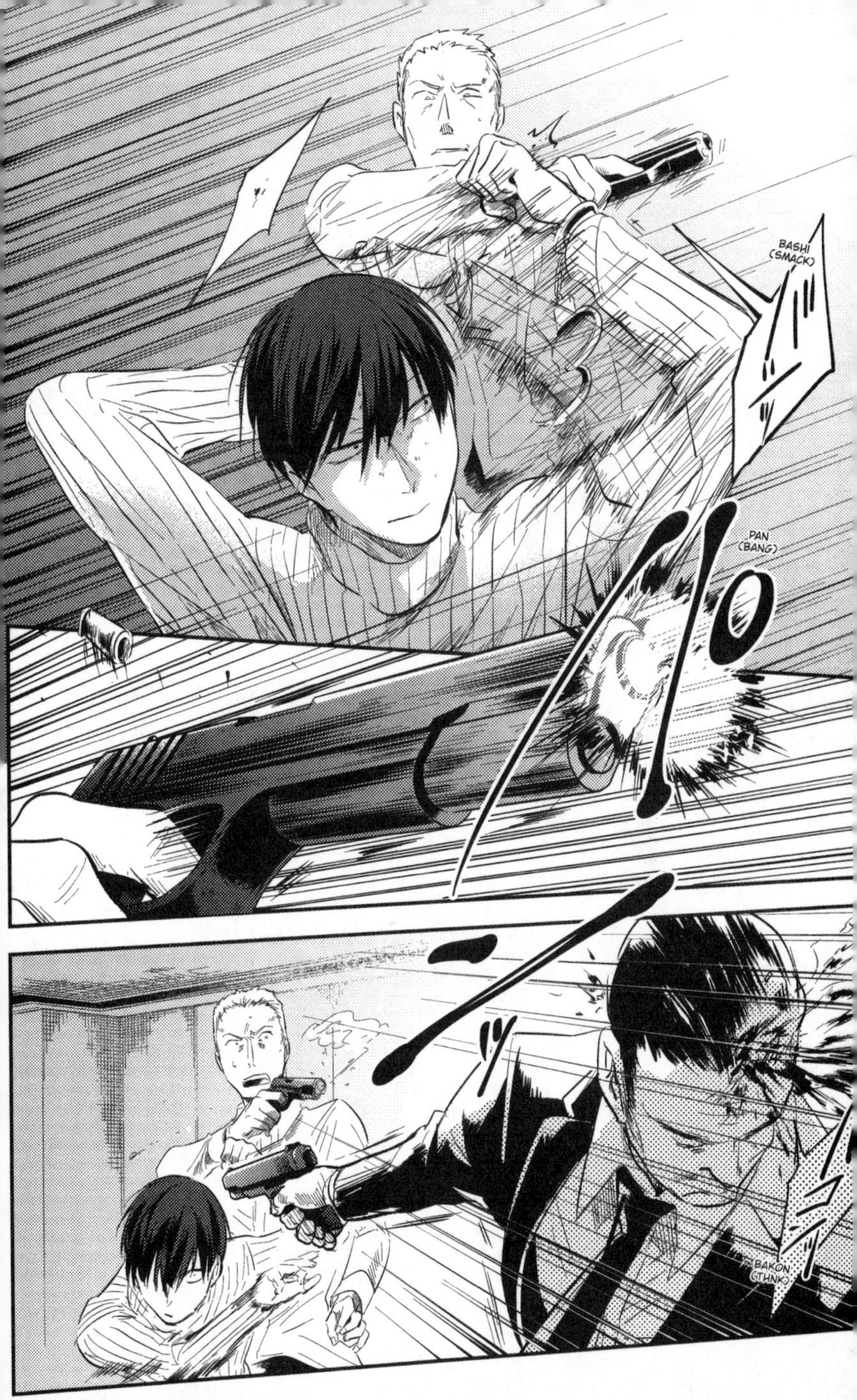
BASHI
(SMACK)
PAN
(BANG)
BAKON
(THNK)

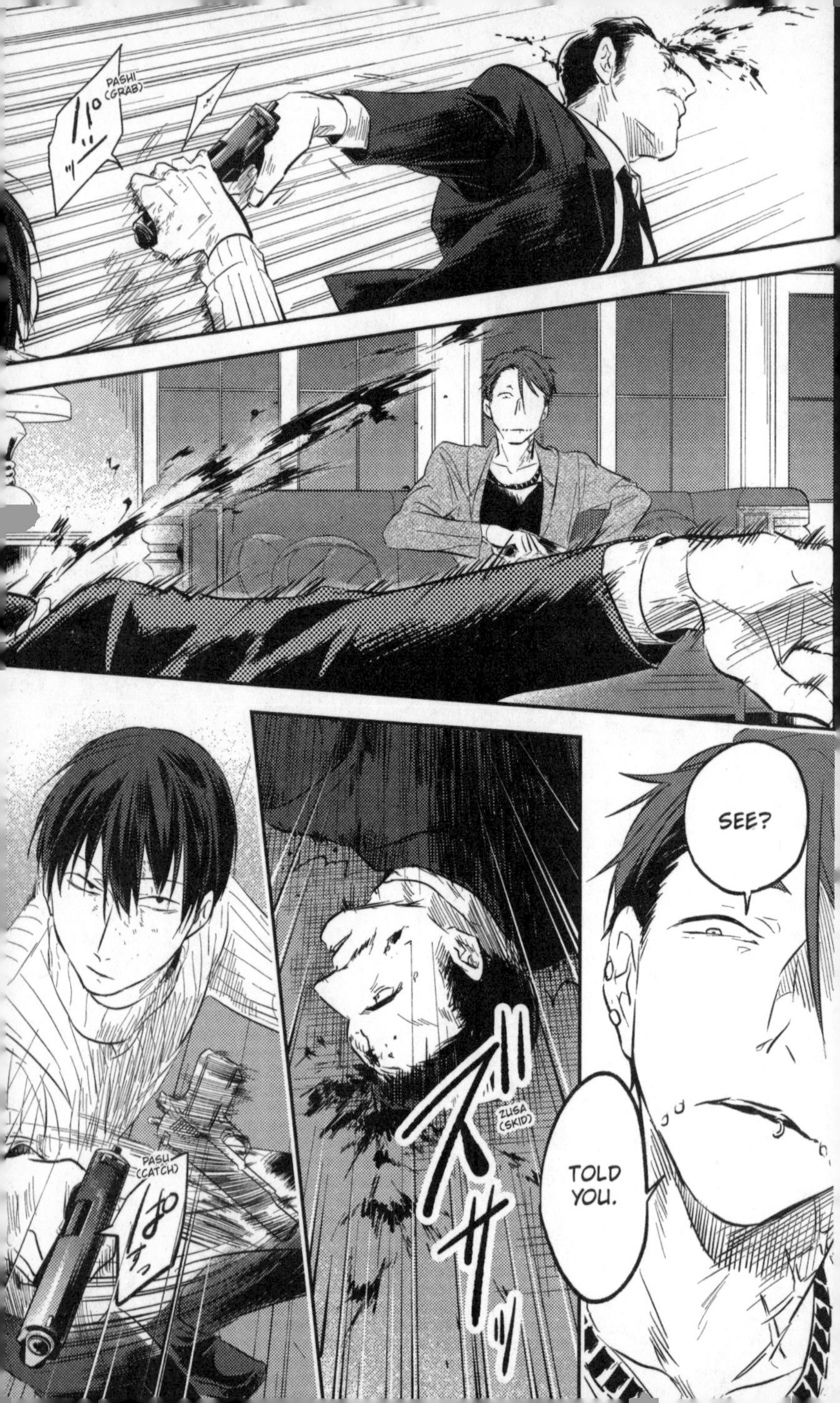
PASHI (GRAB)
PASU (CATCH)
ZUSA (SKID)
SEE?
TOLD YOU.

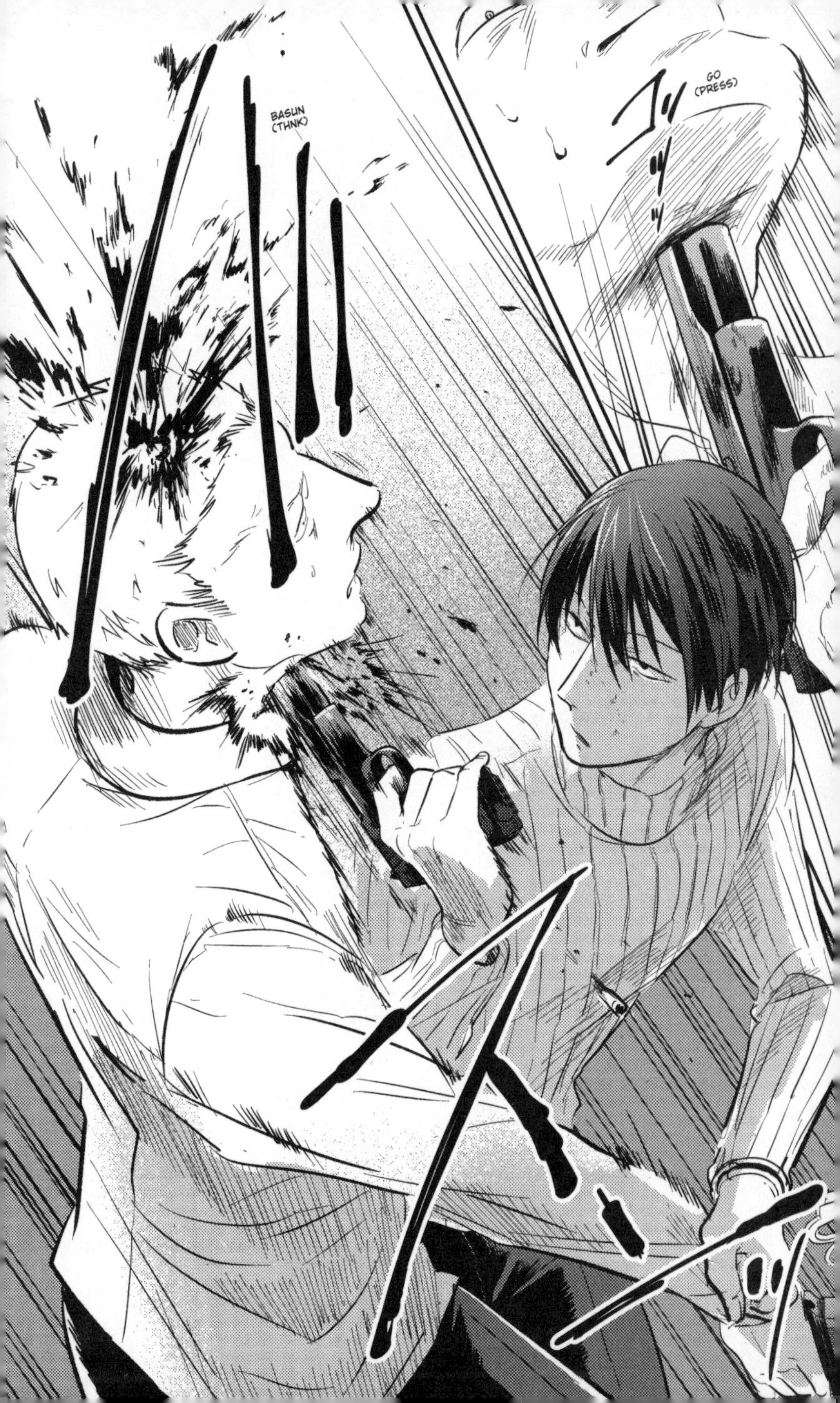
GO (PRESS)
BASUN (THNK)

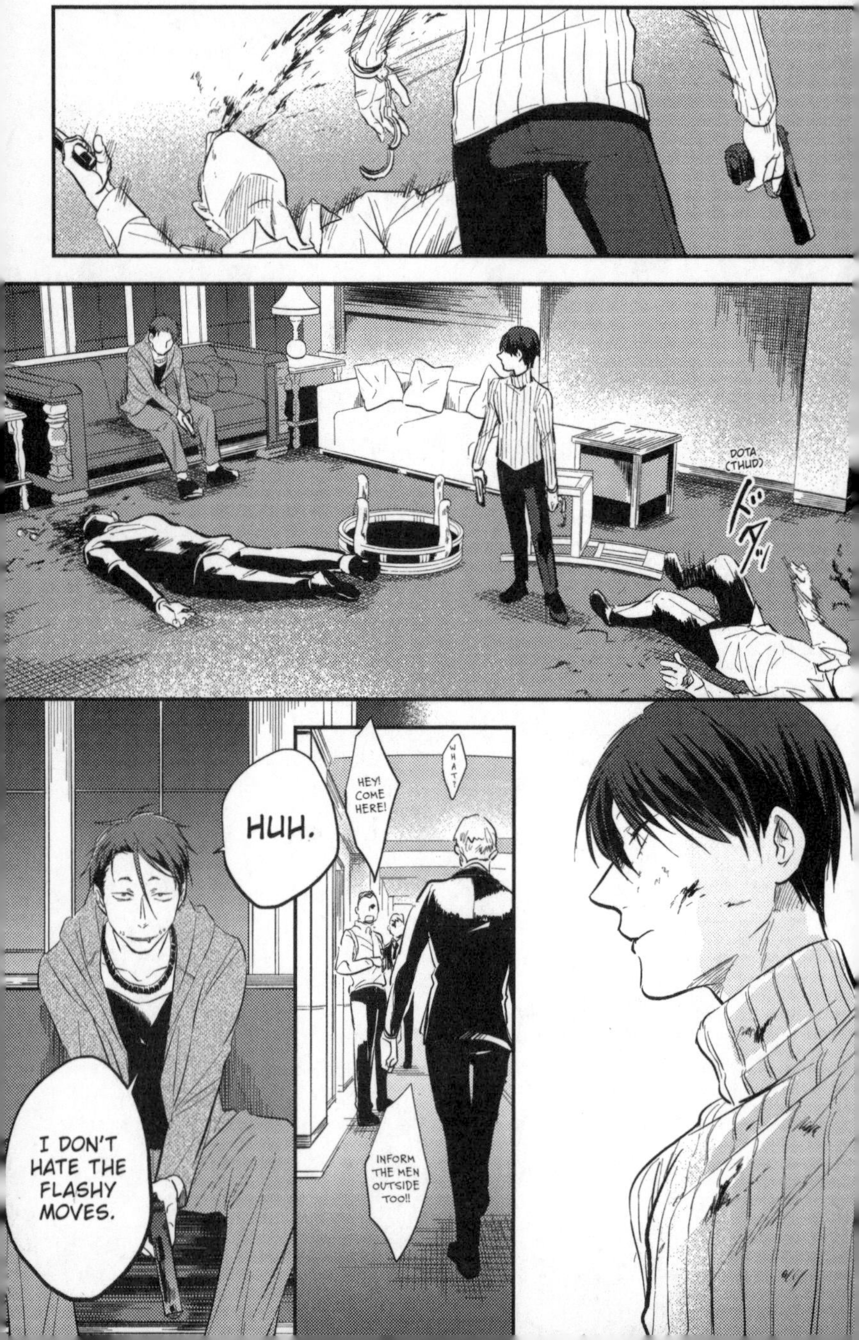
DOTA (THUD)
ドダッ
WHAT?
HEY! COME HERE!
INFORM THE MEN OUTSIDE TOO!!
HUH.
I DON'T HATE THE FLASHY MOVES.

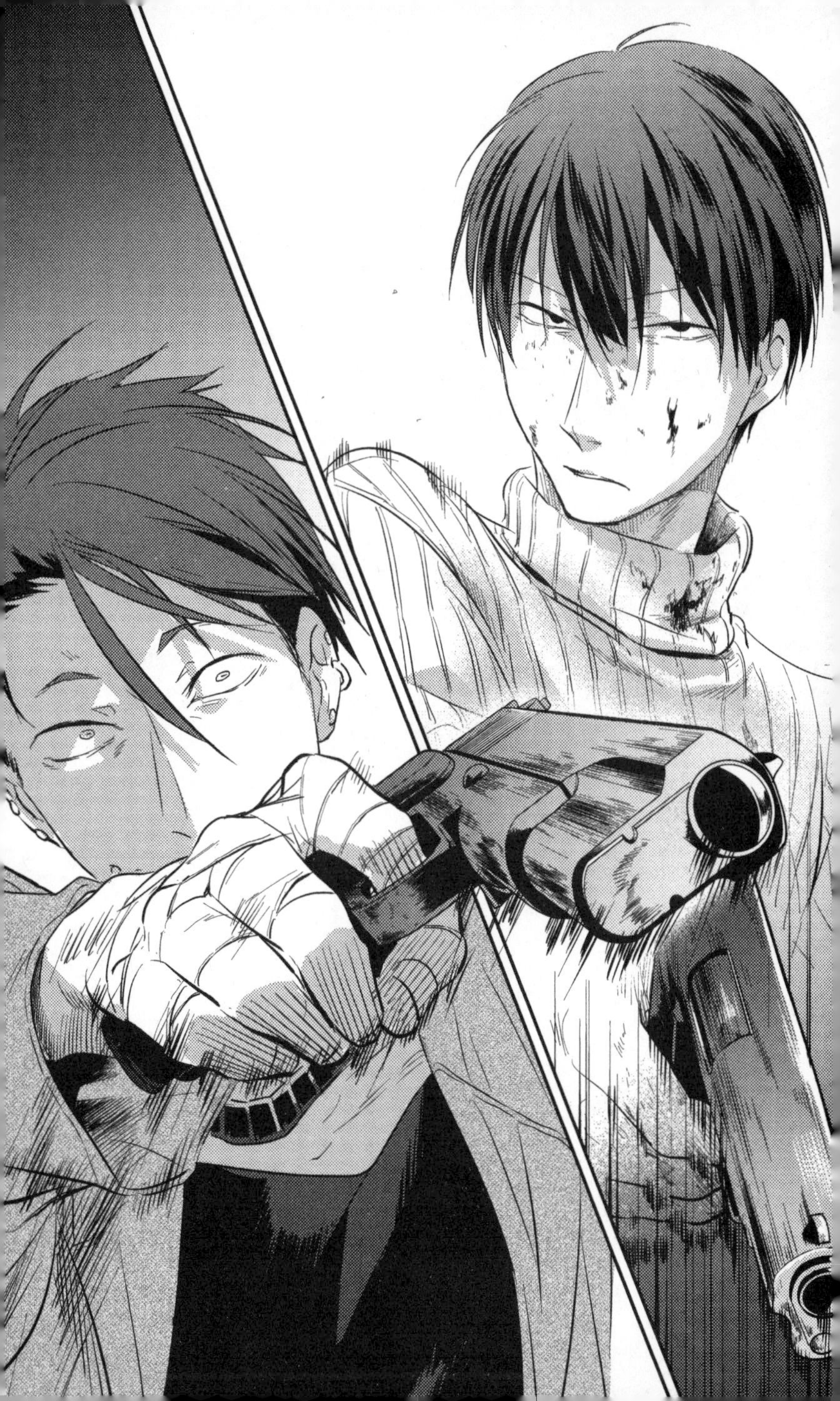

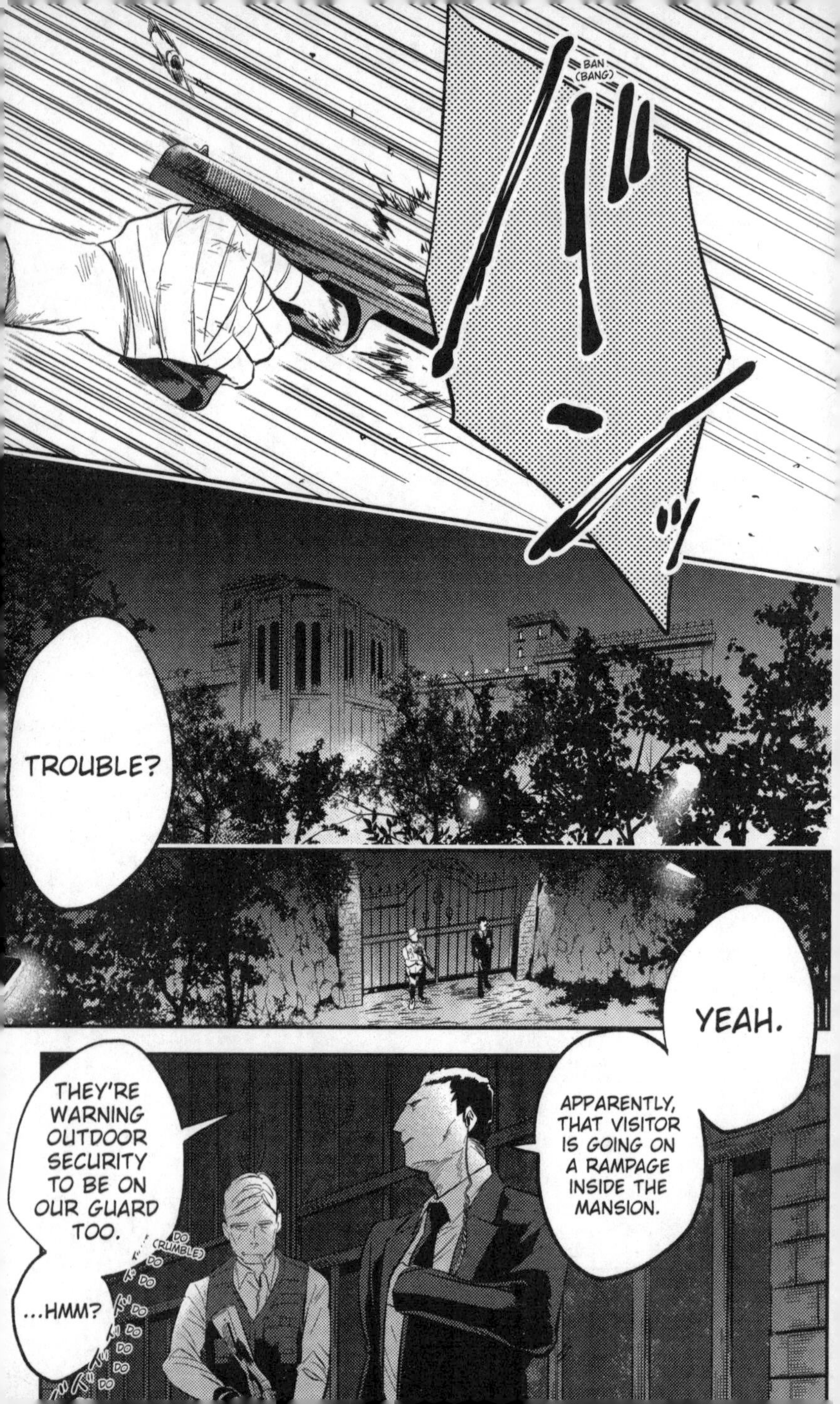
BAN (BANG)
TROUBLE?
YEAH.
APPARENTLY, THAT VISITOR IS GOING ON A RAMPAGE INSIDE THE MANSION.
THEY'RE WARNING OUTDOOR SECURITY TO BE ON OUR GUARD TOO.
DO (RUMBLE)
DO DO DO DO DO DO DO
...HMM?

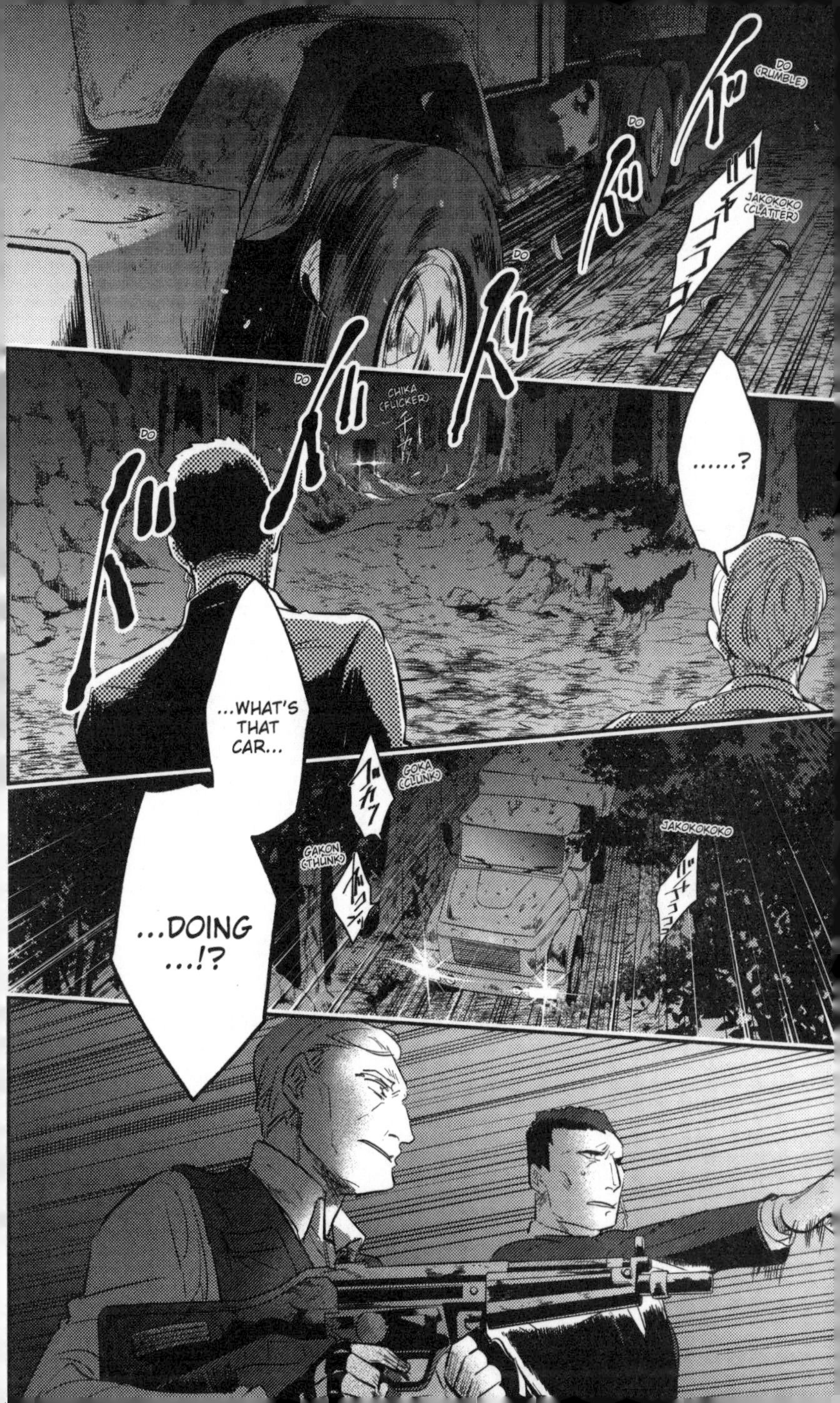
DO (RUMBLE)
JAKOKOKO (CLATTER)
DO
DO
DO
DO
CHIKA (FLICKER)
......?
...WHAT'S THAT CAR...
JAKOKOKOKO
GOKA (CLUNK)
GAKON (THUNK)
...DOING ...!?

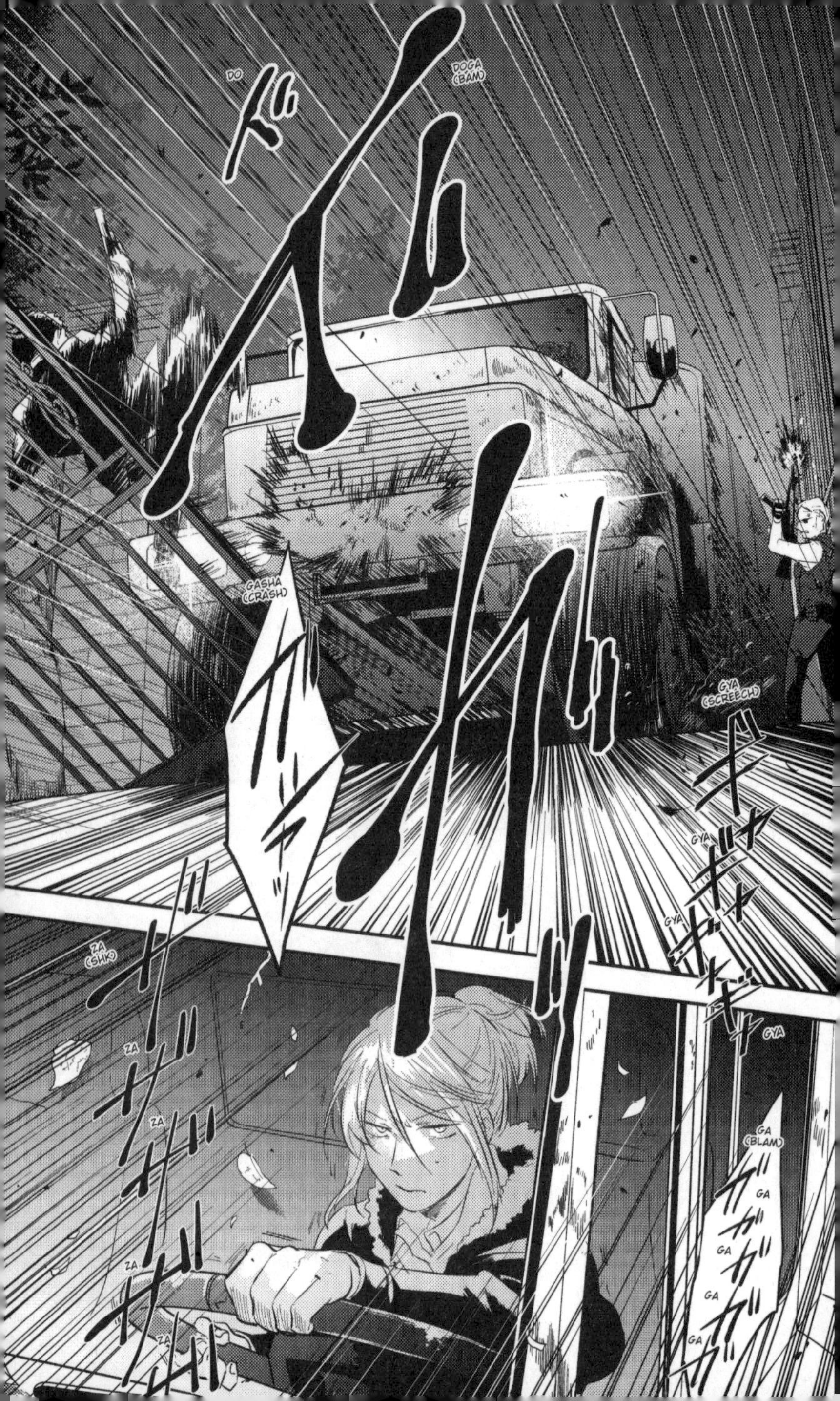
DOGA (BAM)
DO
GASHA (CRASH)
GYA (SCREECH)
GYA
GYA
GYA
GA (BLAM)
GA
GA
GA
GA
ZA (SHK)
ZA
ZA
ZA
ZA

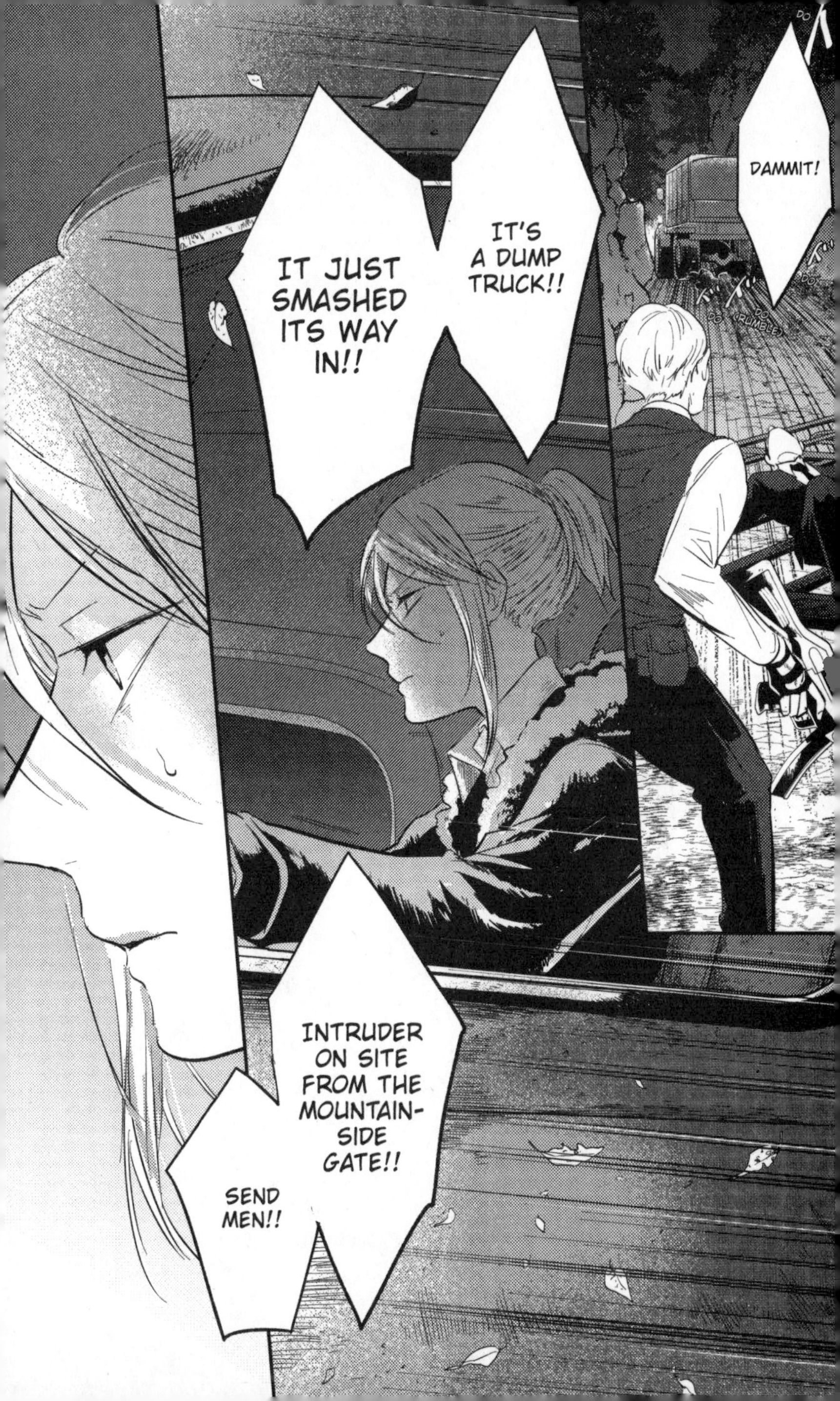
DO
DAMMIT!
DO
DO (RUMBLE)
IT'S A DUMP TRUCK!!
IT JUST SMASHED ITS WAY IN!!
INTRUDER ON SITE FROM THE MOUNTAIN-SIDE GATE!!
SEND MEN!!

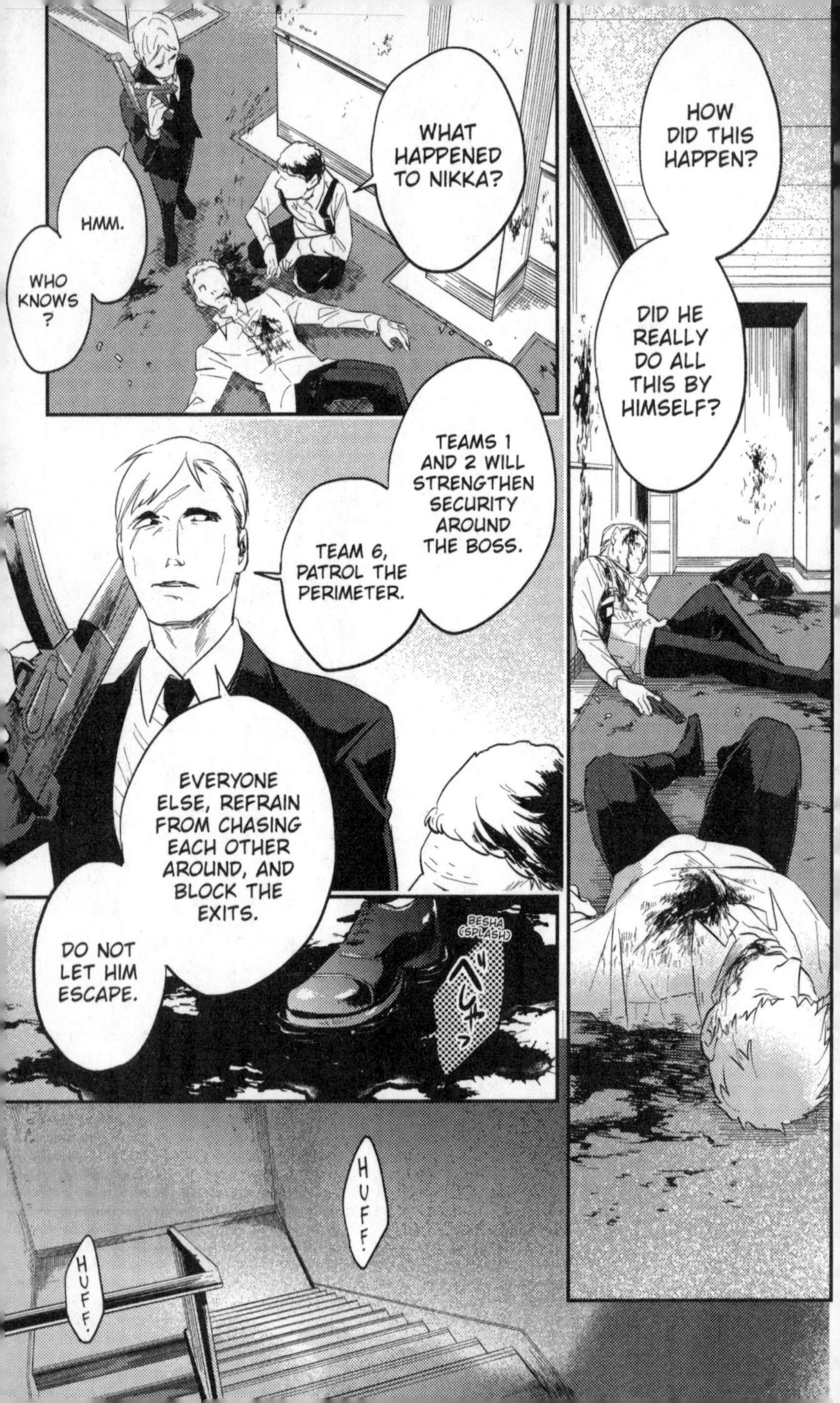
HOW DID THIS HAPPEN?
DID HE REALLY DO ALL THIS BY HIMSELF?
WHAT HAPPENED TO NIKKA?
HMM.
WHO KNOWS?
TEAMS 1 AND 2 WILL STRENGTHEN SECURITY AROUND THE BOSS.
TEAM 6, PATROL THE PERIMETER.
EVERYONE ELSE, REFRAIN FROM CHASING EACH OTHER AROUND, AND BLOCK THE EXITS.
DO NOT LET HIM ESCAPE.
BESHA (SPLASH)
HUFF.
HUFF.

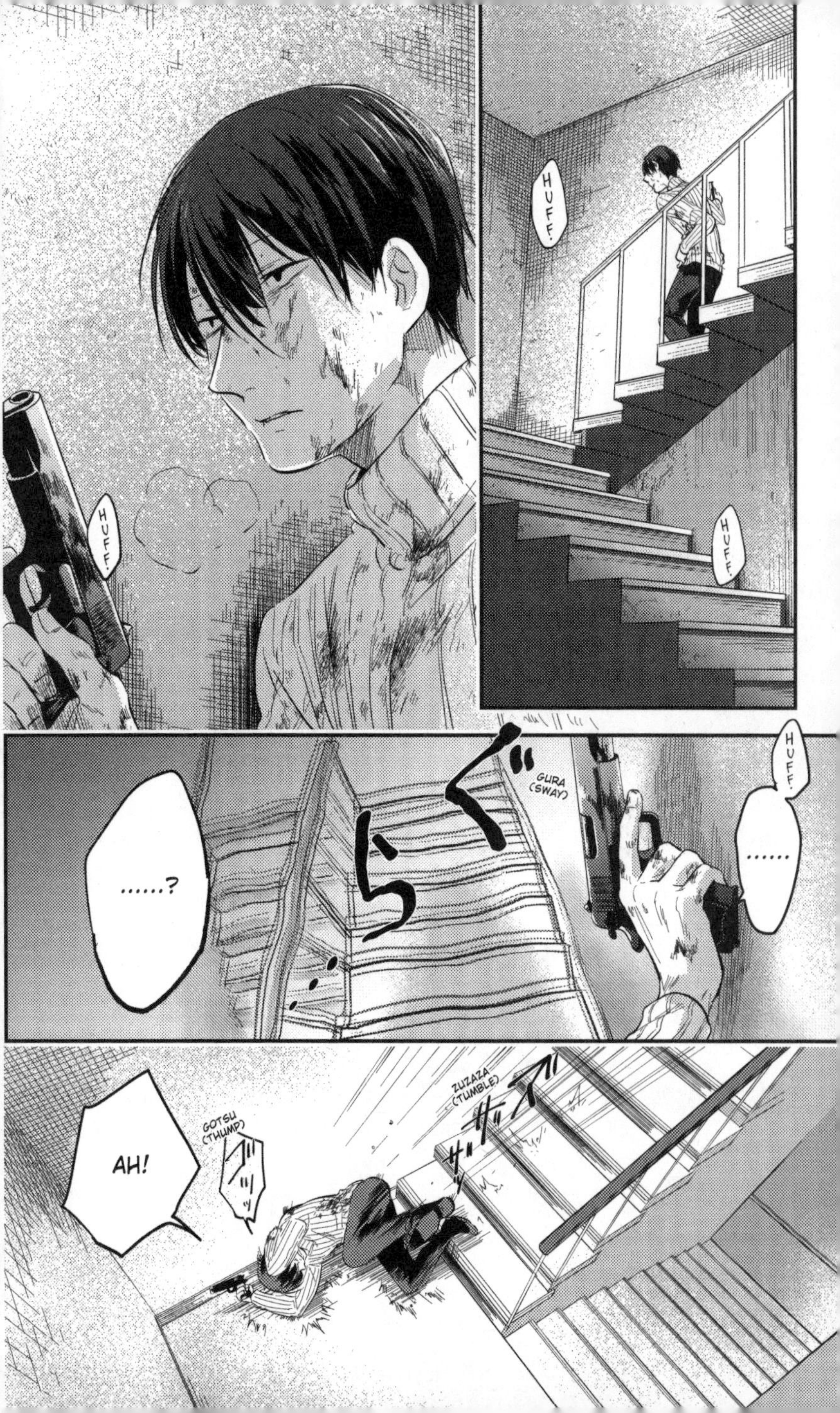
HUFF.
HUFF.
HUFF.
HUFF.
......
GURA (SWAY)
......?
ZUZAZA (TUMBLE)
GOTSU (THUMP)
AH!

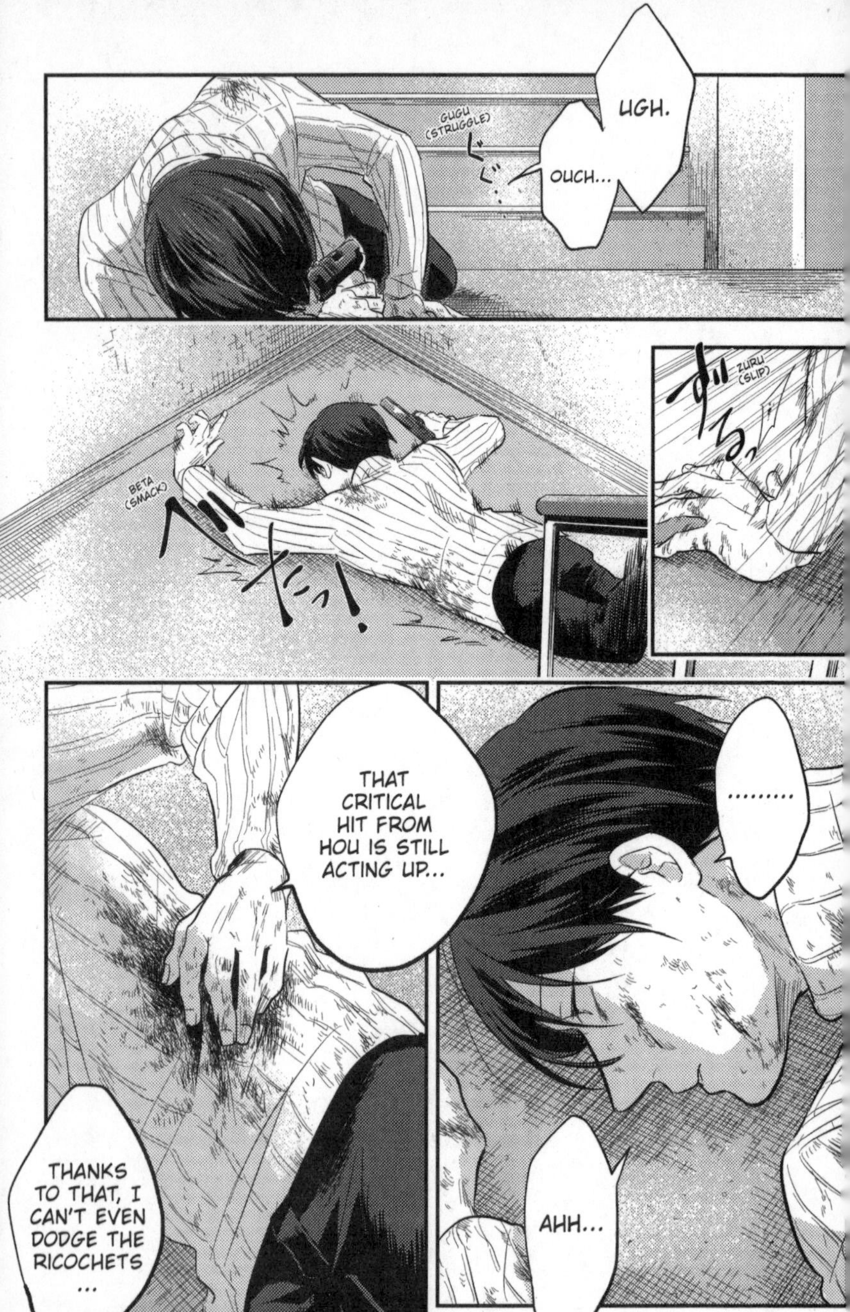
UGH.
OUCH...
GUGU (STRUGGLE)
ZURU (SLIP)
BETA (SMACK)
....
AHH...
THAT CRITICAL HIT FROM HOU IS STILL ACTING UP...
THANKS TO THAT, I CAN'T EVEN DODGE THE RICOCHETS ...

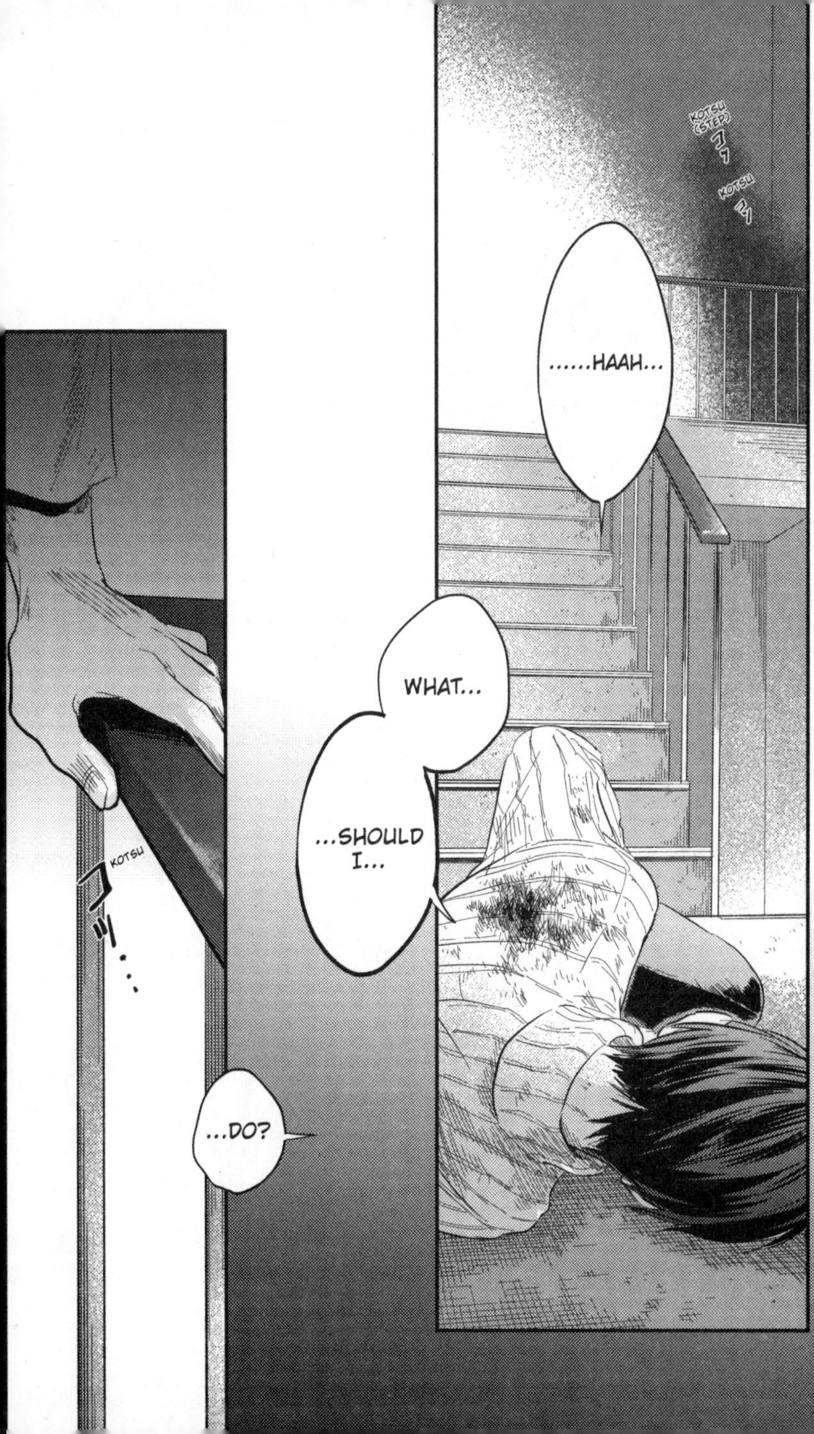
KOTSU (STEP)
KOTSU
......HAAH...
WHAT...
...SHOULD I...
KOTSU
...DO?

AND NOW, A COMPLETE RIP-OFF OF A (PAST) REGULAR SEGMENT FROM *COMIC GENE*!

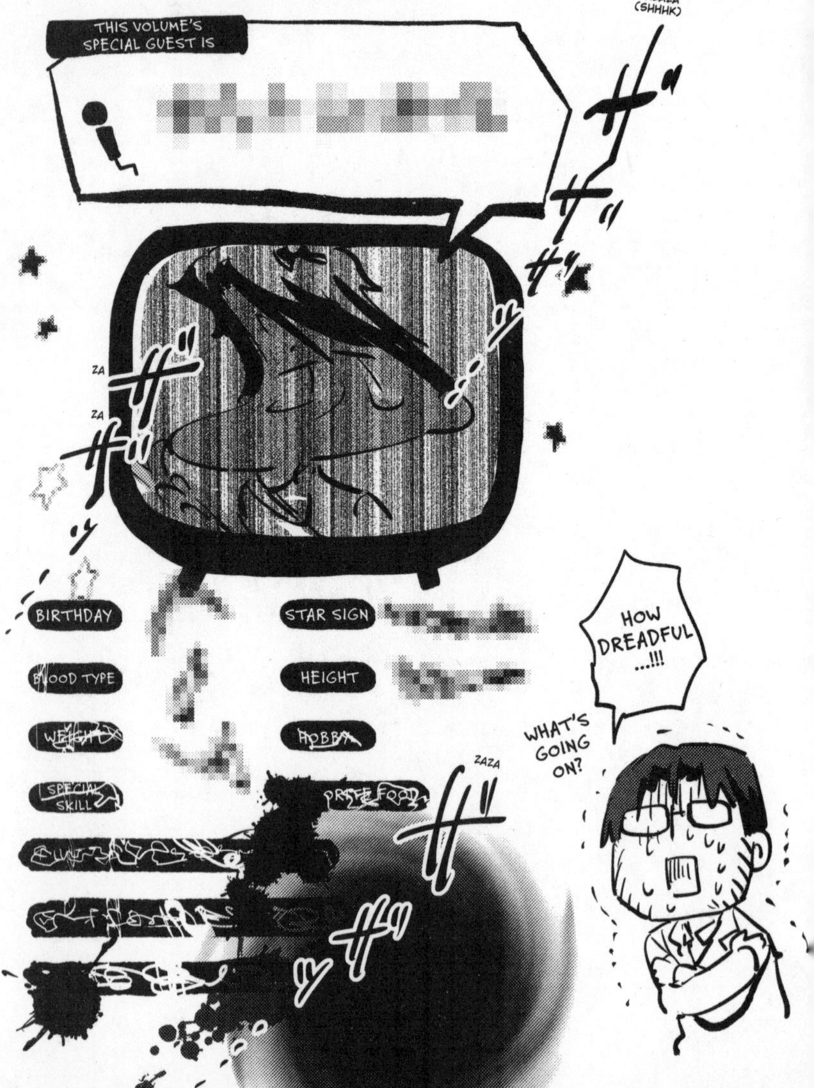
ZAZAZA (SHHHK)
THIS VOLUME'S SPECIAL GUEST IS
ZA
ZA
BIRTHDAY
STAR SIGN
BLOOD TYPE
HEIGHT
SPECIAL SKILL
HOW DREADFUL ...!!!
WHAT'S GOING ON?
ZAZA

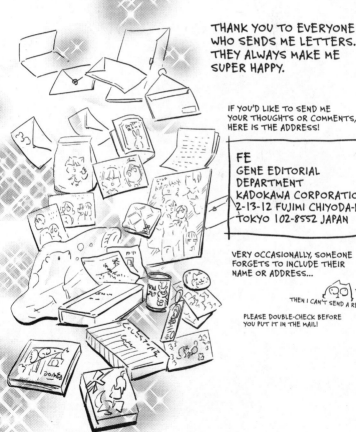

THANK YOU TO EVERYONE WHO SENDS ME LETTERS. ♡ THEY ALWAYS MAKE ME SUPER HAPPY.

IF YOU'D LIKE TO SEND ME YOUR THOUGHTS OR COMMENTS, HERE IS THE ADDRESS!

FE
GENE EDITORIAL DEPARTMENT
KADOKAWA CORPORATION
2-13-12 FUJIMI CHIYODA-KU
TOKYO 102-8552 JAPAN

VERY OCCASIONALLY, SOMEONE FORGETS TO INCLUDE THEIR NAME OR ADDRESS...

THEN I CAN'T SEND A REPLY...

PLEASE DOUBLE-CHECK BEFORE YOU PUT IT IN THE MAIL!

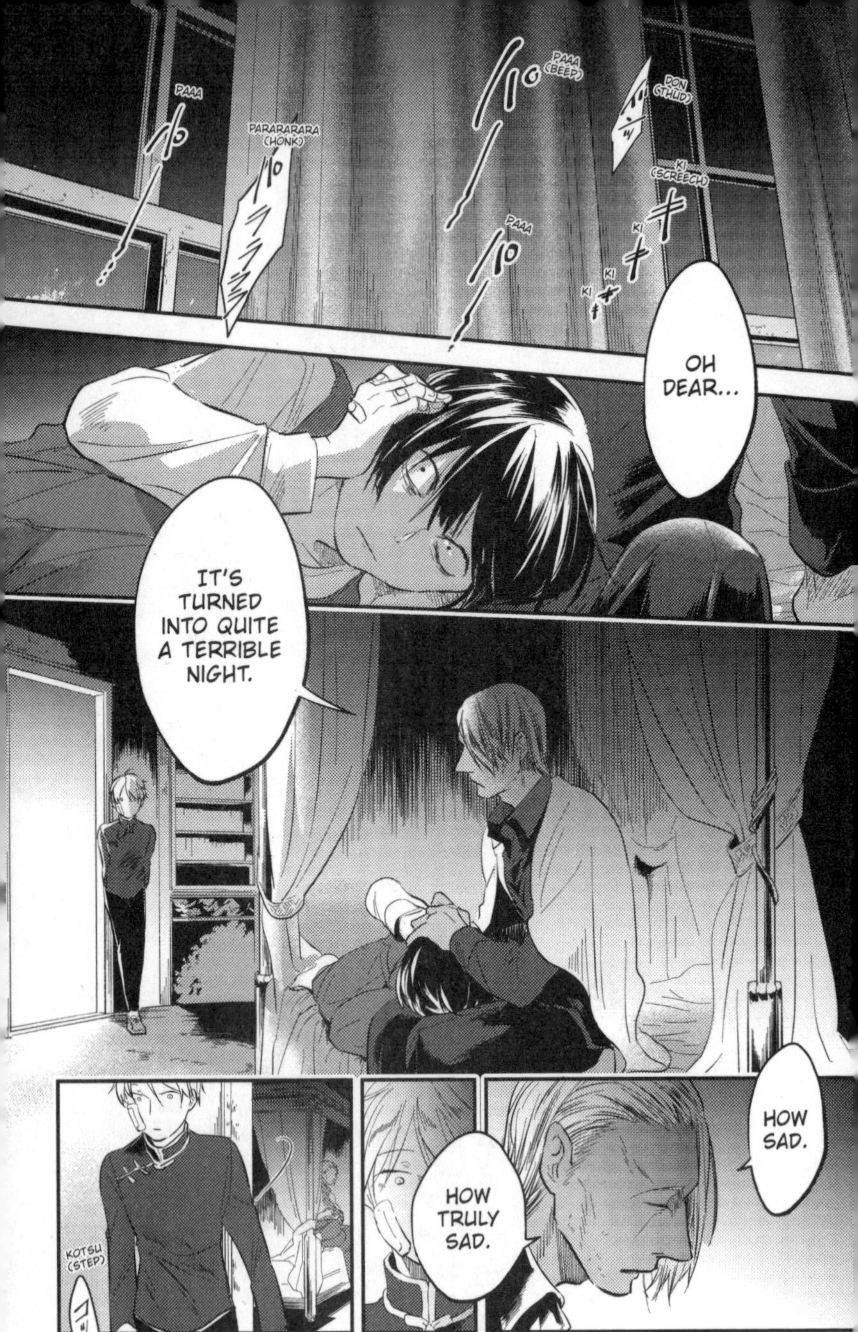
DON (THUD)
KI (SCREECH)
KI
KI
KI
PAAA (BEEP)
PAAA
PARARARARA (HONK)
PAAA
OH DEAR...
IT'S TURNED INTO QUITE A TERRIBLE NIGHT.
HOW SAD.
HOW TRULY SAD.
KOTSU (STEP)

FILE 30 REUNION

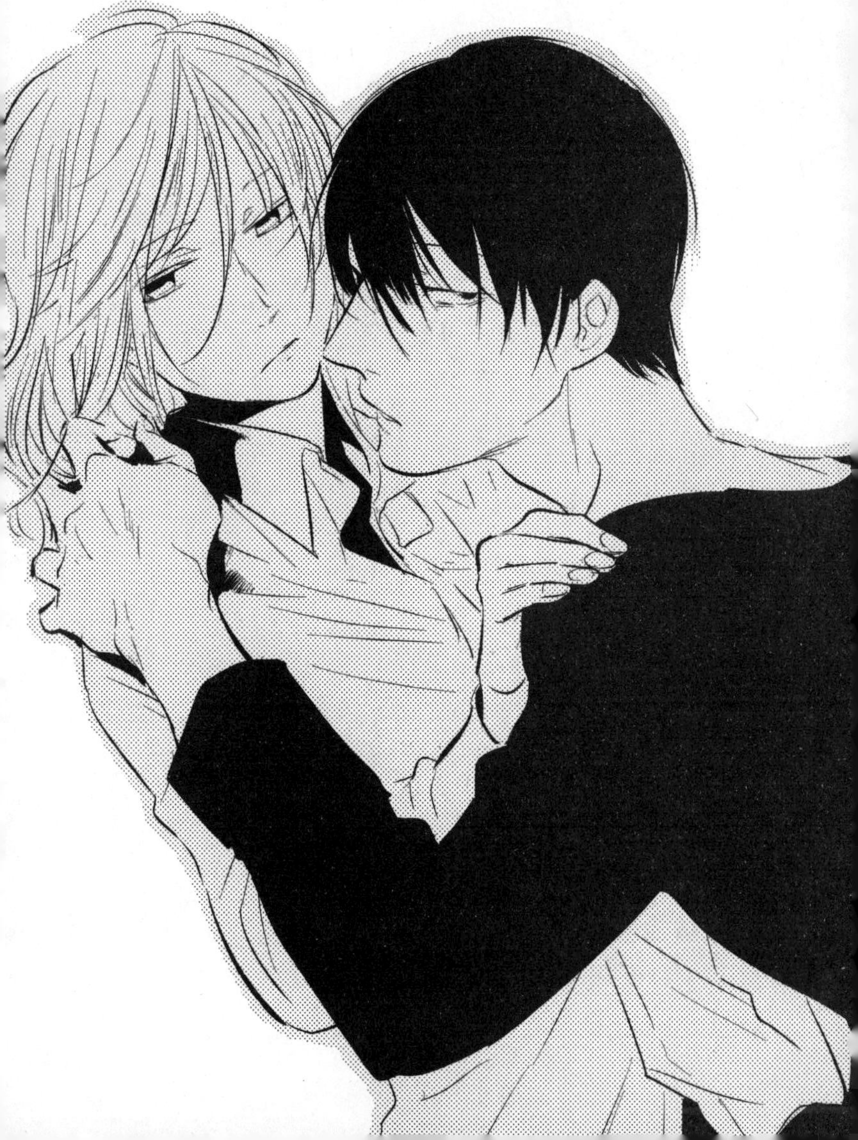

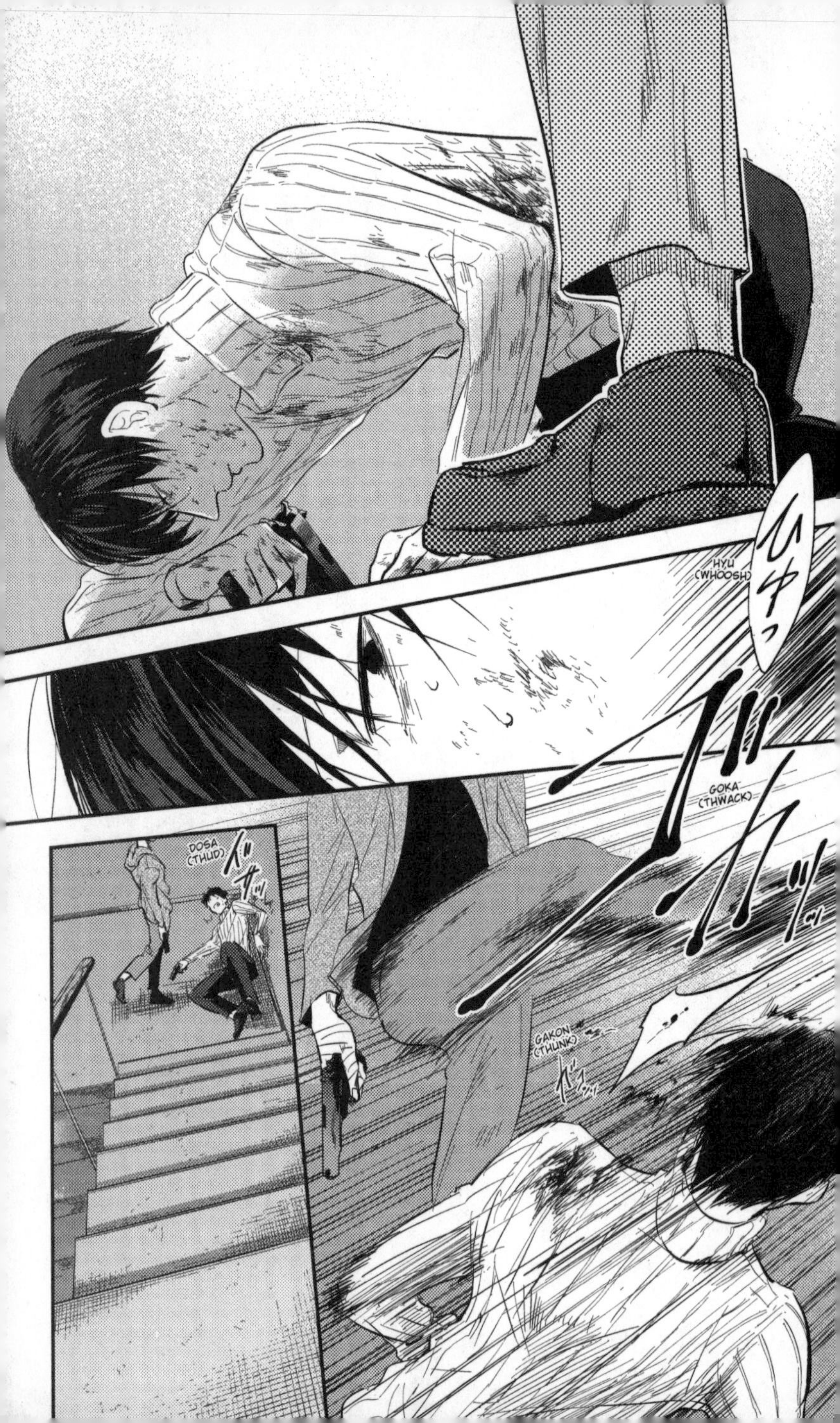
ひゅっ
HYU (WHOOSH)
GOKA (THWACK)
GAKON (THUNK)
DOSA (THUD)

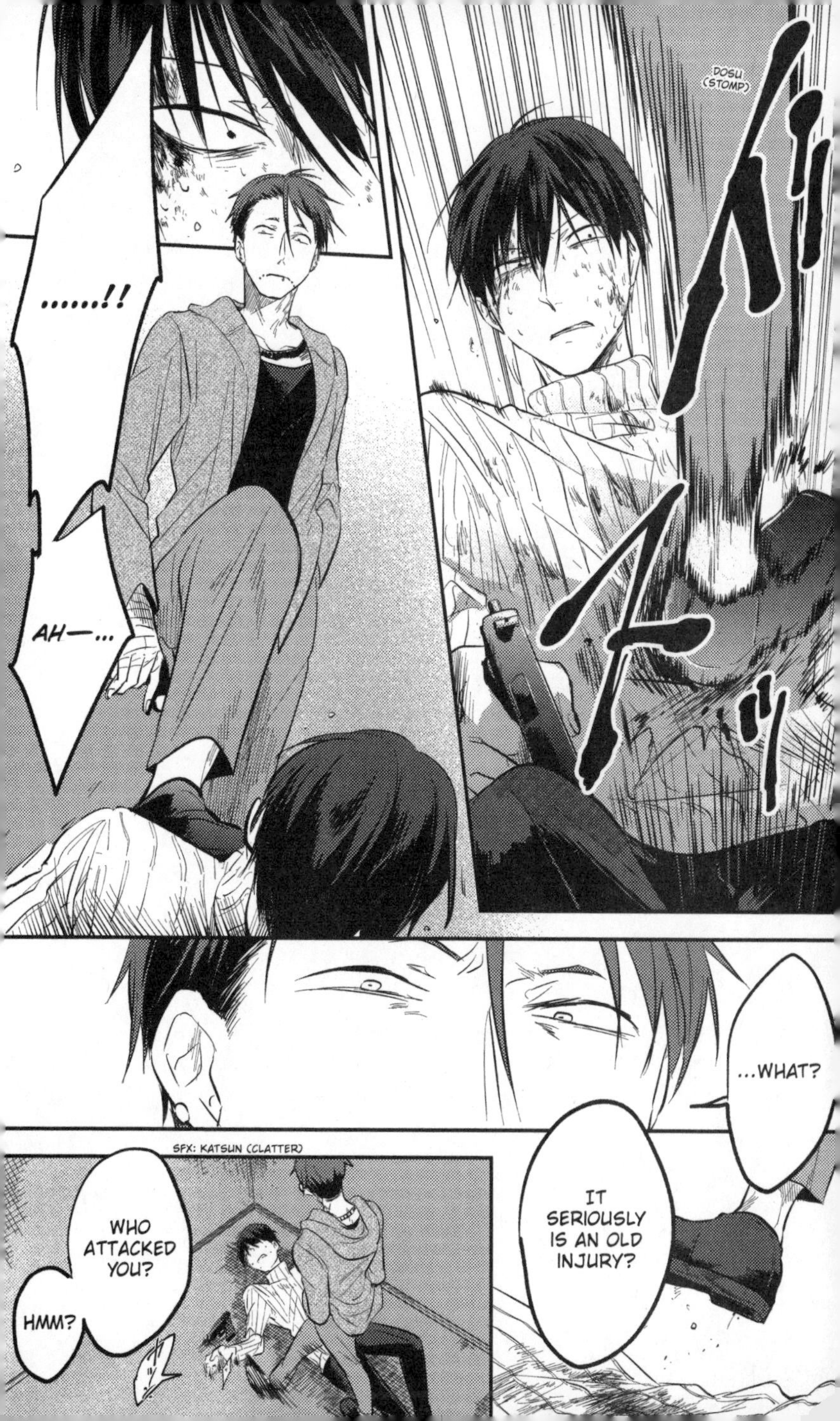
DOSU (STOMP)
......!!
AH—...
...WHAT?
IT SERIOUSLY IS AN OLD INJURY?
SFX: KATSUN (CLATTER)
WHO ATTACKED YOU?
HMM?

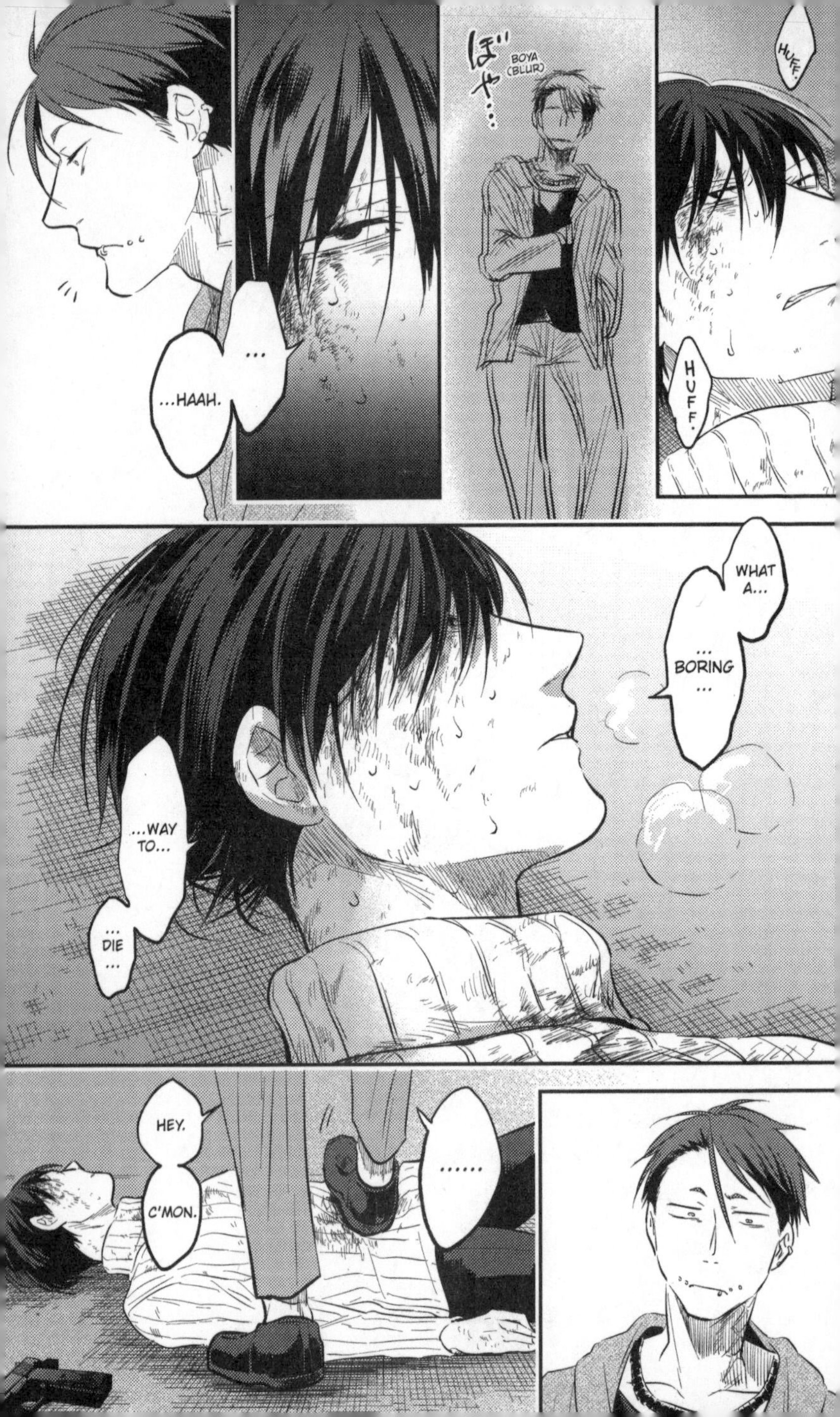
HUFF.
HUFF.
ぼや…
BOYA (BLUR)
...
...HAAH.
WHAT A...
...BORING...
...WAY TO...
...DIE...
......
HEY.
C'MON.

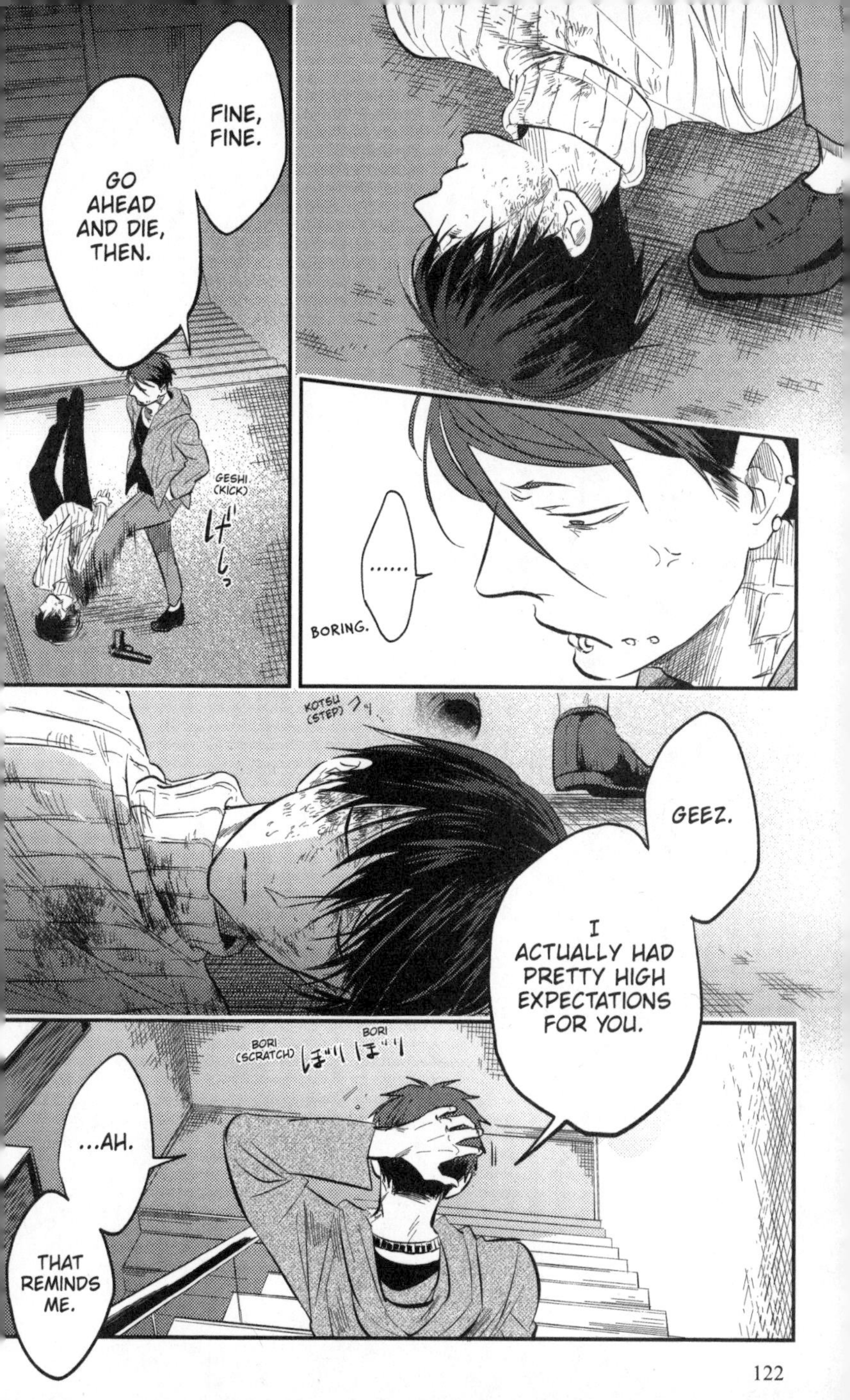
......
BORING.
FINE, FINE.
GO AHEAD AND DIE, THEN.
GESHI (KICK)
げしっ
KOTSU (STEP)
コツ...
GEEZ.
I ACTUALLY HAD PRETTY HIGH EXPECTATIONS FOR YOU.
BORI (SCRATCH) BORI
ぼりぼり
...AH.
THAT REMINDS ME.

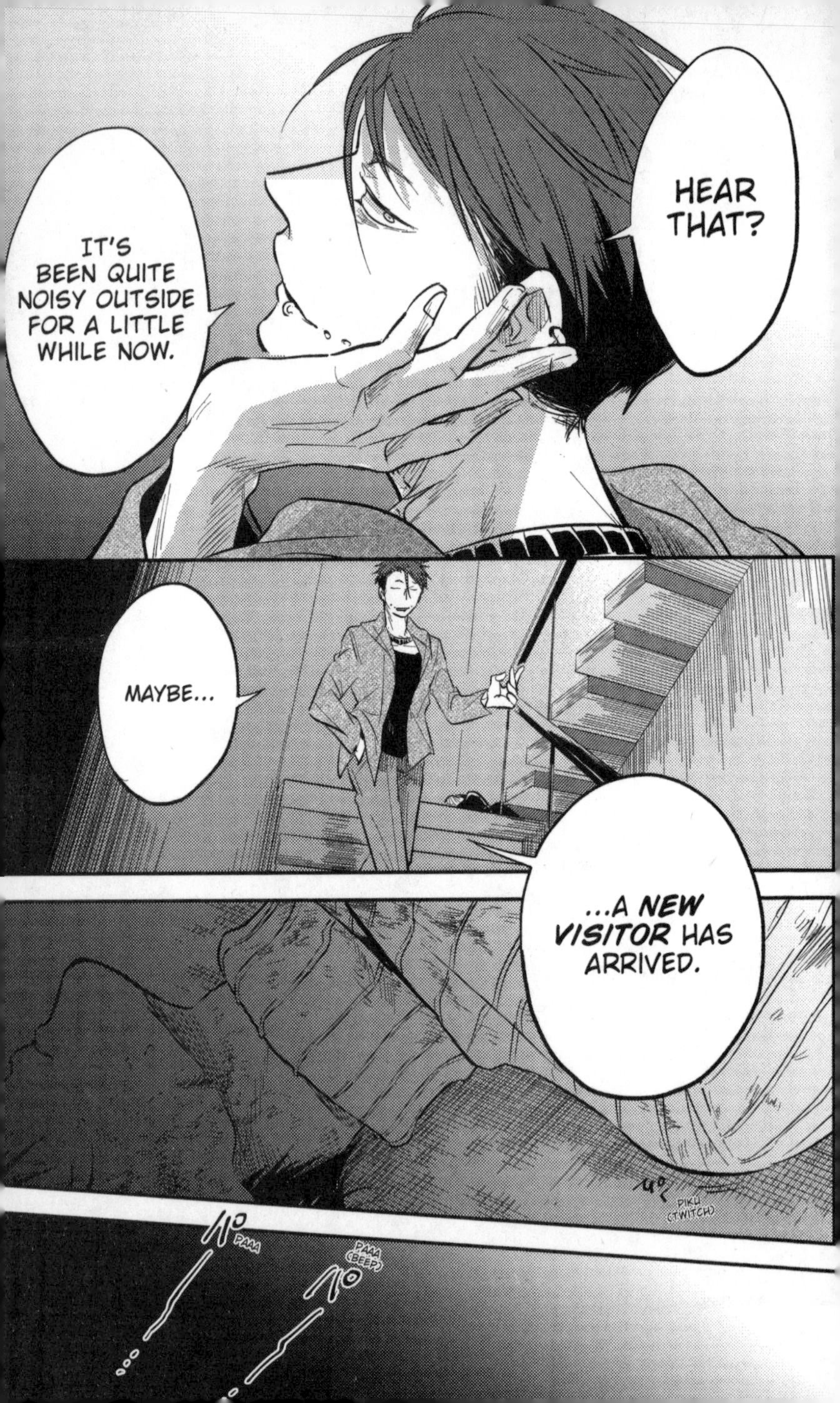
HEAR THAT?
IT'S BEEN QUITE NOISY OUTSIDE FOR A LITTLE WHILE NOW.
MAYBE...
...A NEW VISITOR HAS ARRIVED.
PIKU (TWITCH)
PAAA
PAAA (BEEP)

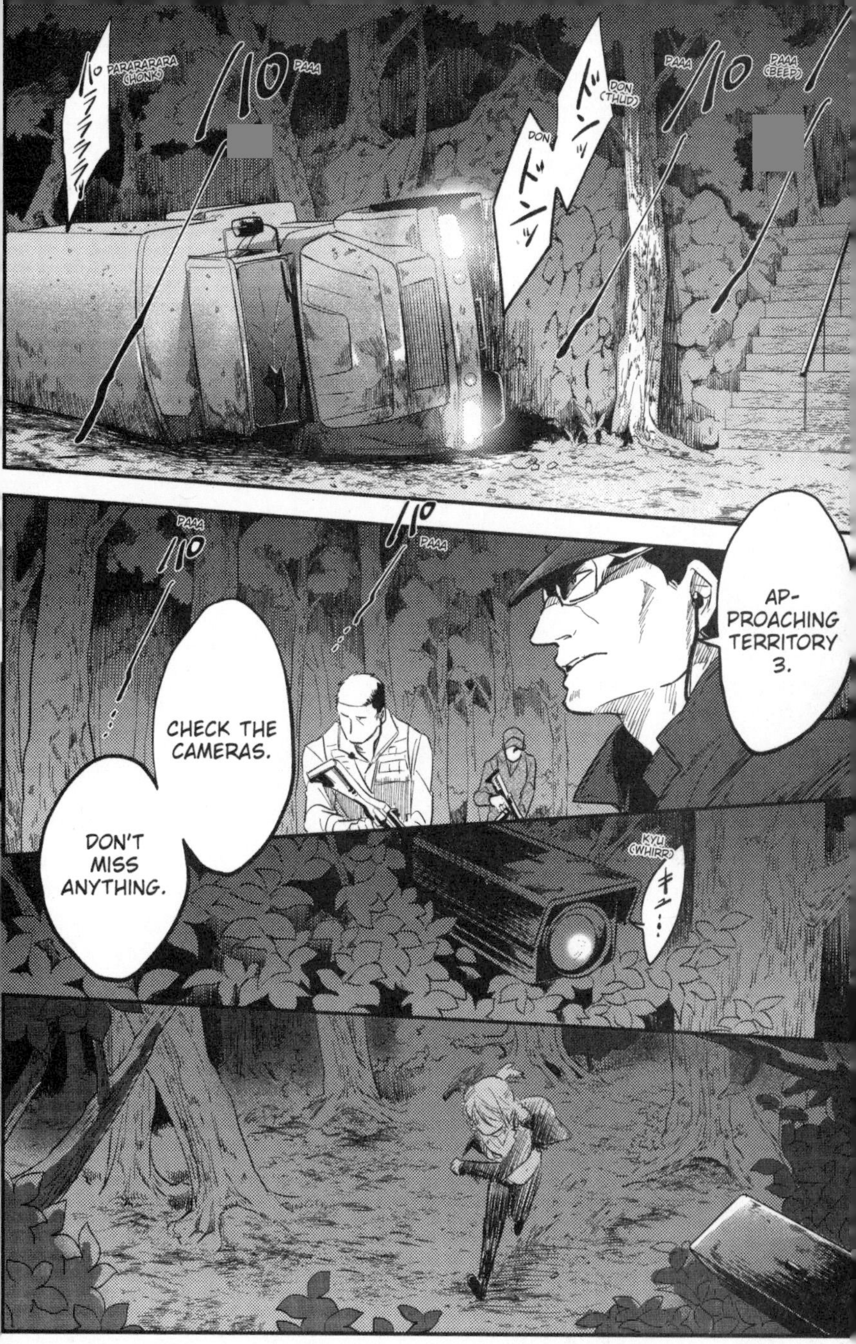
PAAA (BEEP)
PAAA
DON (THUD)
DON
PAAA
PARARARARA (HONK)
AP-PROACHING TERRITORY 3.
PAAA
PAAA
CHECK THE CAMERAS.
KYU (WHIRR)
DON'T MISS ANYTHING.

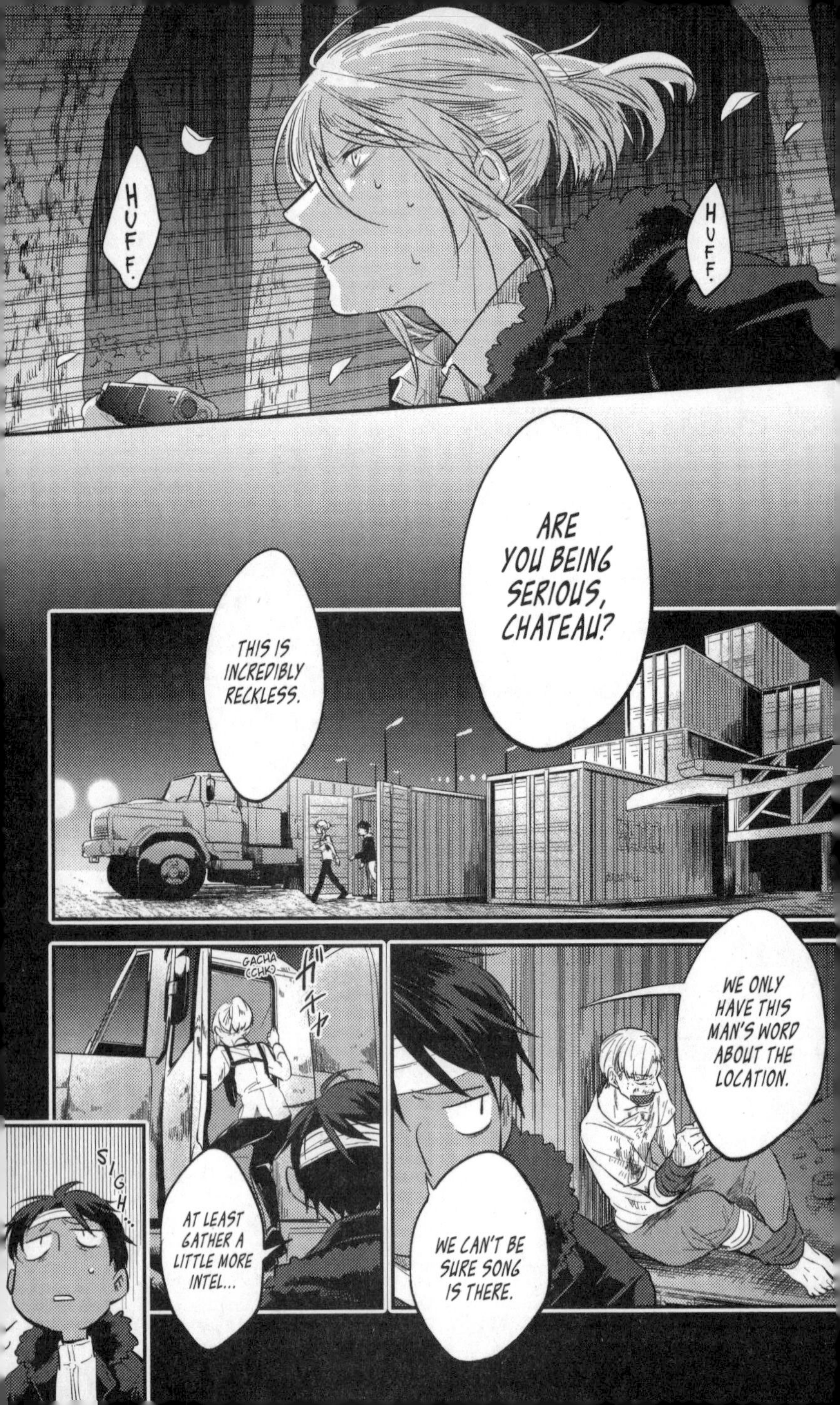
HUFF.
HUFF.
ARE YOU BEING SERIOUS, CHATEAU?
THIS IS INCREDIBLY RECKLESS.
WE ONLY HAVE THIS MAN'S WORD ABOUT THE LOCATION.
WE CAN'T BE SURE SONG IS THERE.
GACHA (CHK)
ガチャ
AT LEAST GATHER A LITTLE MORE INTEL...
SIGH...

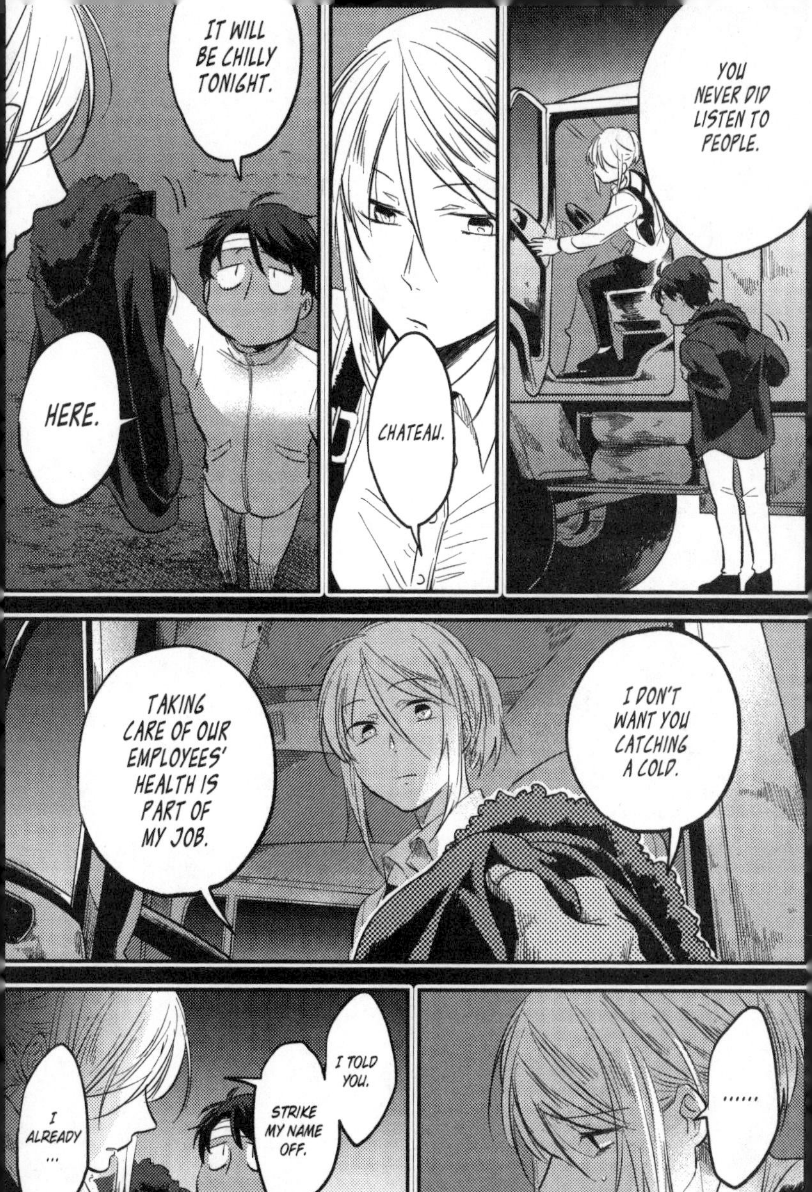
YOU NEVER DID LISTEN TO PEOPLE.
CHATEAU.
IT WILL BE CHILLY TONIGHT.
HERE.
I DON'T WANT YOU CATCHING A COLD.
TAKING CARE OF OUR EMPLOYEES' HEALTH IS PART OF MY JOB.
......
I TOLD YOU.
STRIKE MY NAME OFF.
I ALREADY ...

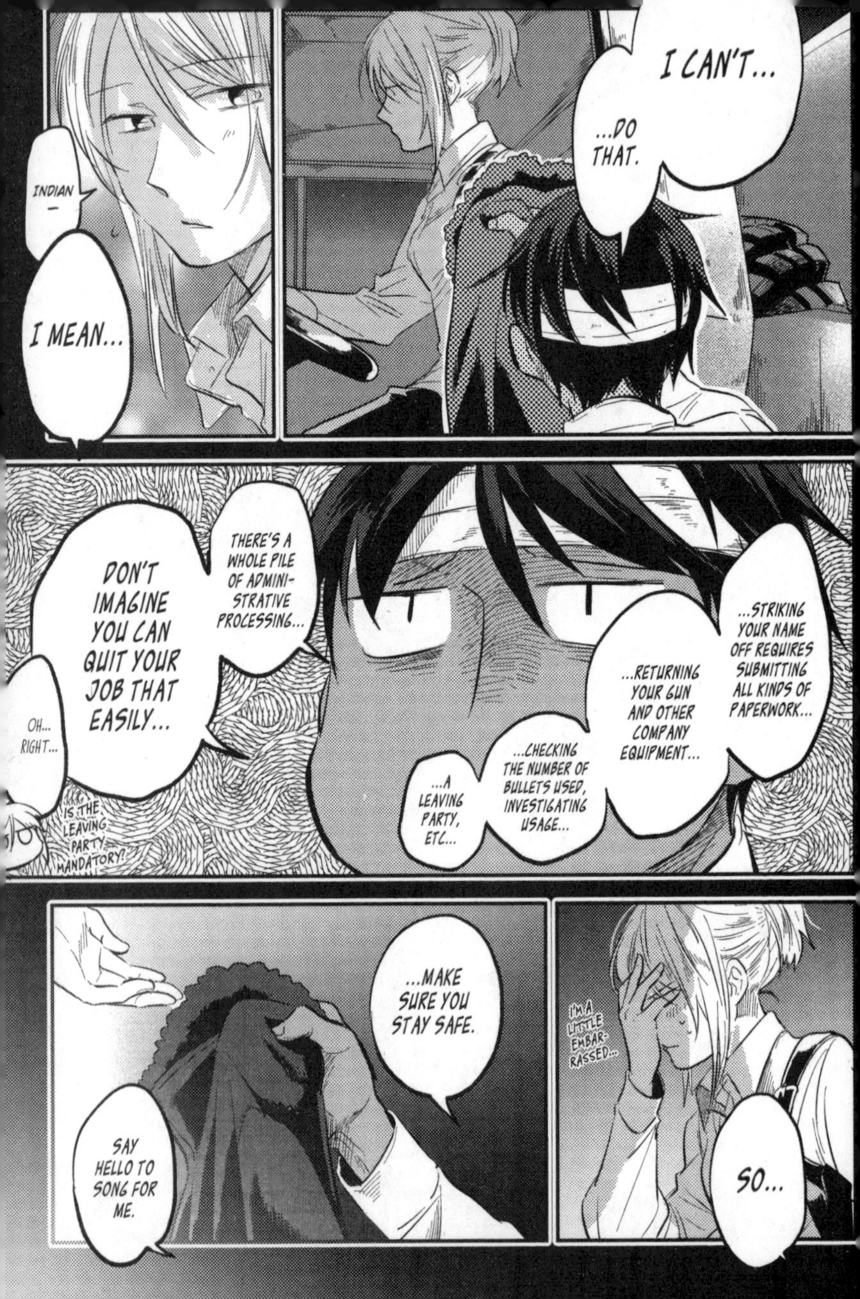
I CAN'T...
...DO THAT.
INDIAN—
I MEAN...
DON'T IMAGINE YOU CAN QUIT YOUR JOB THAT EASILY...
THERE'S A WHOLE PILE OF ADMINI-STRATIVE PROCESSING...
...STRIKING YOUR NAME OFF REQUIRES SUBMITTING ALL KINDS OF PAPERWORK...
...RETURNING YOUR GUN AND OTHER COMPANY EQUIPMENT...
...CHECKING THE NUMBER OF BULLETS USED, INVESTIGATING USAGE...
...A LEAVING PARTY, ETC...
OH... RIGHT...
IS THE LEAVING PARTY MANDATORY?
I'M A LITTLE EMBAR-RASSED...
SO...
...MAKE SURE YOU STAY SAFE.
SAY HELLO TO SONG FOR ME.

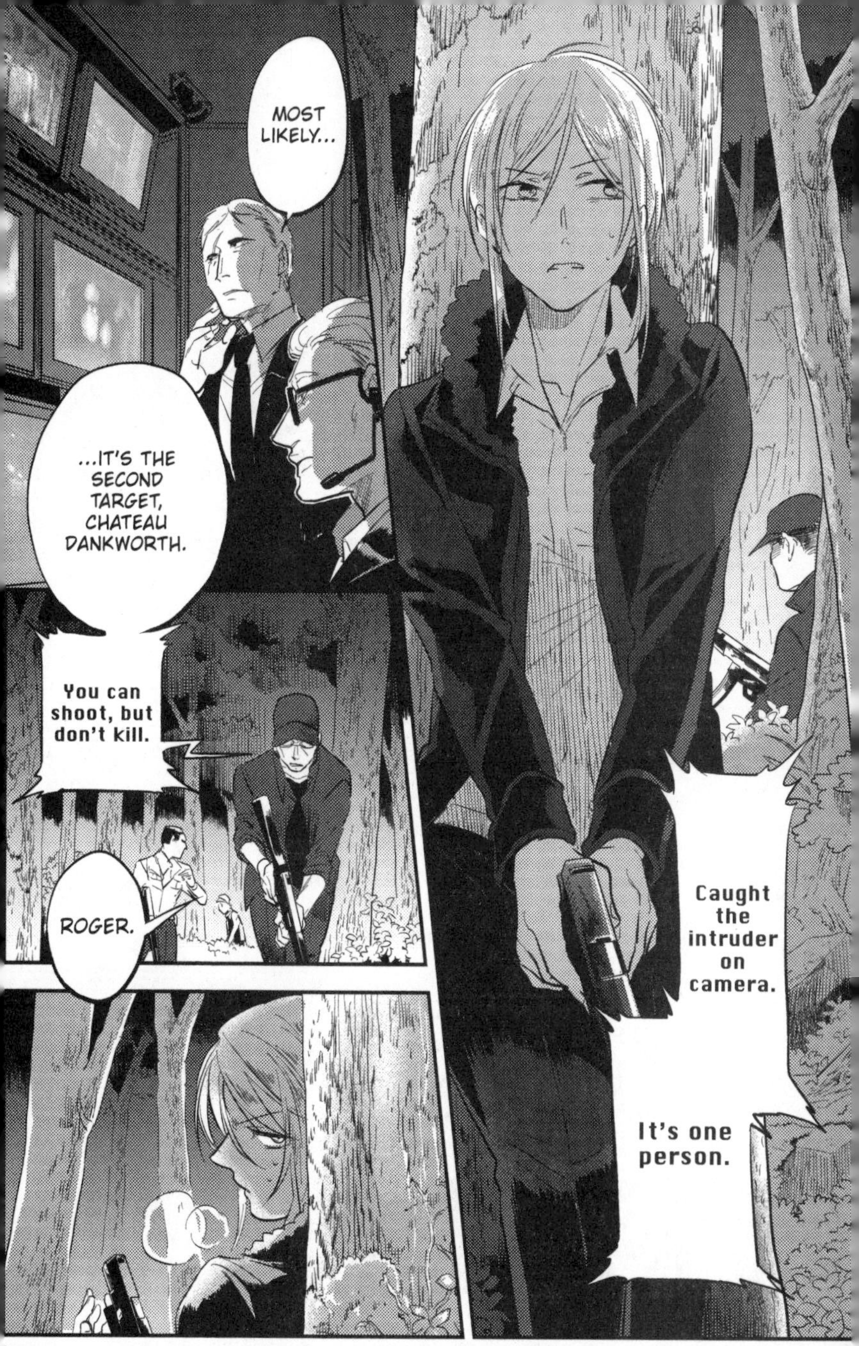

Caught the intruder on camera.
It's one person.
MOST LIKELY...
...IT'S THE SECOND TARGET, CHATEAU DANKWORTH.
You can shoot, but don't kill.
ROGER.

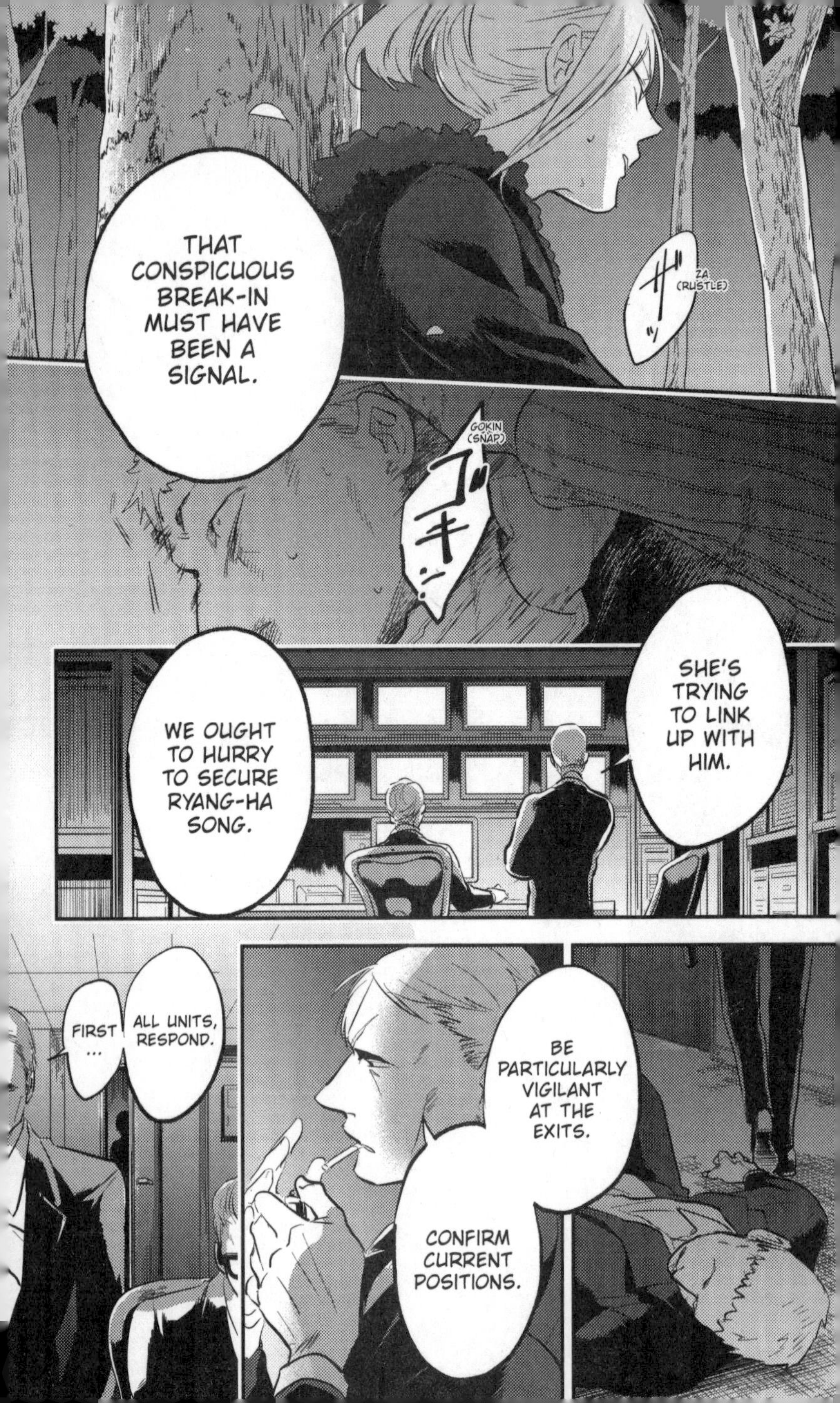
ZA (RUSTLE)
THAT CONSPICUOUS BREAK-IN MUST HAVE BEEN A SIGNAL.
GOKIN (SNAP)
SHE'S TRYING TO LINK UP WITH HIM.
WE OUGHT TO HURRY TO SECURE RYANG-HA SONG.
BE PARTICULARLY VIGILANT AT THE EXITS.
CONFIRM CURRENT POSITIONS.
ALL UNITS, RESPOND.
FIRST ...

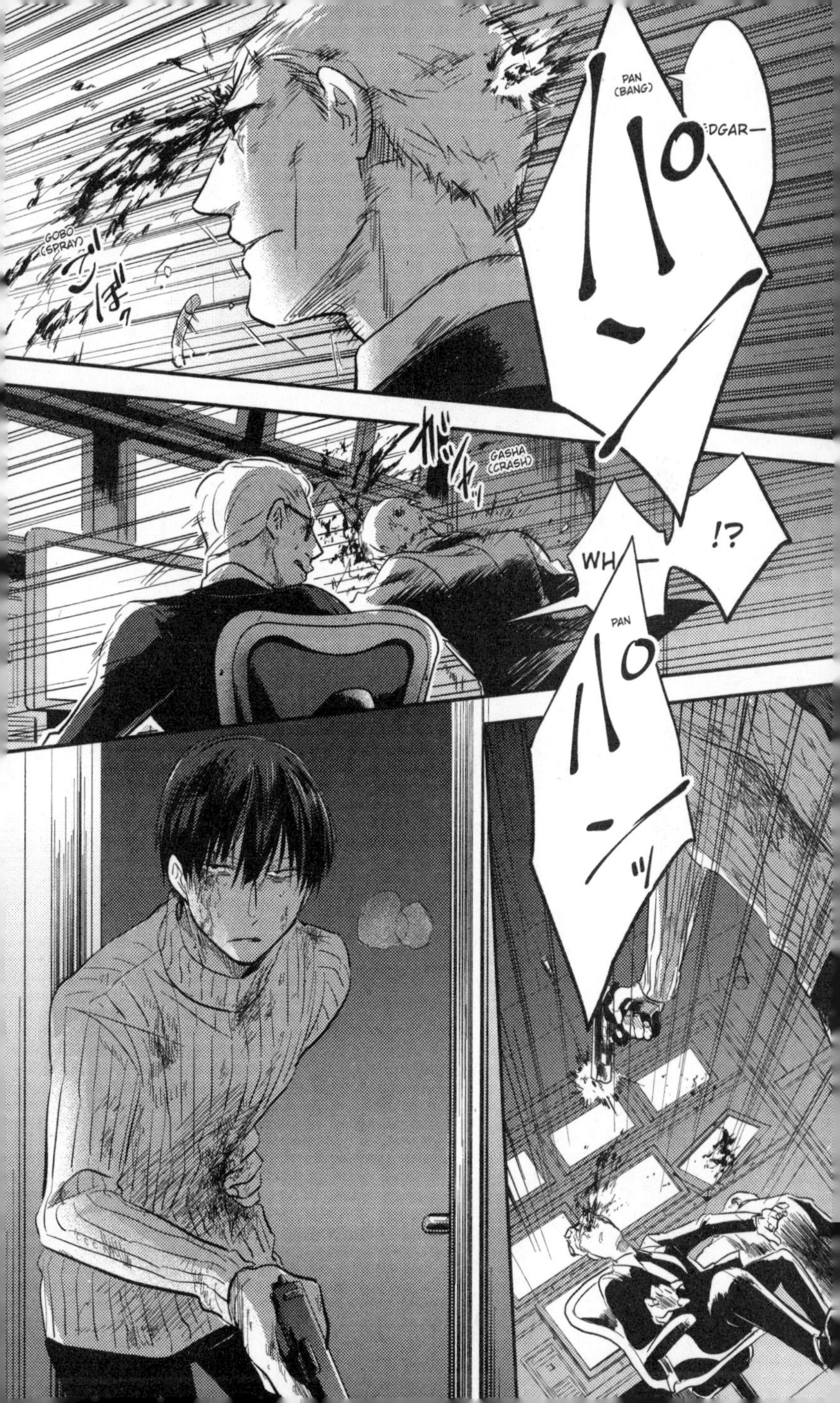
EDGAR—
PAN (BANG)
GOBO (SPRAY)
GASHA (CRASH)
WH—
!?
PAN

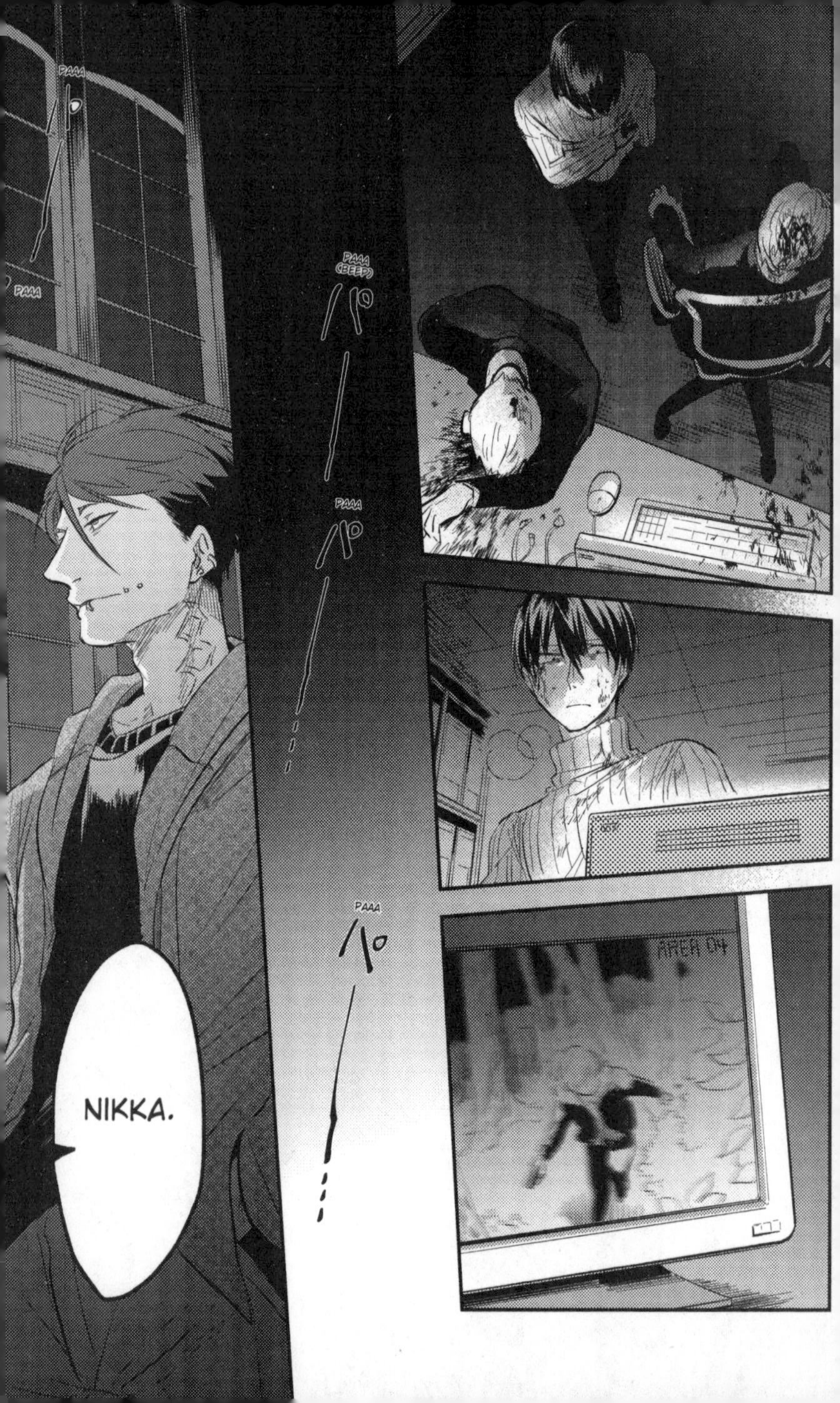
AREA 04
PAAA
PAAA (BEEP)
PAAA
PAAA
PAAA
NIKKA.

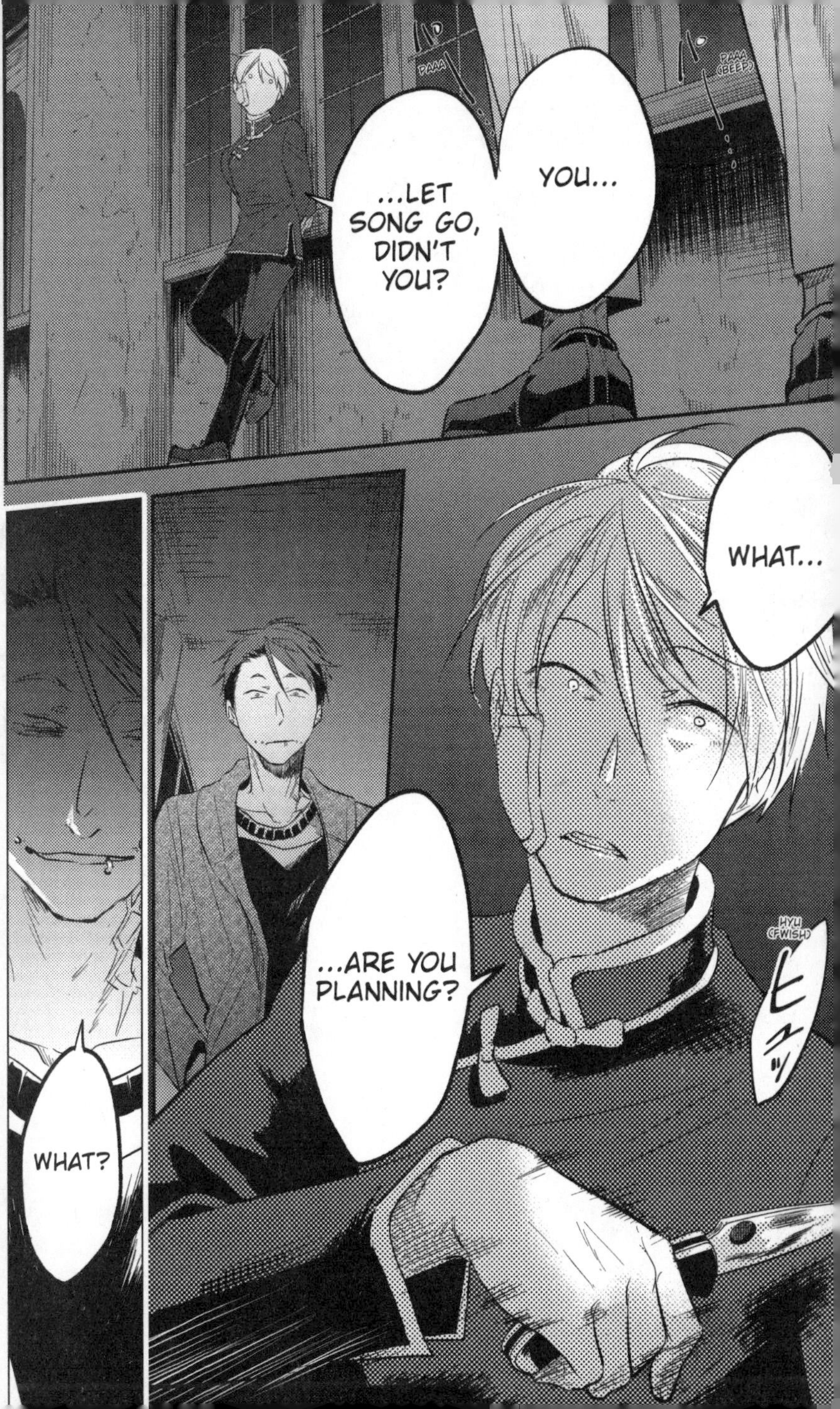
PAAA (BEEP)
YOU...
PAAA
...LET SONG GO, DIDN'T YOU?
WHAT...
...ARE YOU PLANNING?
HYU (FWISH)
ヒュッ
WHAT?

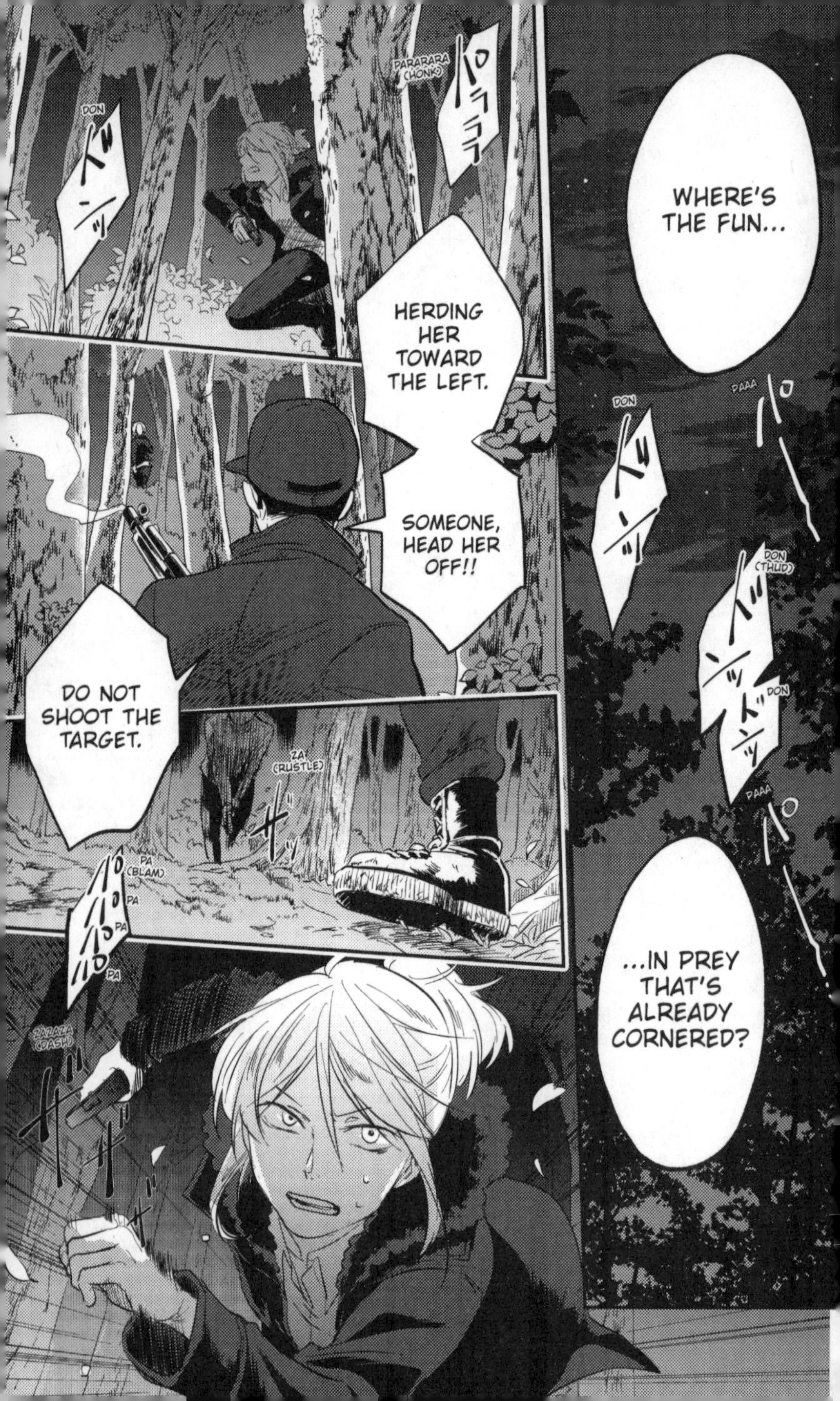
WHERE'S THE FUN...
PAAA
DON
DON (THUD)
DON
PAAA
...IN PREY THAT'S ALREADY CORNERED?
PARARARA (CHONK)
DON
HERDING HER TOWARD THE LEFT.
SOMEONE, HEAD HER OFF!!
DO NOT SHOOT THE TARGET.
ZA (RUSTLE)
PA (BLAM)
PA
PA
PA
ZAZAZA (DASH)

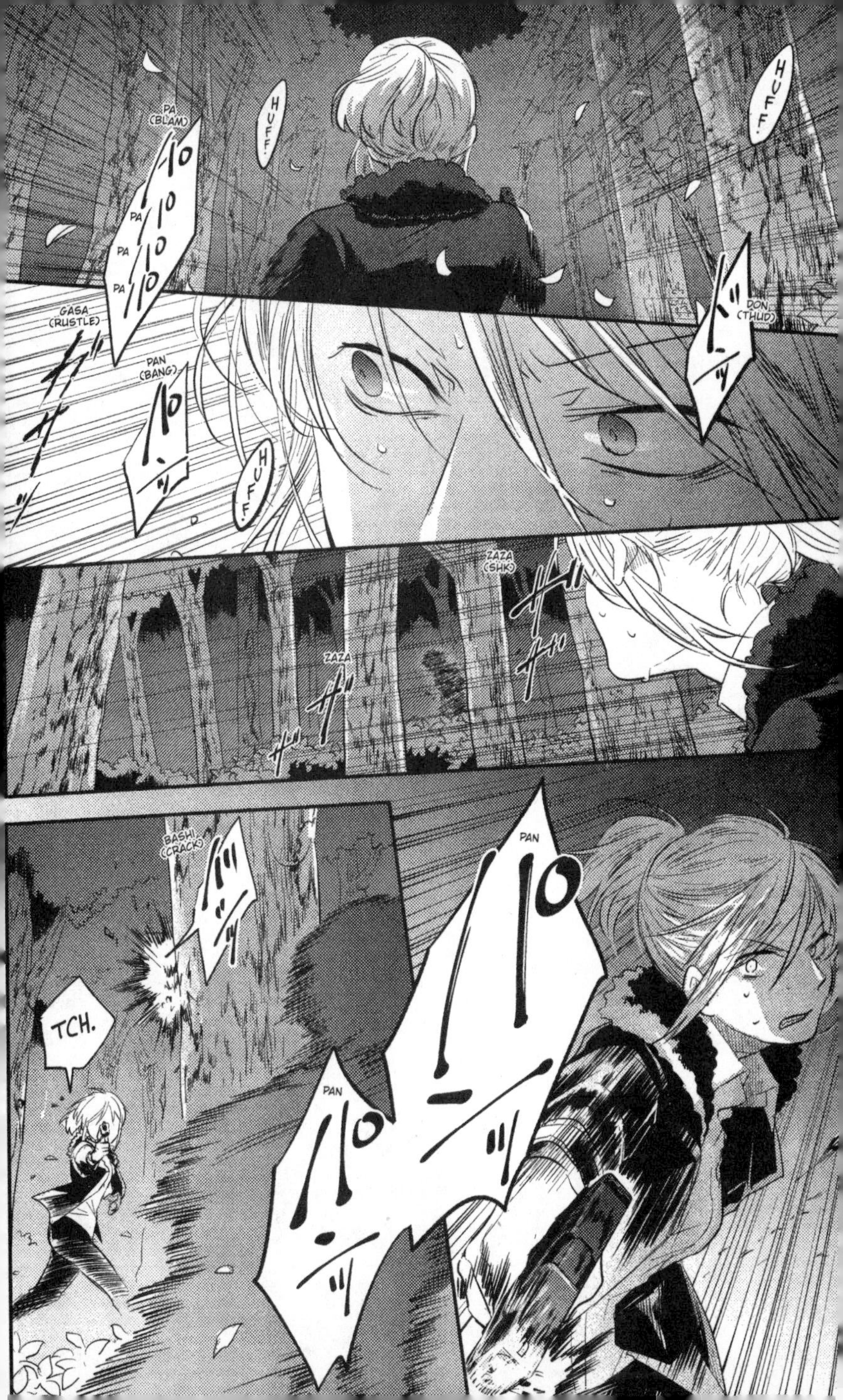
HUFF.
HUFF.
PA (BLAM)
PA
PA
PA
DON (THUD)
HUFF
GASA (RUSTLE)
PAN (BANG)
ZAZA (SHK)
ZAZA
PAN
PAN
BASHI (CRACK)
TCH.

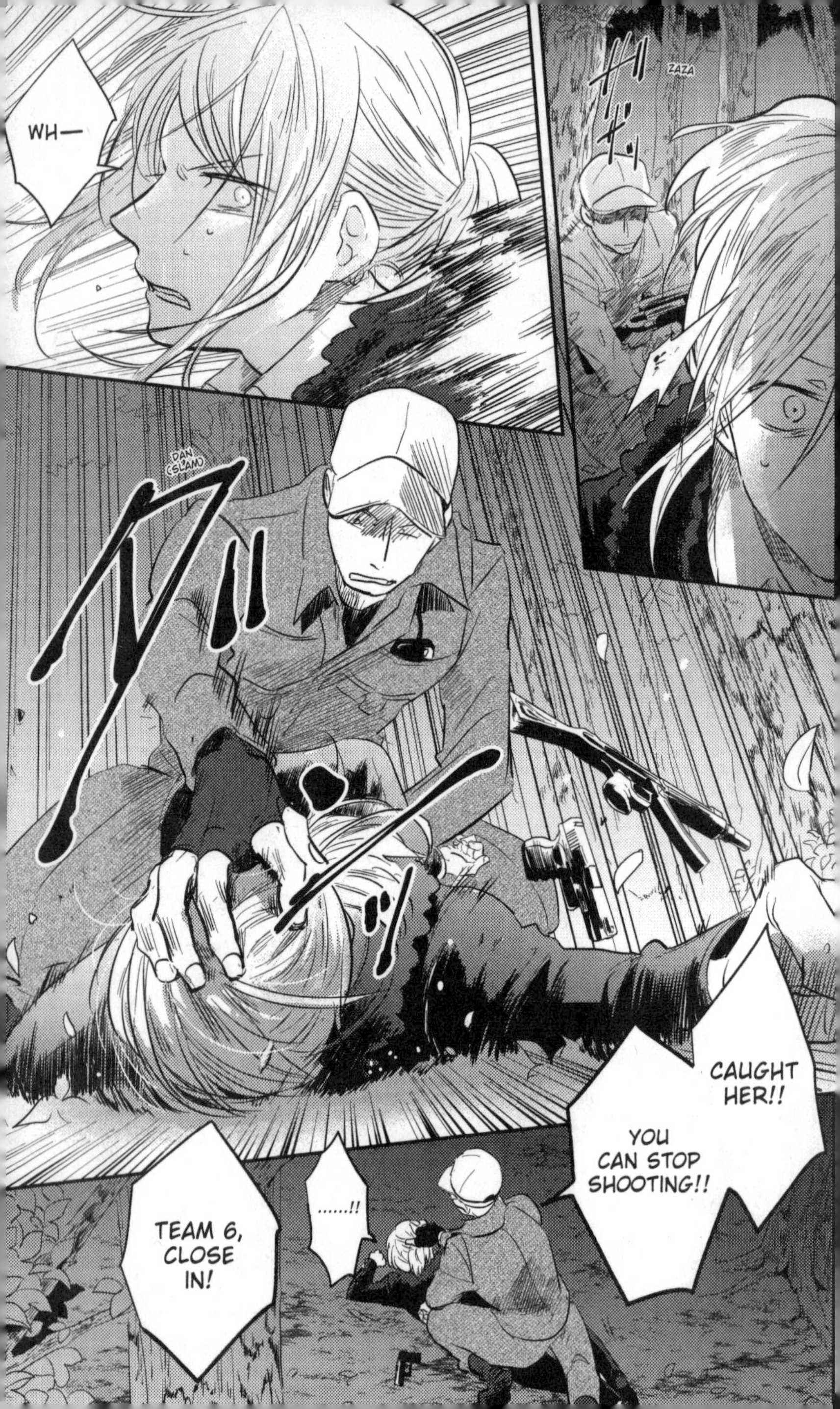
ZAZA
WH—
DAN (SLAM)
CAUGHT HER!!
YOU CAN STOP SHOOTING!!
......!!
TEAM 6, CLOSE IN!

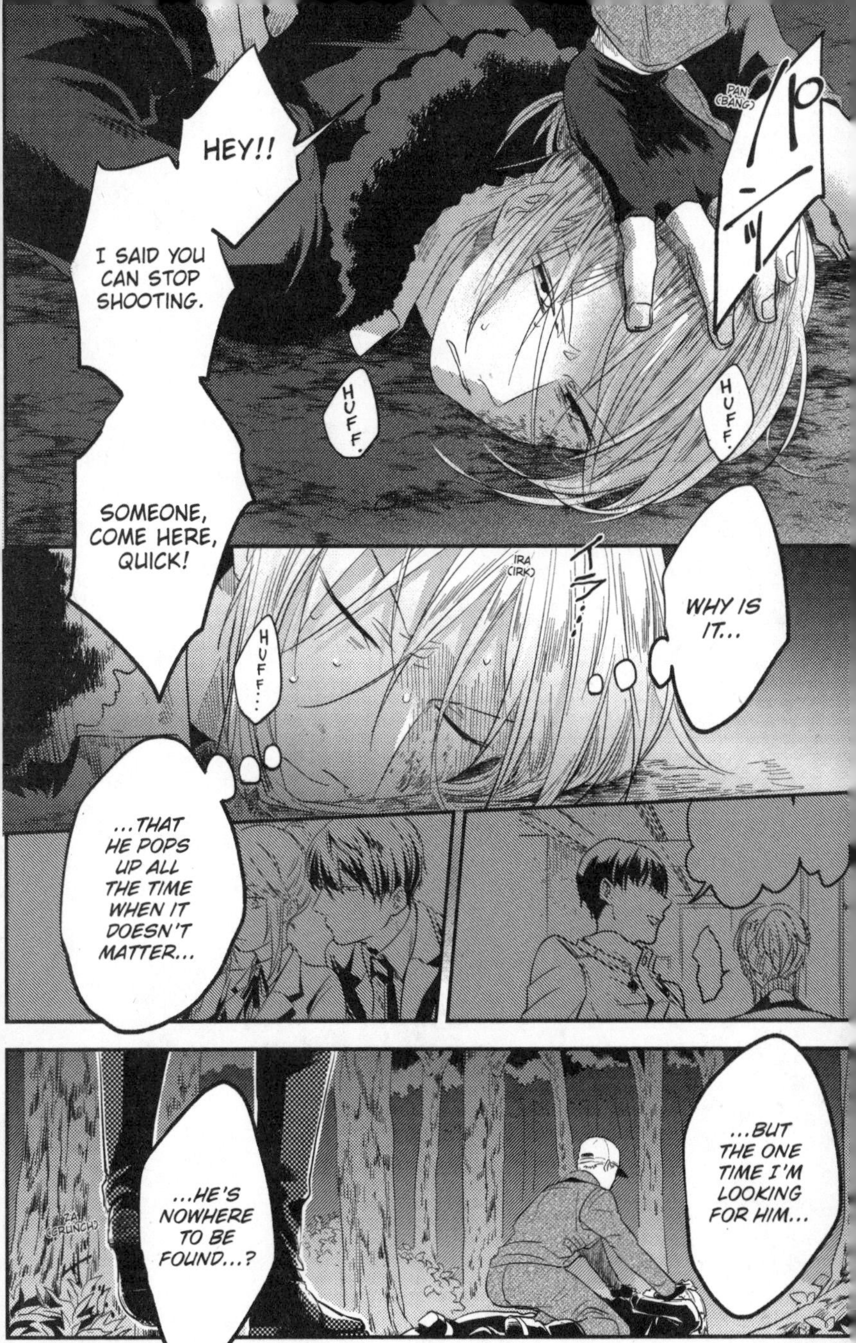
PAN (BANG)
HEY!!
I SAID YOU CAN STOP SHOOTING.
HUFF.
HUFF.
SOMEONE, COME HERE, QUICK!
WHY IS IT...
IRA (IRK)
HUFF...
...THAT HE POPS UP ALL THE TIME WHEN IT DOESN'T MATTER...
...BUT THE ONE TIME I'M LOOKING FOR HIM...
...HE'S NOWHERE TO BE FOUND...?
ZA (CRUNCH)

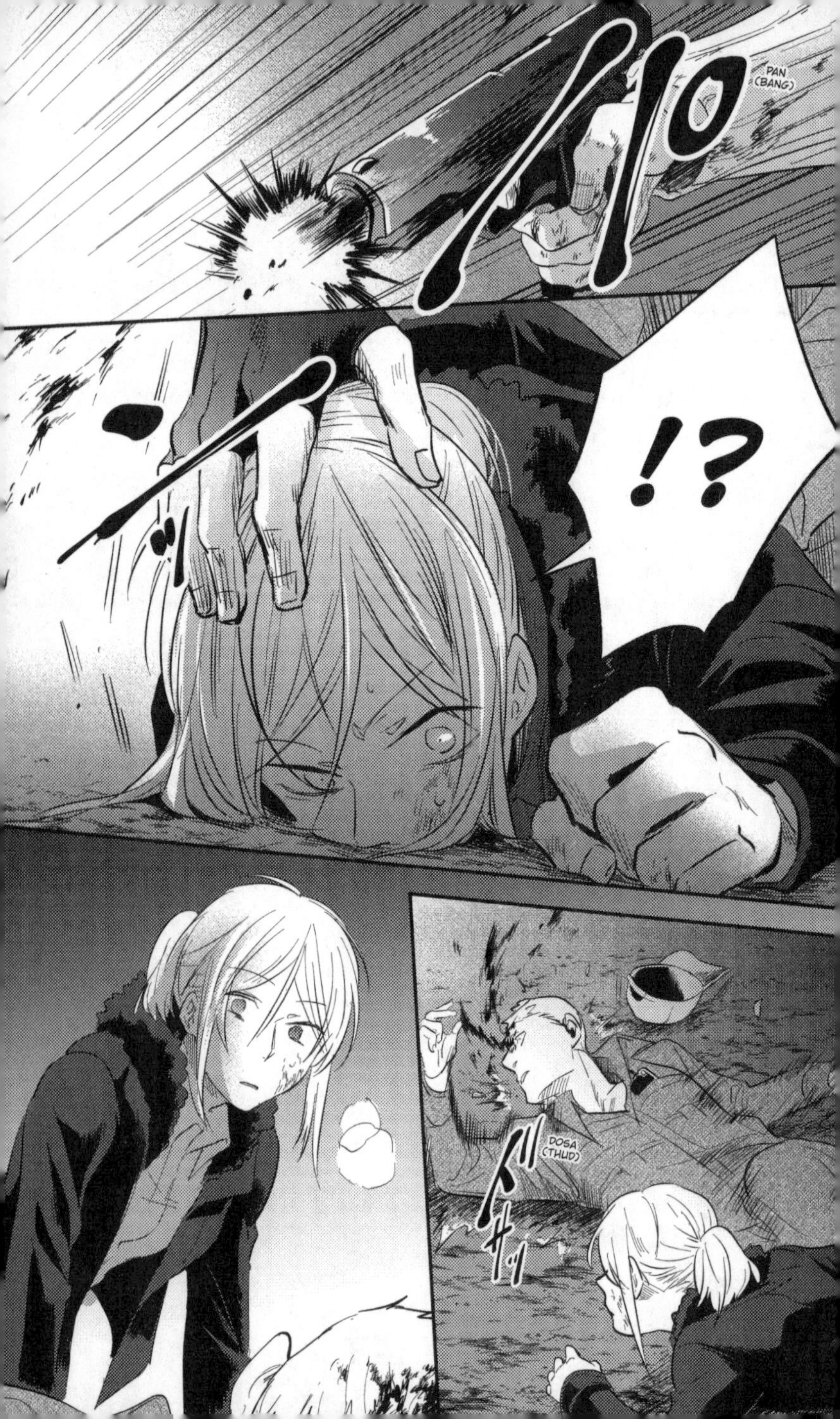
PAN
(BANG)
!?
DOSA
(THUD)

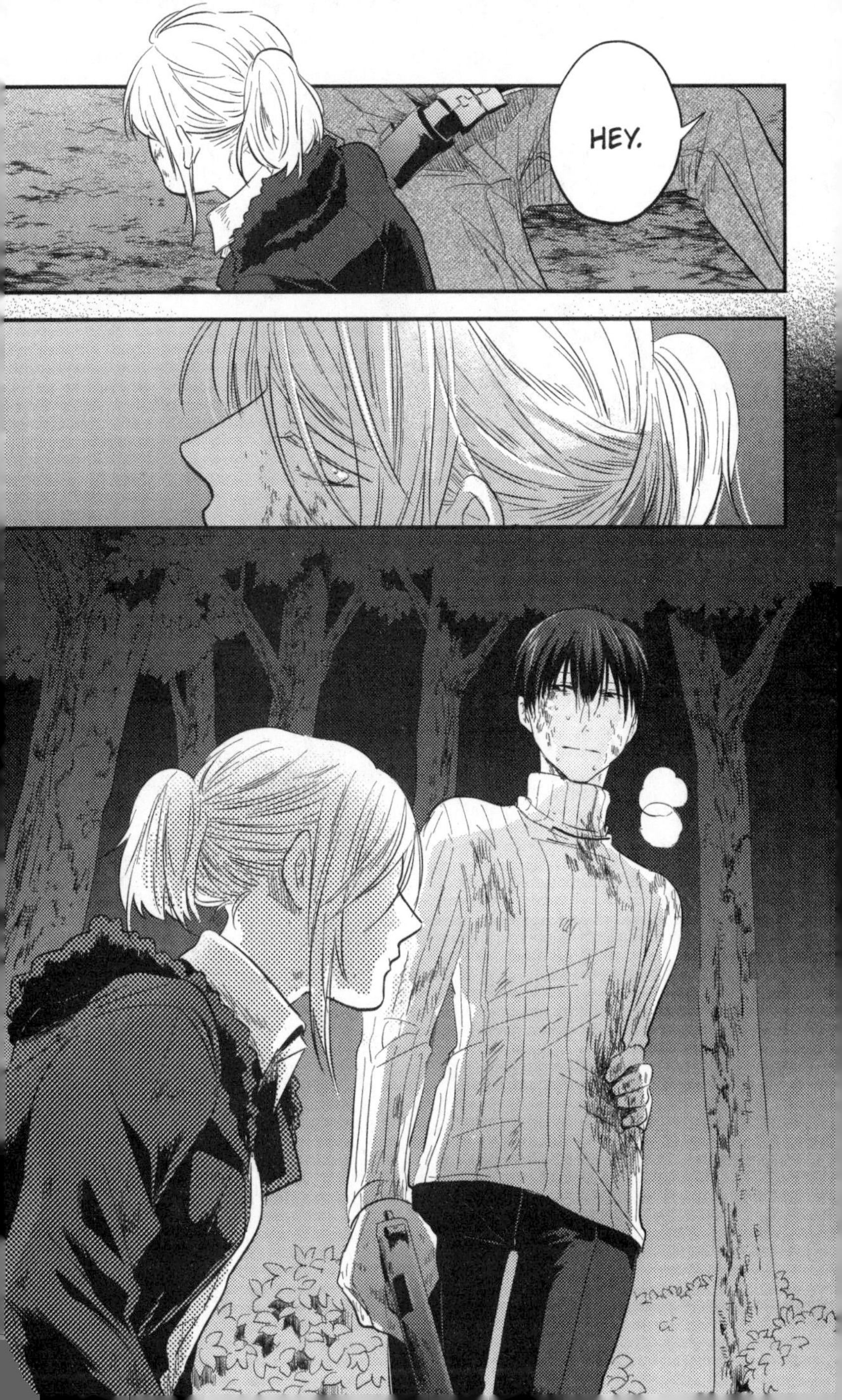
HEY.

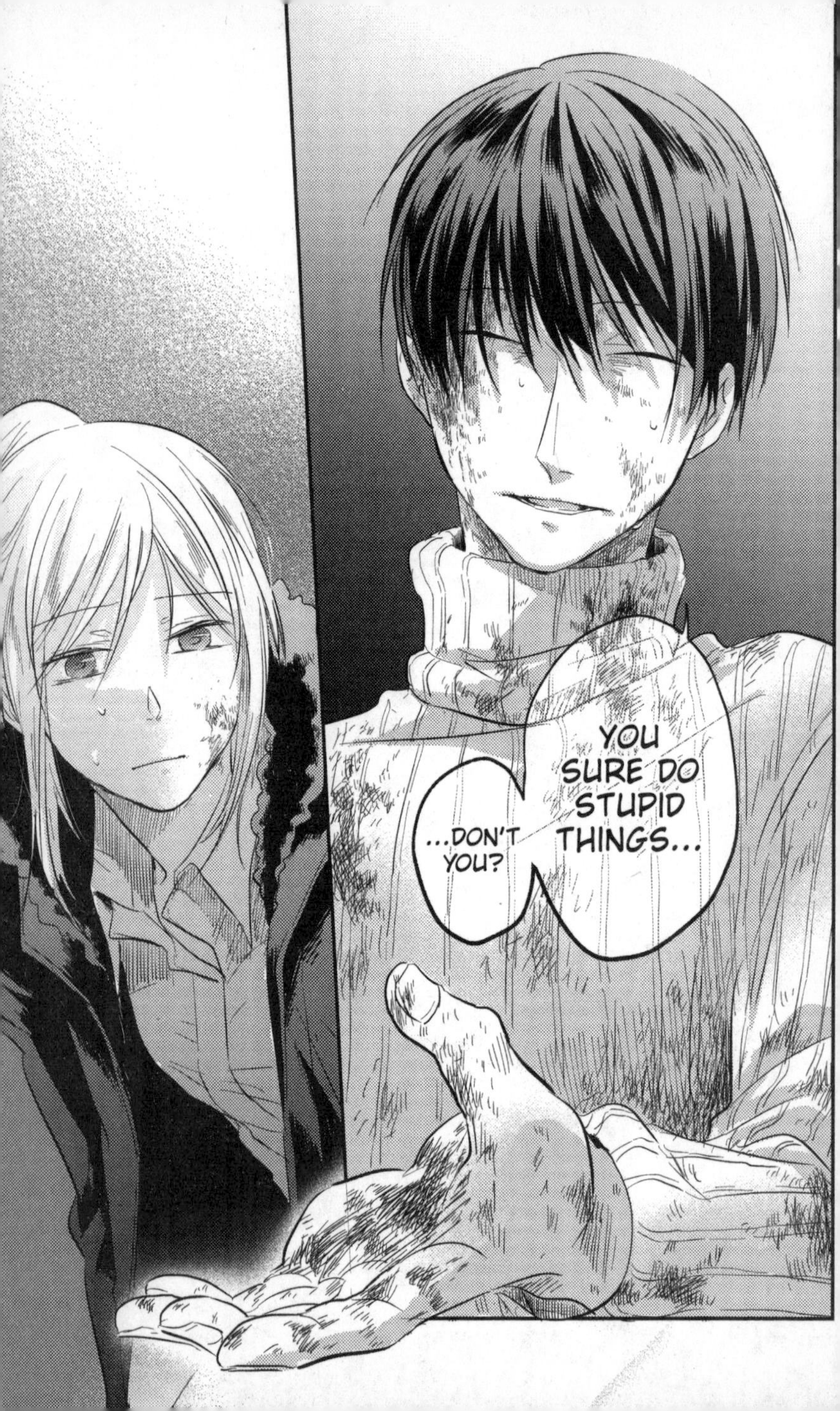
YOU SURE DO STUPID THINGS...
...DON'T YOU?

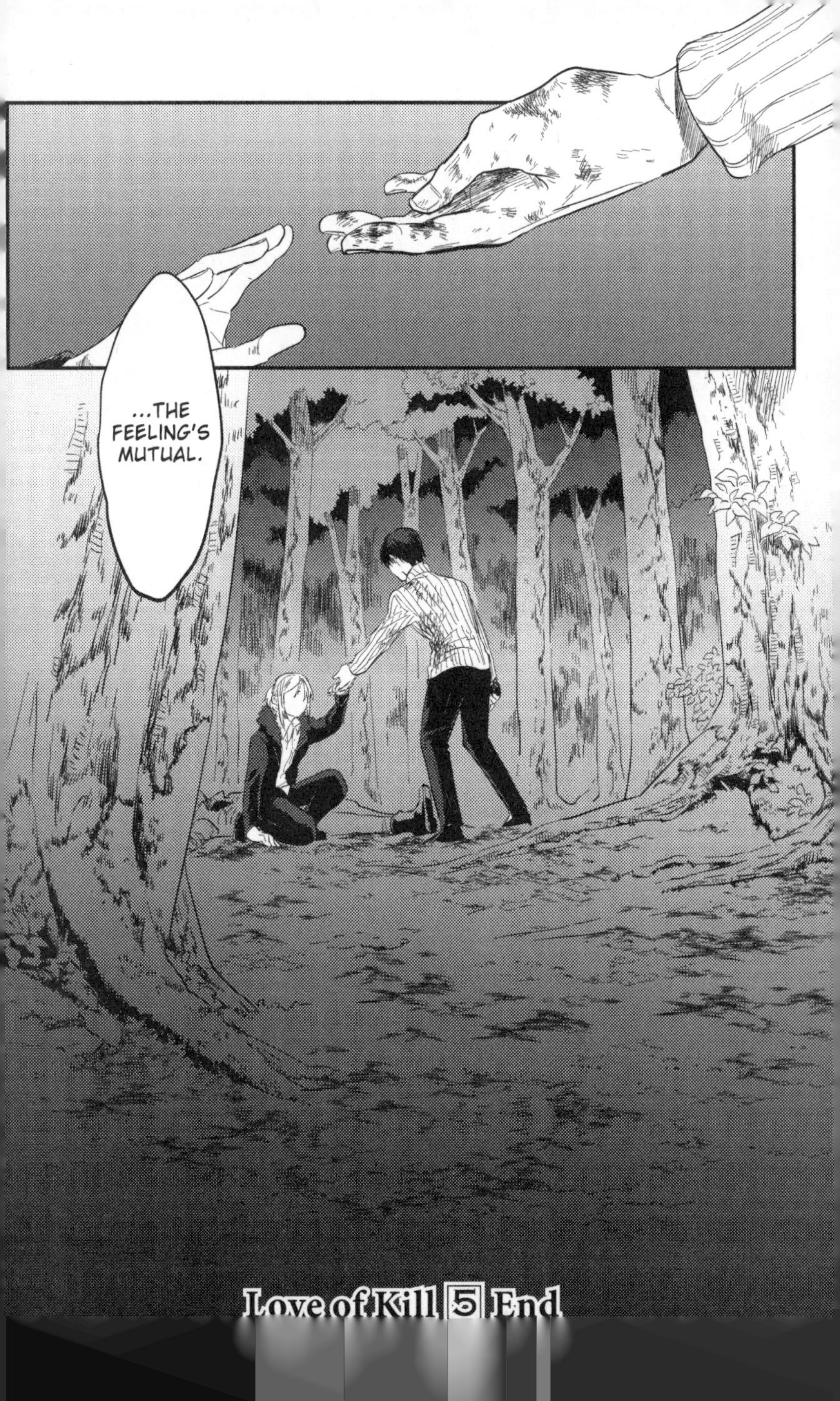
...THE FEELING'S MUTUAL.
Love of Kill 5 End

FILE 28: A WAR TRIGGER

I MILDLY REGRET INTRODUCING A NAME THAT SUGGESTS SUCH A LARGE SCALE, LOL. CAN I TAKE IT BACK...? AFTER ALL, THE WORLD OF THIS MANGA USES THE PRESENT-DAY REAL WORLD THAT WE LIVE IN AS A BASIS. IT FEELS LIKE I'D BE PILING TOO MUCH FICTION ON TOP OF THAT. SO BIG THINGS LIKE WORLD WARS THAT AFFECT THE COURSE OF HISTORY WOULD ALSO BE BASED IN REALITY.

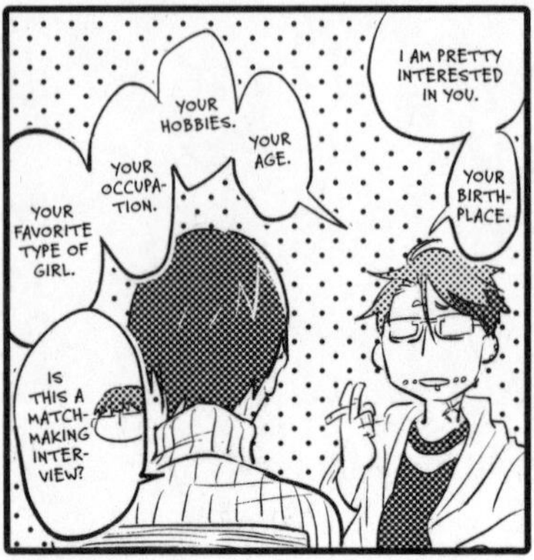
I AM PRETTY INTERESTED IN YOU.
YOUR BIRTHPLACE.
YOUR AGE.
YOUR HOBBIES.
YOUR OCCUPATION.
YOUR FAVORITE TYPE OF GIRL.
IS THIS A MATCHMAKING INTERVIEW?

FILE 29: CRISIS

THIS CHAPTER CAUSED CONTROVERSY INSIDE MY HEAD. I THOUGHT, "AM I REALLY GOING TO MAKE CHATEAU CHARGE IN IN A DUMP TRUCK...!!?" BUT IN THE END, I SERIOUSLY HAD HER DO IT... SO I GUESS CHATEAU HAS A HEAVY VEHICLE LICENSE...? WOW...

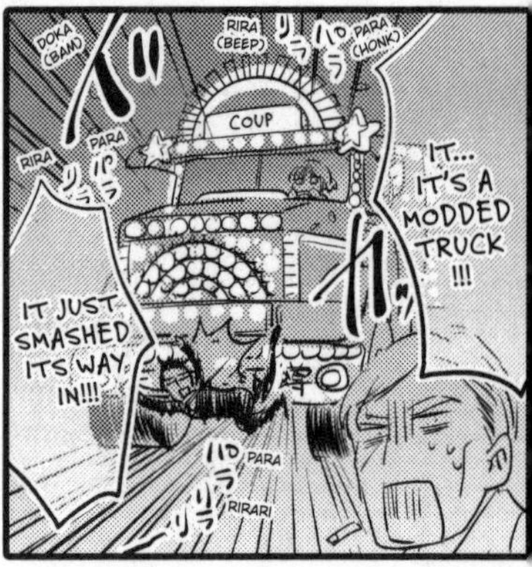
PARA (HONK)
RIRA (BEEP)
DOKA (BAM)
COUP
IT... IT'S A MODDED TRUCK!!!
PARA
RIRA
IT JUST SMASHED ITS WAY IN!!!
PARA
RIRARI

FILE 30: REUNION

AT THE END OF VOLUME 5, THE TWO LEADS FINALLY PROGRESSED IN THEIR RELATIONSHIP TO A POINT WHERE THEY HOLD HANDS, LOL. CONSIDERING THE IMPRESSION THE LAST PANEL MAKES, I COULDN'T HELP BUT WONDER, "WOULD IT BE BETTER TO END IT HERE AND MAKE THIS THE FINAL CHAPTER...?" ANYWAY, THEY FINALLY LINKED UP.

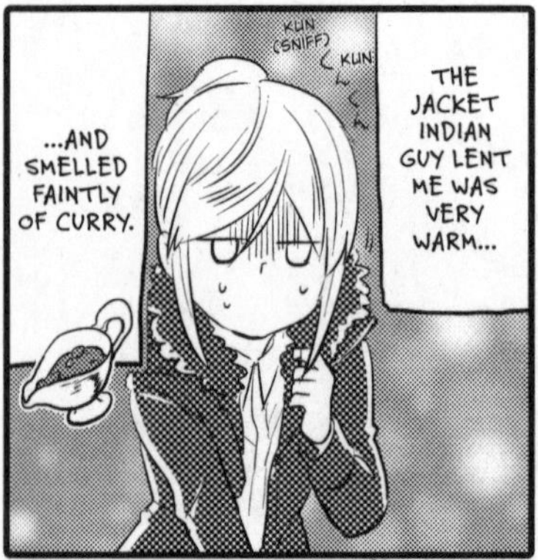
KUN (SNIFF)
KUN
THE JACKET INDIAN GUY LENT ME WAS VERY WARM...
...AND SMELLED FAINTLY OF CURRY.

BECAUSE THAT'S WHAT I ATE FOR LUNCH.

THE FOLLOWING IS A SPECIAL COMIC FOR THE COLLECTED VOLUME.

IT IS SET AFTER THE SITUATION WITH HOU, BETWEEN FILE 15 AND FILE 16. SOME OF IT CROSSES OVER A LITTLE WITH THE STORY IN THE ANIMATE SPECIAL EDITION BOOKLET "BLACK CAT" THAT CAME WITH VOLUME 4.

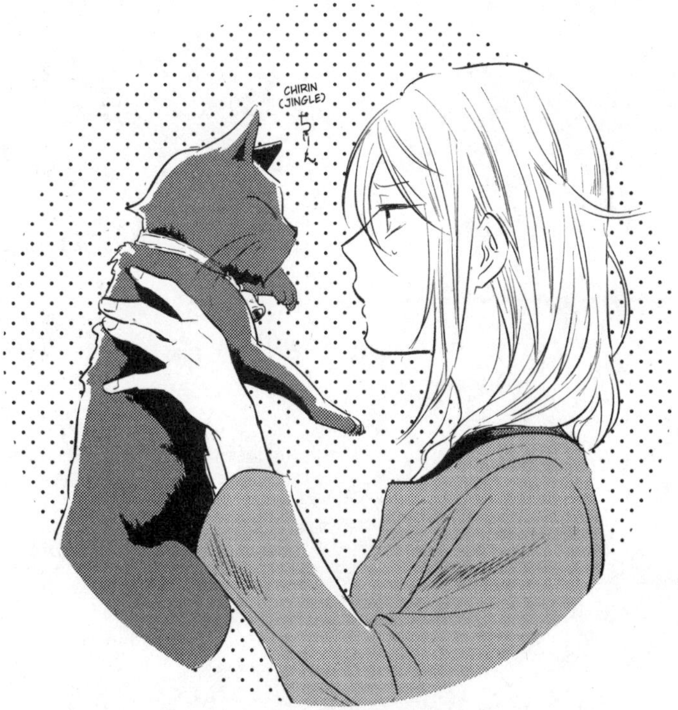
CHIRIN (JINGLE)
ちりん

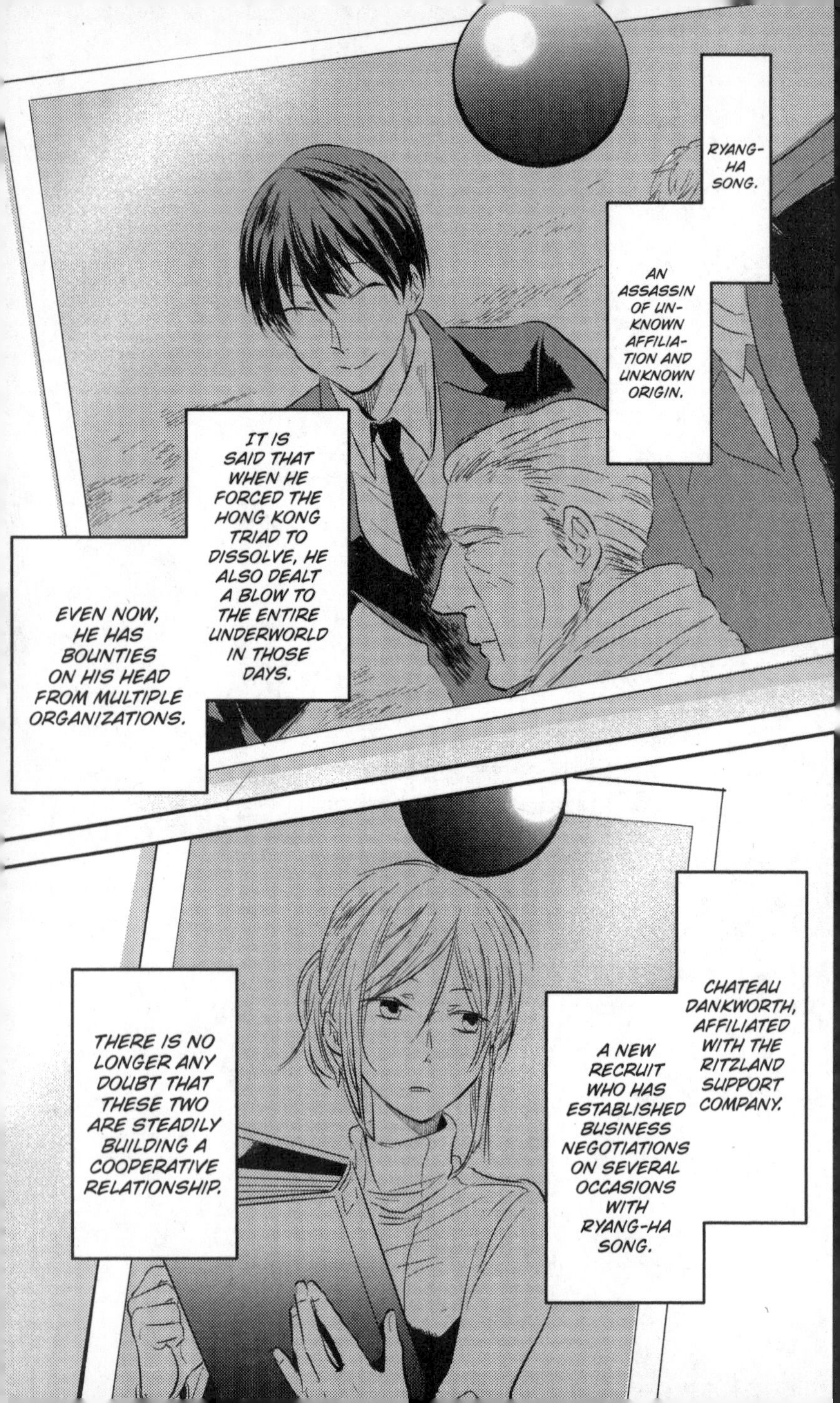
RYANG-HA SONG.
AN ASSASSIN OF UNKNOWN AFFILIATION AND UNKNOWN ORIGIN.
IT IS SAID THAT WHEN HE FORCED THE HONG KONG TRIAD TO DISSOLVE, HE ALSO DEALT A BLOW TO THE ENTIRE UNDERWORLD IN THOSE DAYS.
EVEN NOW, HE HAS BOUNTIES ON HIS HEAD FROM MULTIPLE ORGANIZATIONS.
CHATEAU DANKWORTH, AFFILIATED WITH THE RITZLAND SUPPORT COMPANY.
A NEW RECRUIT WHO HAS ESTABLISHED BUSINESS NEGOTIATIONS ON SEVERAL OCCASIONS WITH RYANG-HA SONG.
THERE IS NO LONGER ANY DOUBT THAT THESE TWO ARE STEADILY BUILDING A COOPERATIVE RELATIONSHIP.

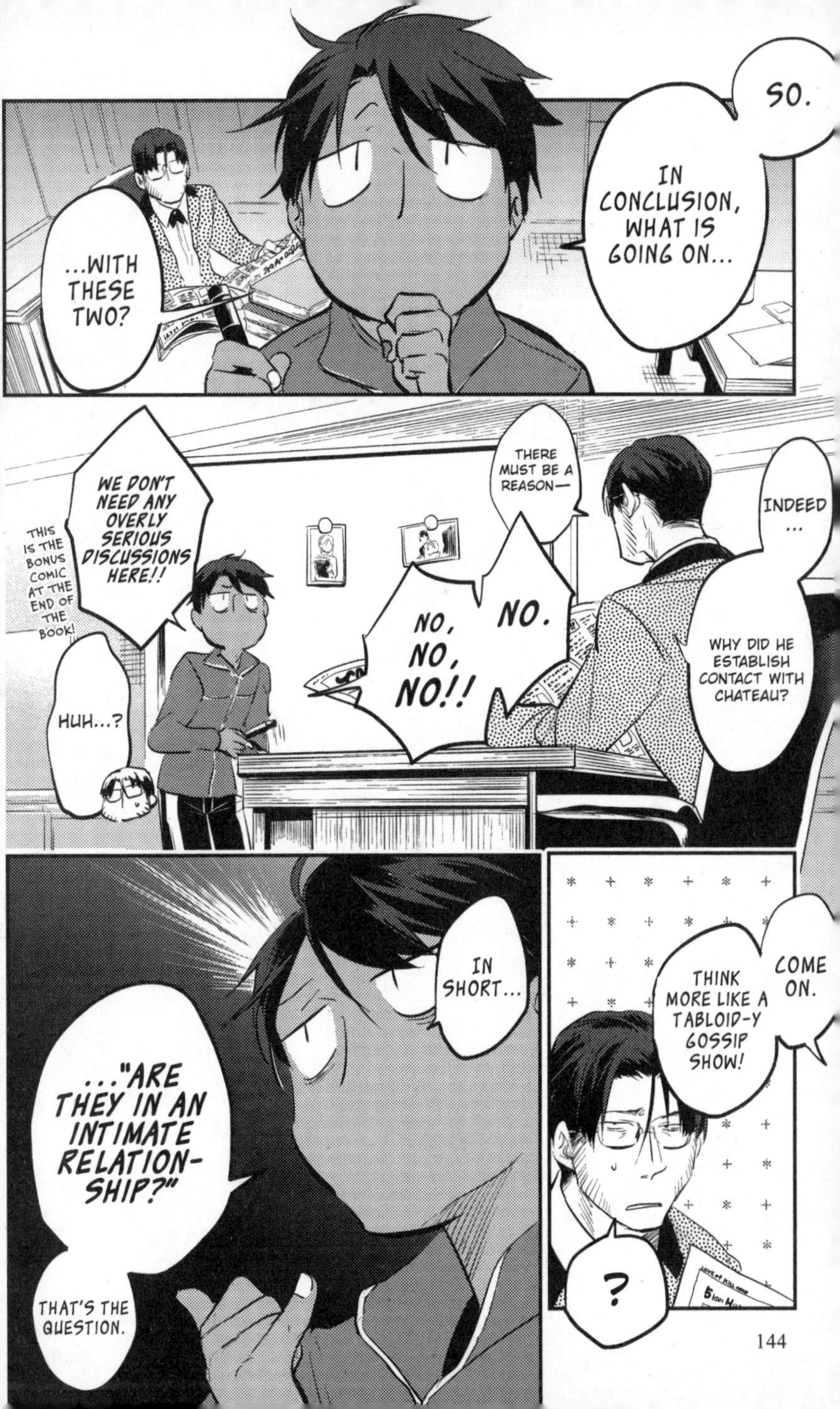
SO.
IN CONCLUSION, WHAT IS GOING ON...
...WITH THESE TWO?
INDEED...
WHY DID HE ESTABLISH CONTACT WITH CHATEAU?
THERE MUST BE A REASON—
NO.
NO, NO, NO!!
WE DON'T NEED ANY OVERLY SERIOUS DISCUSSIONS HERE!!
THIS IS THE BONUS COMIC AT THE END OF THE BOOK!
HUH...?
COME ON.
THINK MORE LIKE A TABLOID-Y GOSSIP SHOW!
?
IN SHORT...
..."ARE THEY IN AN INTIMATE RELATIONSHIP?"
THAT'S THE QUESTION.

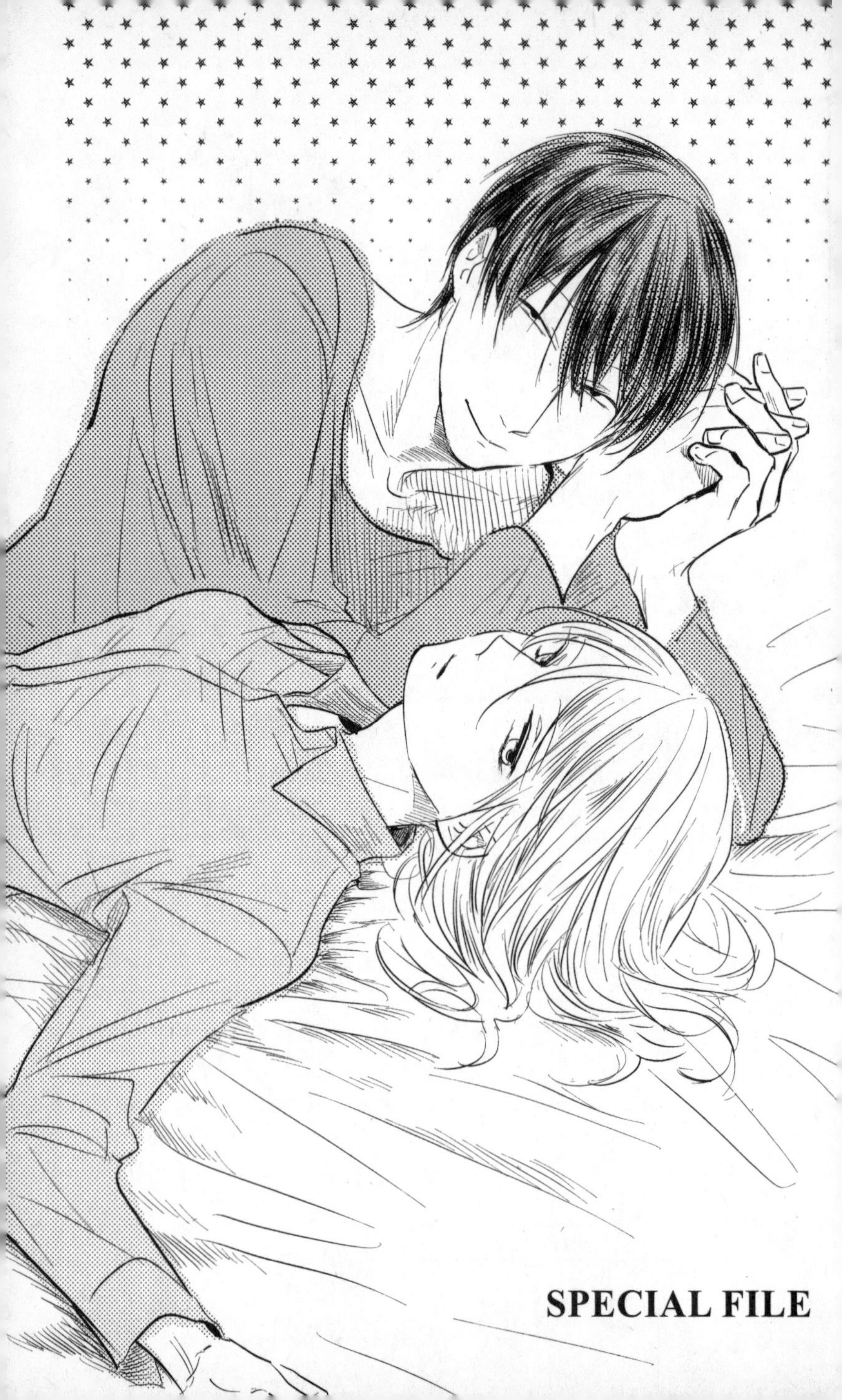

SPECIAL FILE

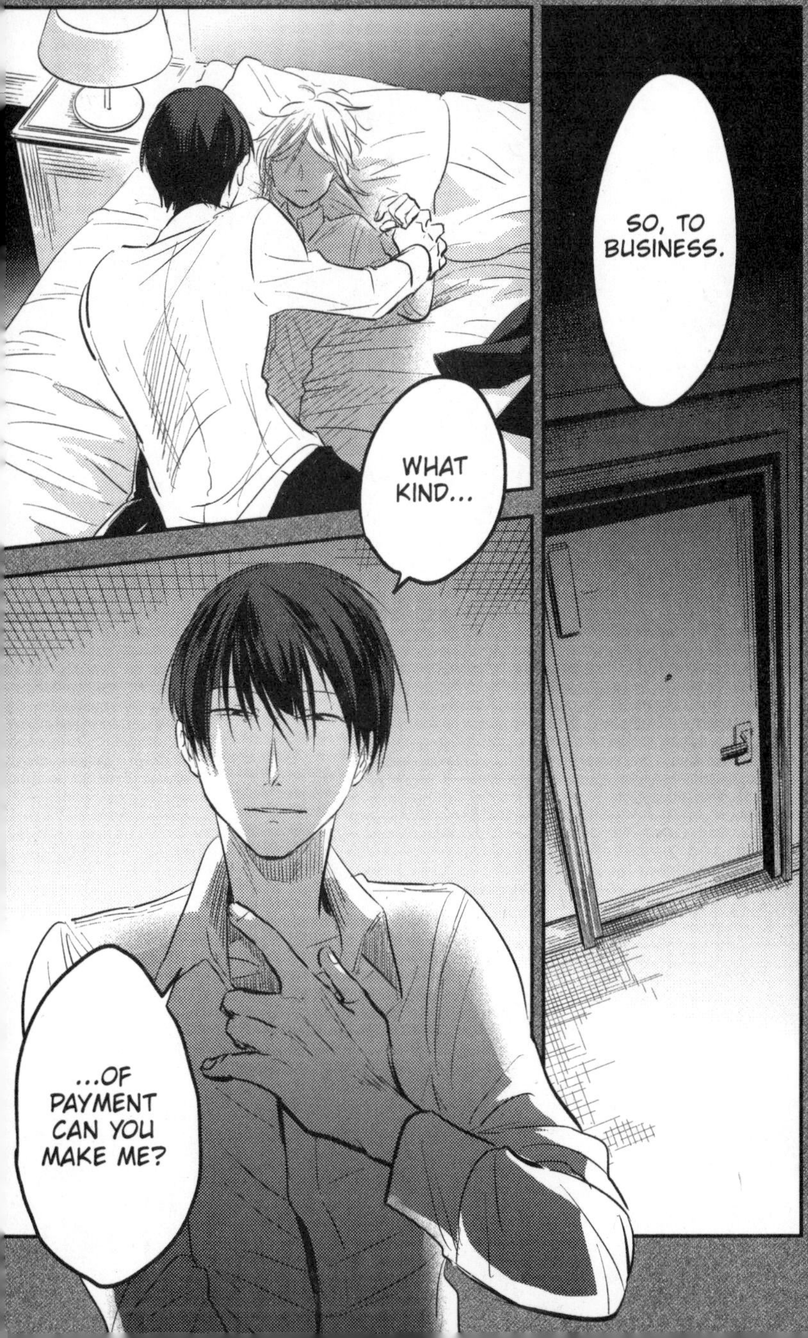
SO, TO BUSINESS.
WHAT KIND...
...OF PAYMENT CAN YOU MAKE ME?

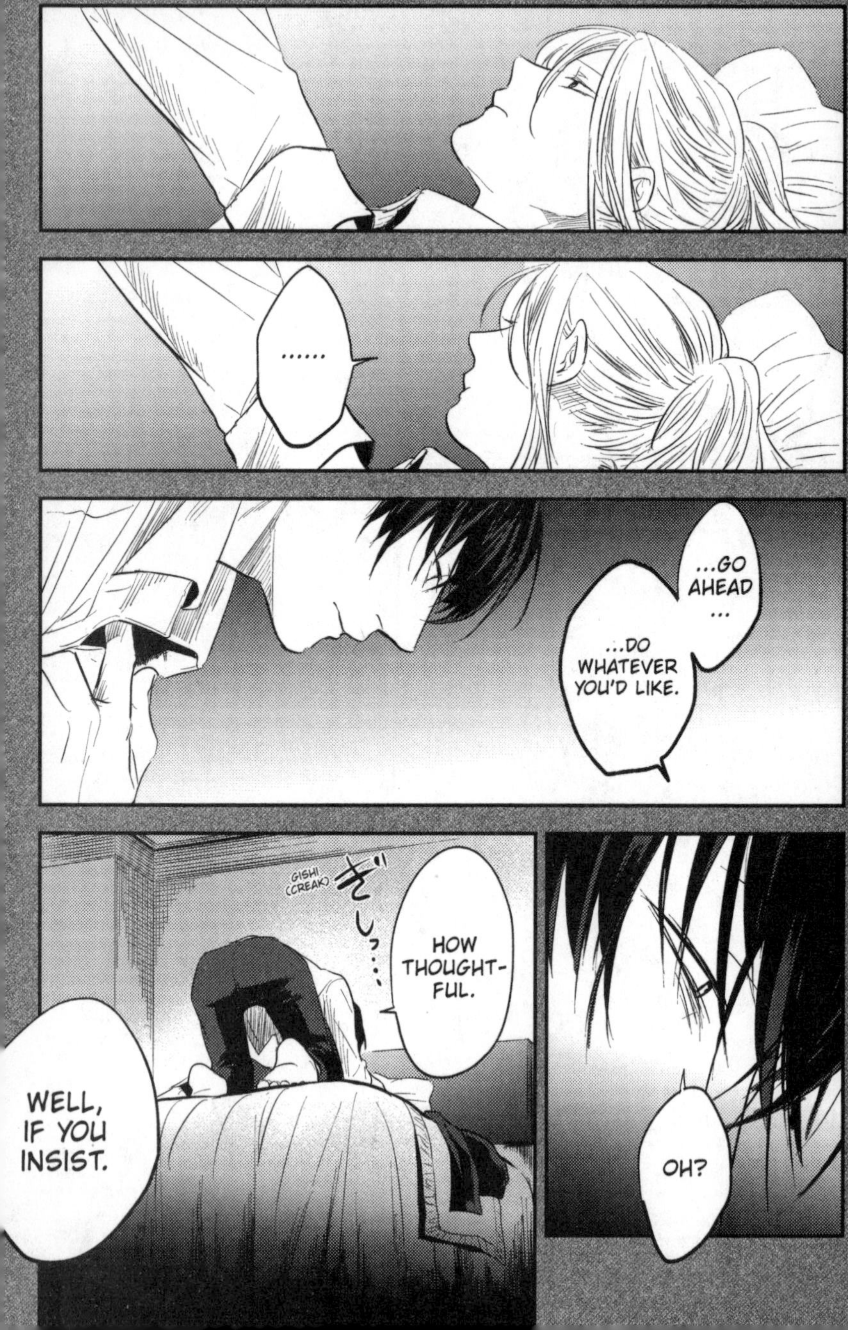
......
...GO AHEAD ...
...DO WHATEVER YOU'D LIKE.
OH?
ぎしっ…
GISHI (CREAK)
HOW THOUGHT-FUL.
WELL, IF YOU INSIST.

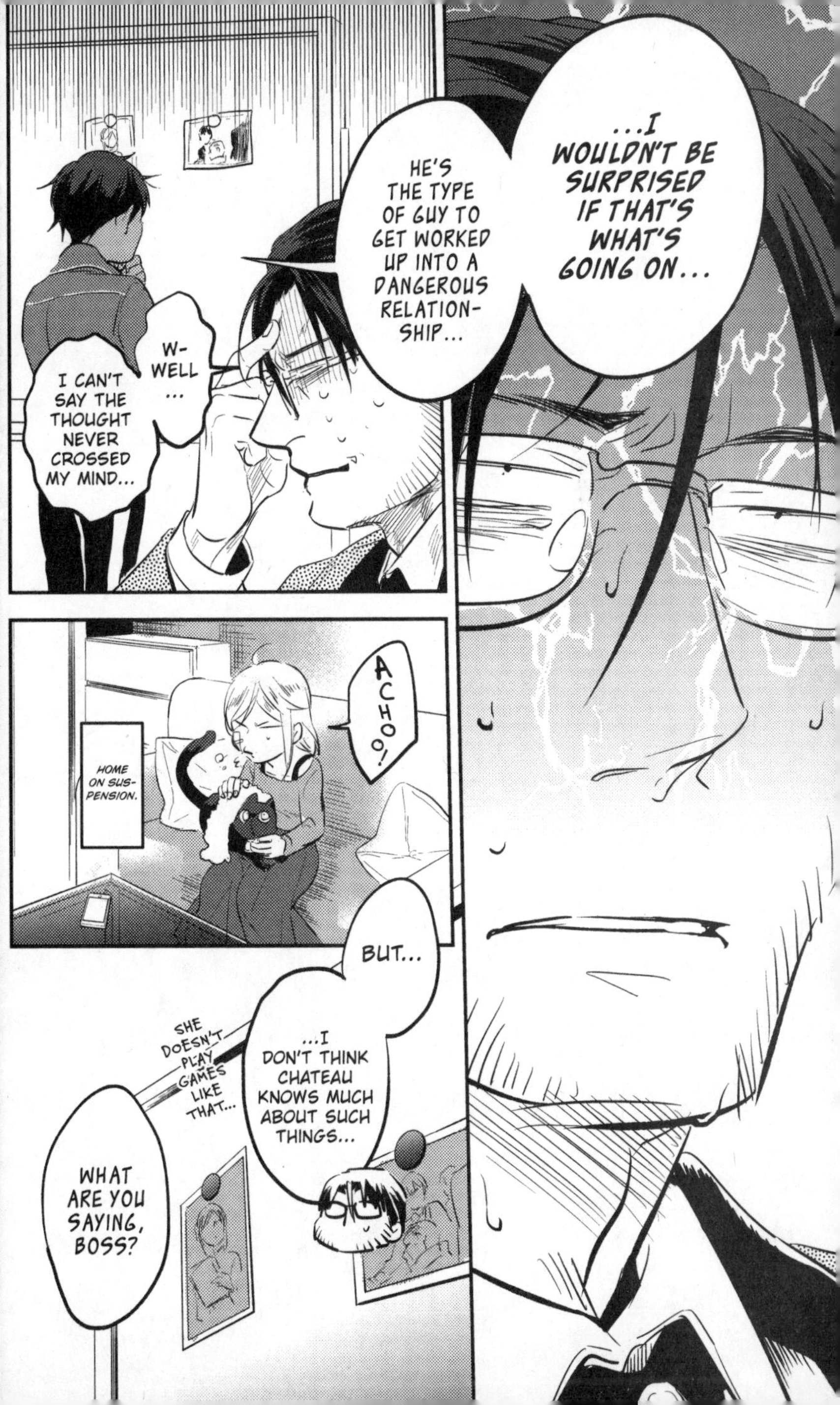
...I WOULDN'T BE SURPRISED IF THAT'S WHAT'S GOING ON...
HE'S THE TYPE OF GUY TO GET WORKED UP INTO A DANGEROUS RELATION-SHIP...
W-WELL...
I CAN'T SAY THE THOUGHT NEVER CROSSED MY MIND...
ACHOO!
HOME ON SUS-PENSION.
BUT...
...I DON'T THINK CHATEAU KNOWS MUCH ABOUT SUCH THINGS...
SHE DOESN'T PLAY GAMES LIKE THAT...
WHAT ARE YOU SAYING, BOSS?

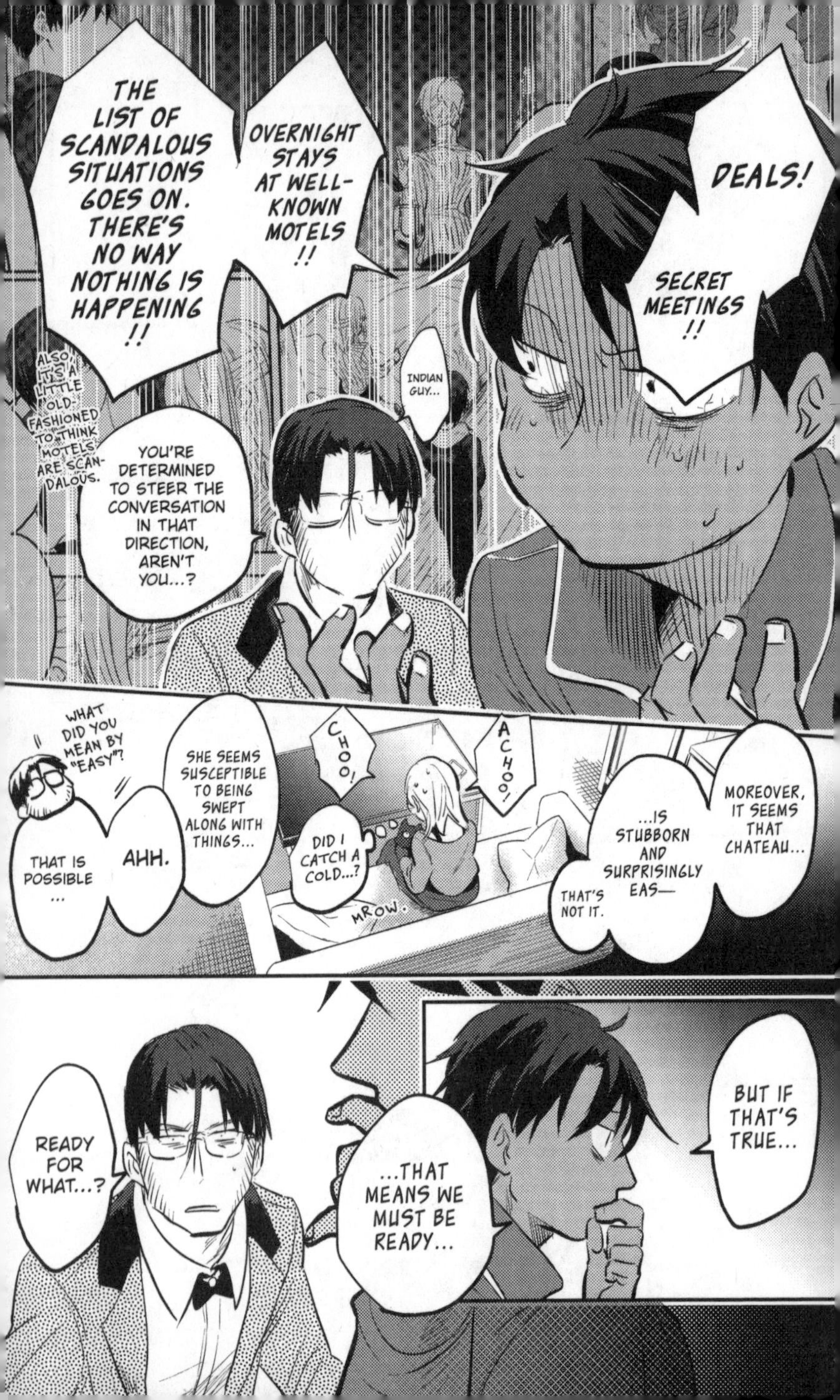
DEALS!
SECRET MEETINGS !!
OVERNIGHT STAYS AT WELL-KNOWN MOTELS !!
THE LIST OF SCANDALOUS SITUATIONS GOES ON. THERE'S NO WAY NOTHING IS HAPPENING !!
INDIAN GUY...
YOU'RE DETERMINED TO STEER THE CONVERSATION IN THAT DIRECTION, AREN'T YOU...?
ALSO, IT'S A LITTLE OLD-FASHIONED TO THINK MOTELS ARE SCAN-DALOUS.
MOREOVER, IT SEEMS THAT CHATEAU...
...IS STUBBORN AND SURPRISINGLY EAS—
THAT'S NOT IT.
ACHOO!
CHOO!
DID I CATCH A COLD...?
MROW.
SHE SEEMS SUSCEPTIBLE TO BEING SWEPT ALONG WITH THINGS...
AHH.
WHAT DID YOU MEAN BY "EASY"?
THAT IS POSSIBLE ...
BUT IF THAT'S TRUE...
...THAT MEANS WE MUST BE READY...
READY FOR WHAT...?

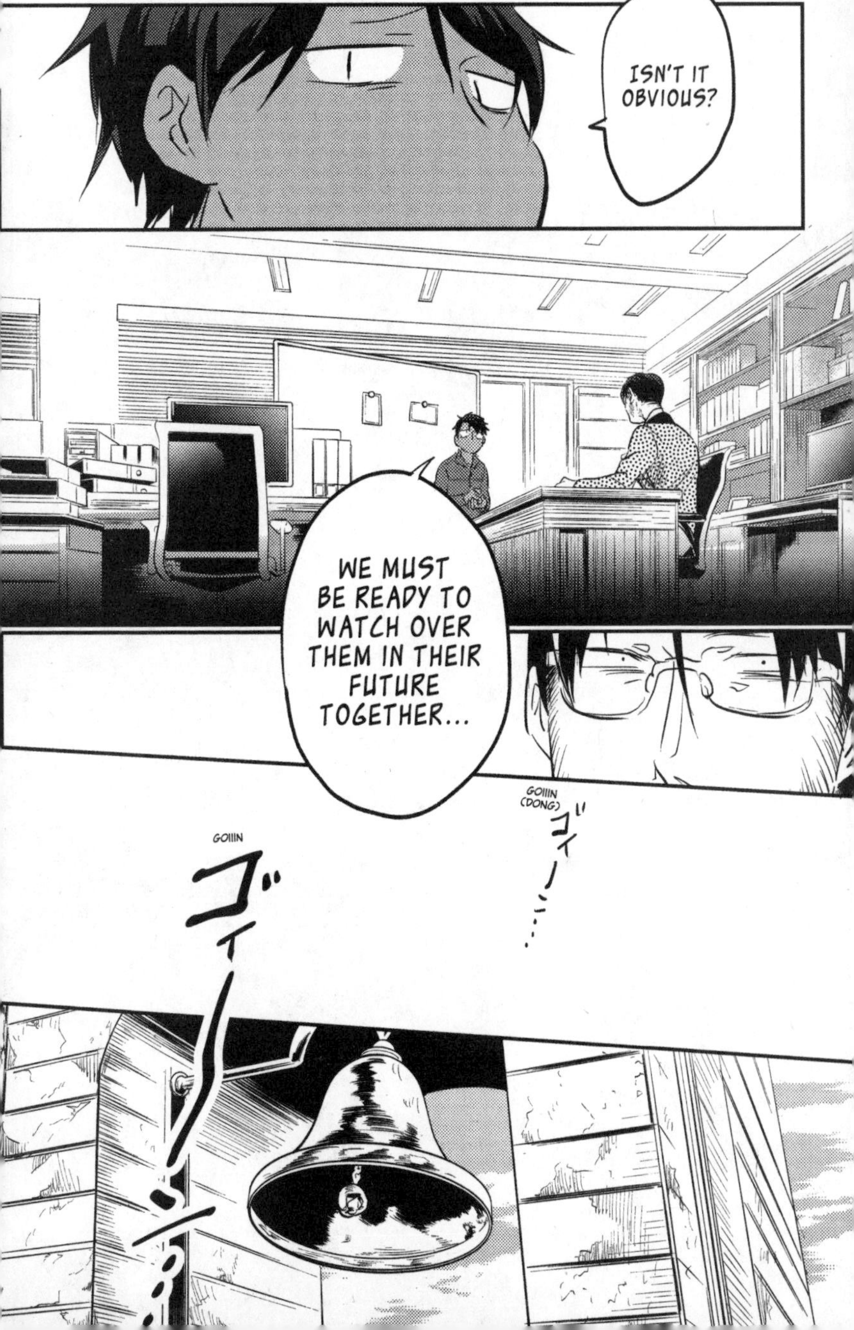
ISN'T IT OBVIOUS?
WE MUST BE READY TO WATCH OVER THEM IN THEIR FUTURE TOGETHER...
GOIIIN (DONG)
ゴイーン…
GOIIIN
ゴイーン…

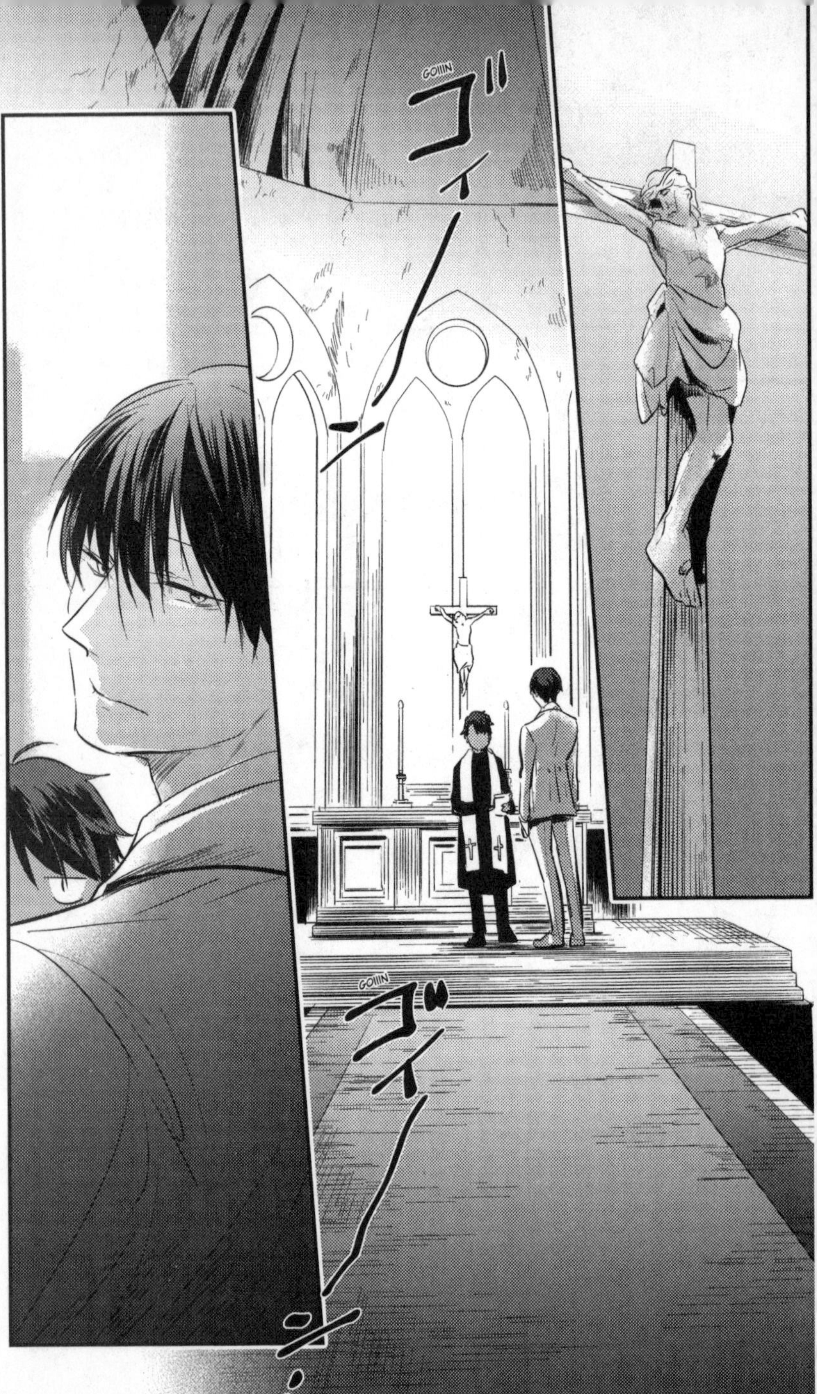
GOIIIN
ゴィーン
GOIIIN
ゴィーーン……

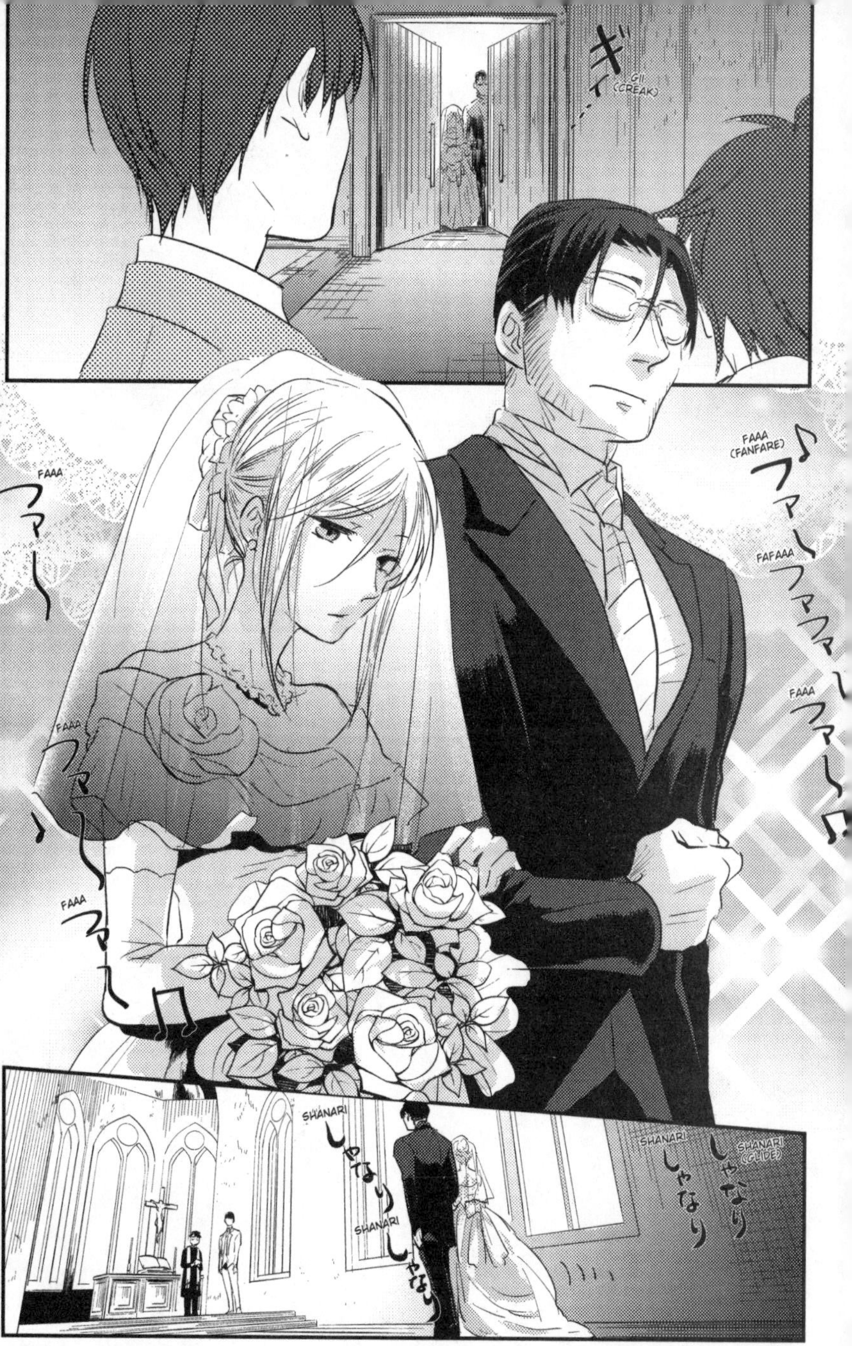
ギイ…
GII (CREAK)
FAAA (FANFARE)
♪ファ～
FAFAAA
ファファファ～
FAAA
ファ～♪
FAAA
ファ～
FAAA
ファ～～♪
FAAA
ファ～
SHANARI (GLIDE)
しゃなり
SHANARI
しゃなり
SHANARI
しゃなり
SHANARI
しゃなし

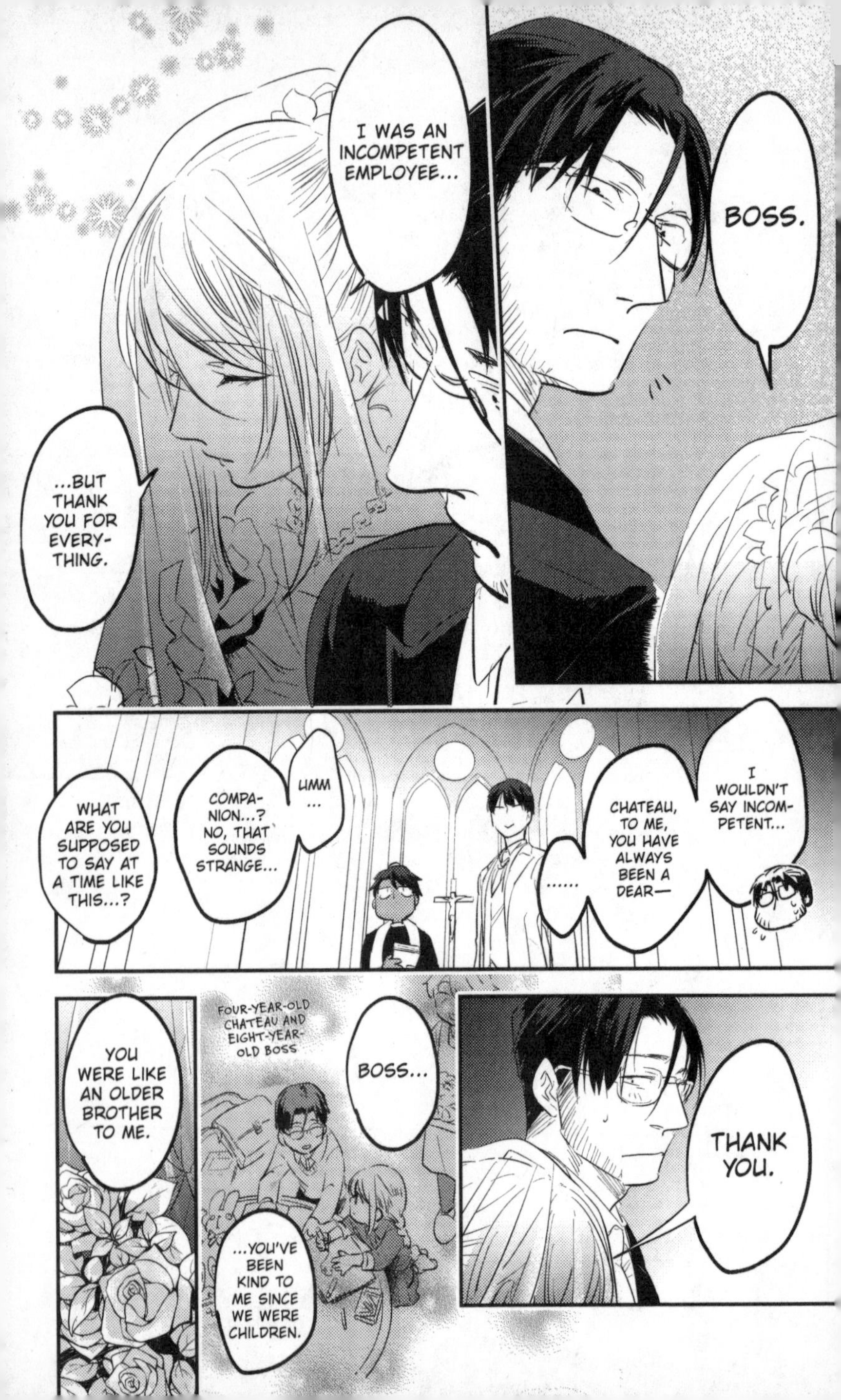
BOSS.
I WAS AN INCOMPETENT EMPLOYEE...
...BUT THANK YOU FOR EVERY-THING.
I WOULDN'T SAY INCOMPETENT...
CHATEAU, TO ME, YOU HAVE ALWAYS BEEN A DEAR—
......
UMM ...
COMPANION...? NO, THAT SOUNDS STRANGE...
WHAT ARE YOU SUPPOSED TO SAY AT A TIME LIKE THIS...?
THANK YOU.
BOSS...
FOUR-YEAR-OLD CHATEAU AND EIGHT-YEAR-OLD BOSS
...YOU'VE BEEN KIND TO ME SINCE WE WERE CHILDREN.
YOU WERE LIKE AN OLDER BROTHER TO ME.

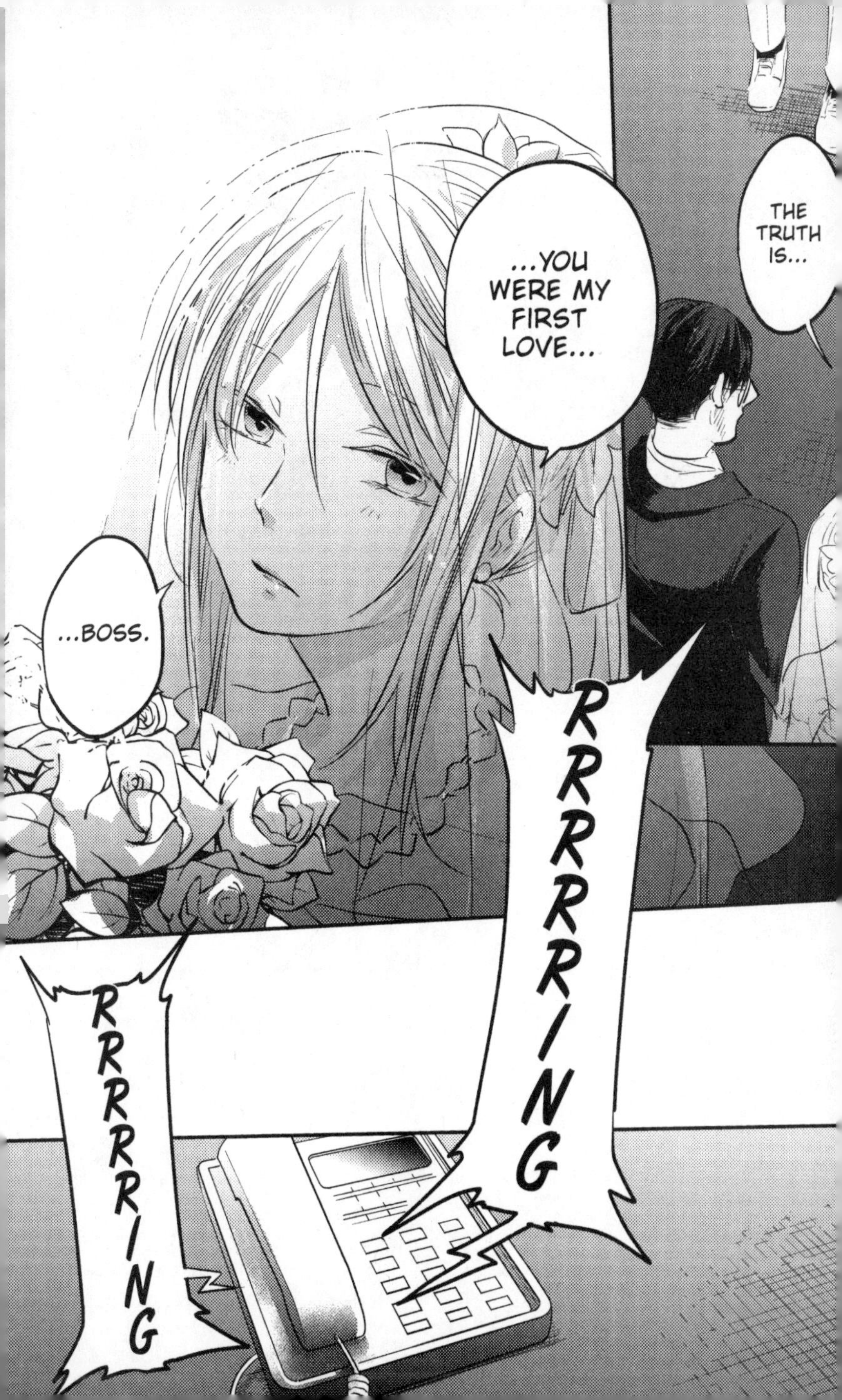
THE TRUTH IS...
...YOU WERE MY FIRST LOVE...
...BOSS.
RRRRRING
RRRRRING

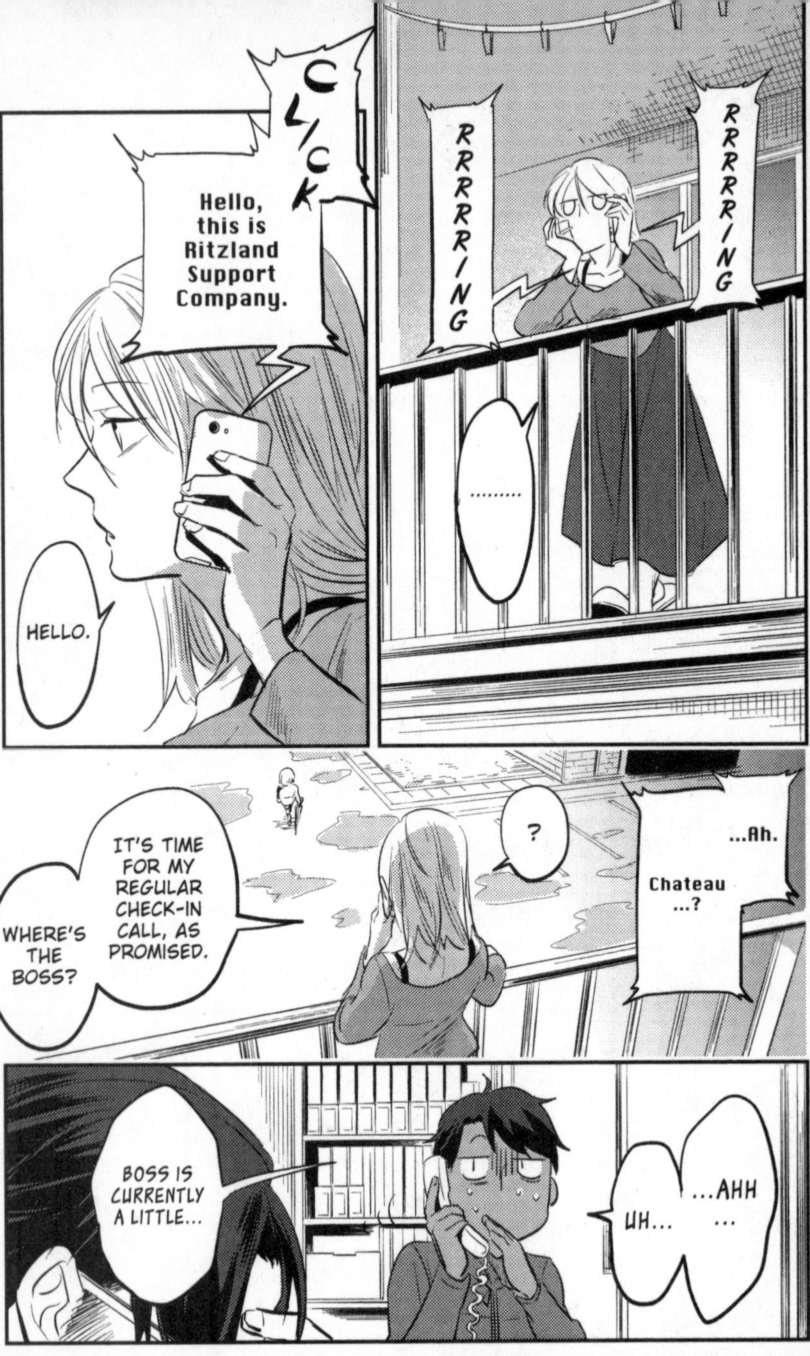
RRRRRING
RRRRRING
....
CLICK
Hello, this is Ritzland Support Company.
HELLO.
...Ah.
Chateau ...?
?
IT'S TIME FOR MY REGULAR CHECK-IN CALL, AS PROMISED.
WHERE'S THE BOSS?
UH... ...AHH ...
BOSS IS CURRENTLY A LITTLE...

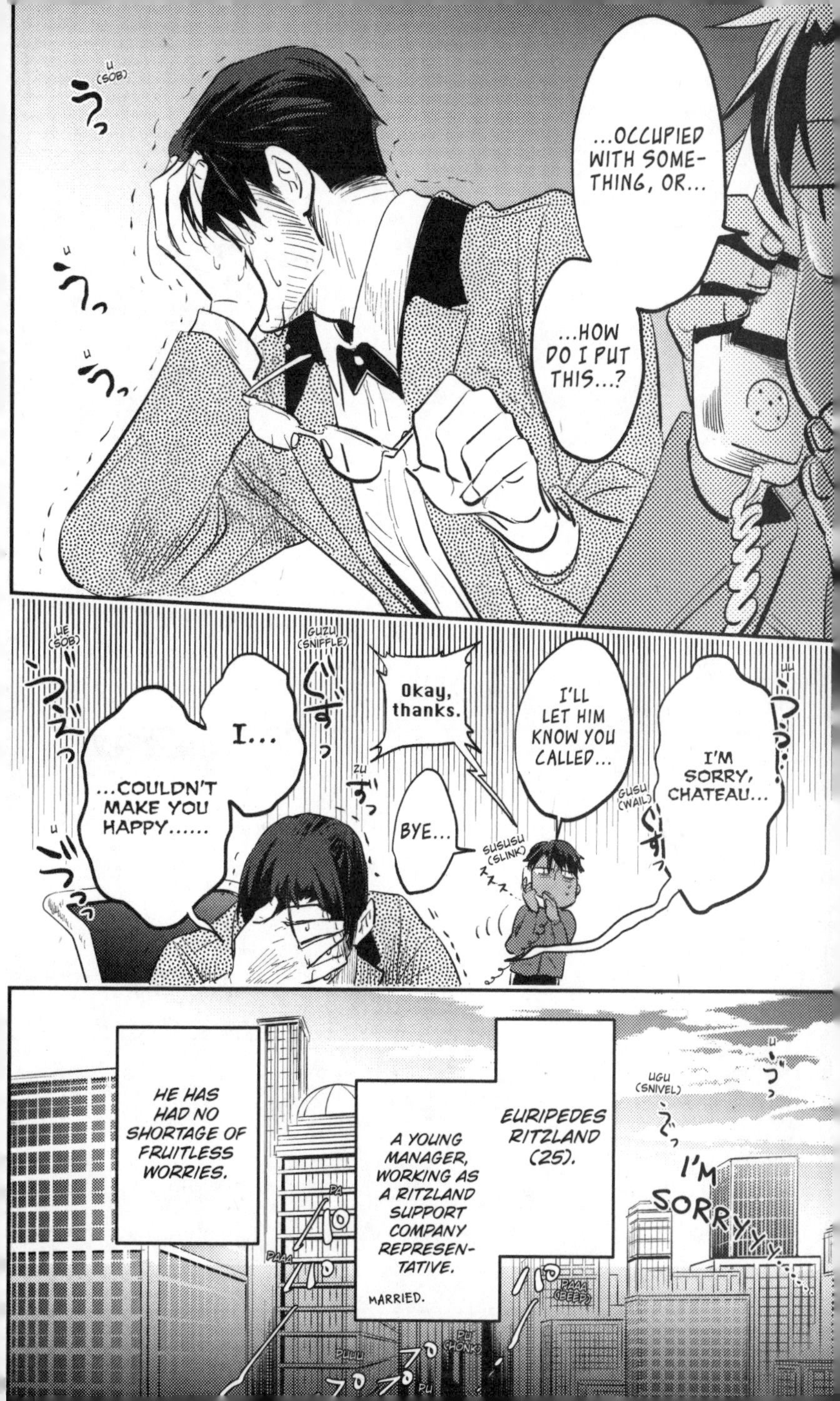

...OCCUPIED WITH SOME-THING, OR...
...HOW DO I PUT THIS...?
U (SOB)
U
U
UU
I'M SORRY, CHATEAU...
GUSU (WAIL)
I'LL LET HIM KNOW YOU CALLED...
SUSUSU (SLINK)
Okay, thanks.
BYE...
ZU
GUZU (SNIFFLE)
I...
...COULDN'T MAKE YOU HAPPY......
UE (SOB)
U
U
UGU (SNIVEL)
I'M SORRYYY...
EURIPEDES RITZLAND (25).
A YOUNG MANAGER, WORKING AS A RITZLAND SUPPORT COMPANY REPRESENTATIVE.
MARRIED.
HE HAS HAD NO SHORTAGE OF FRUITLESS WORRIES.
PAAA (BEEP)
PA
PAAA
PU (HONK)
PUUU
PU

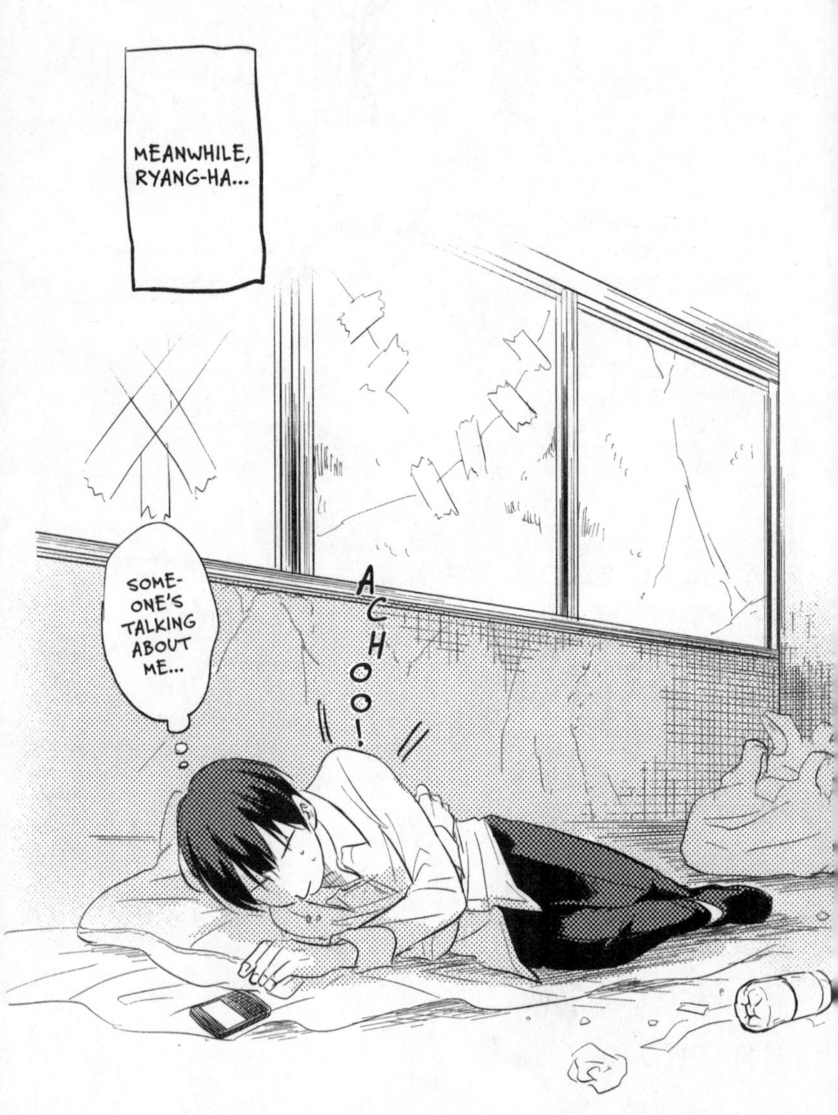
MEANWHILE, RYANG-HA...
SOME-ONE'S TALKING ABOUT ME...
ACHOO!

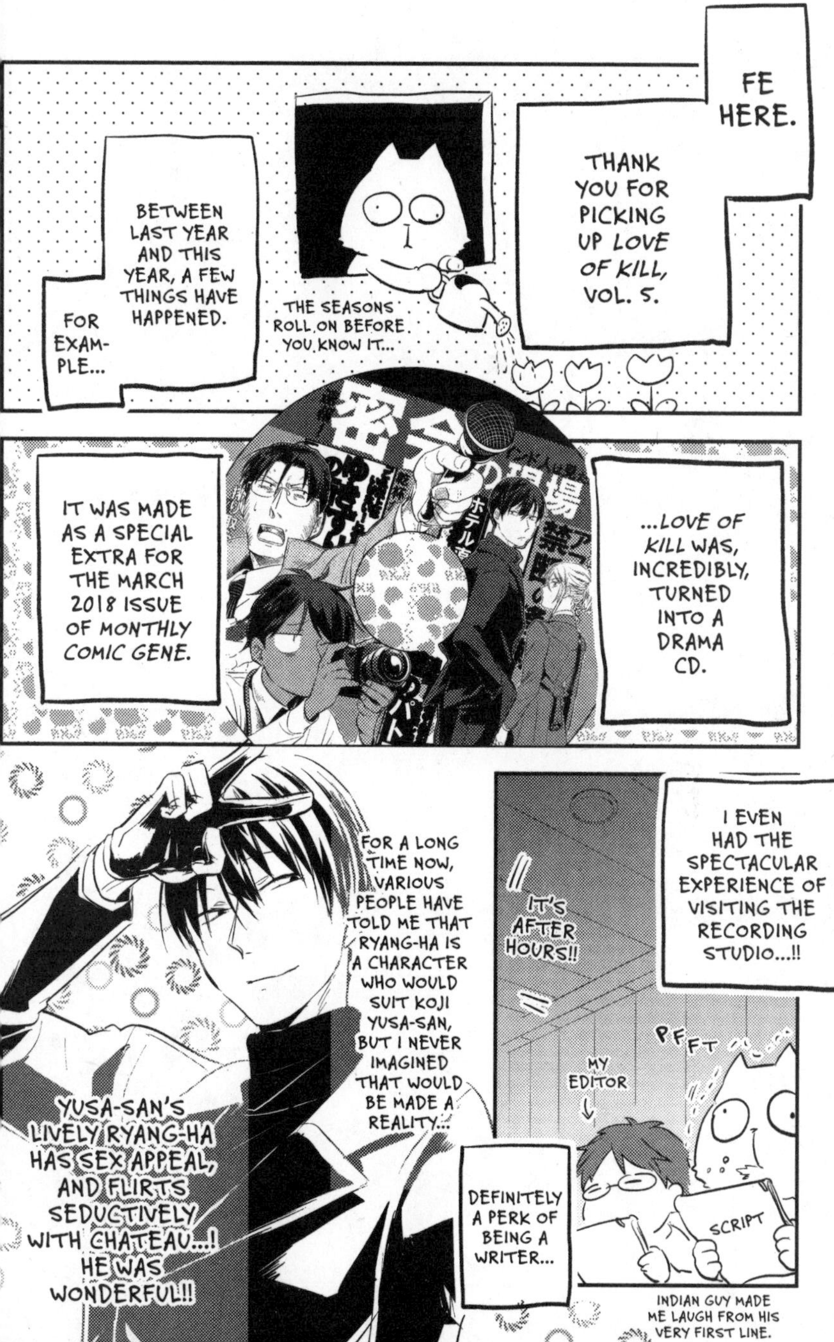
FE HERE.
THANK YOU FOR PICKING UP LOVE OF KILL, VOL. 5.
THE SEASONS ROLL ON BEFORE YOU KNOW IT...
BETWEEN LAST YEAR AND THIS YEAR, A FEW THINGS HAVE HAPPENED.
FOR EXAMPLE...
...LOVE OF KILL WAS, INCREDIBLY, TURNED INTO A DRAMA CD.
IT WAS MADE AS A SPECIAL EXTRA FOR THE MARCH 2018 ISSUE OF MONTHLY COMIC GENE.
I EVEN HAD THE SPECTACULAR EXPERIENCE OF VISITING THE RECORDING STUDIO...!!
IT'S AFTER HOURS!!
PFFT
MY EDITOR
SCRIPT
DEFINITELY A PERK OF BEING A WRITER...
INDIAN GUY MADE ME LAUGH FROM HIS VERY FIRST LINE.
FOR A LONG TIME NOW, VARIOUS PEOPLE HAVE TOLD ME THAT RYANG-HA IS A CHARACTER WHO WOULD SUIT KOJI YUSA-SAN, BUT I NEVER IMAGINED THAT WOULD BE MADE A REALITY...
YUSA-SAN'S LIVELY RYANG-HA HAS SEX APPEAL, AND FLIRTS SEDUCTIVELY WITH CHATEAU...! HE WAS WONDERFUL!!

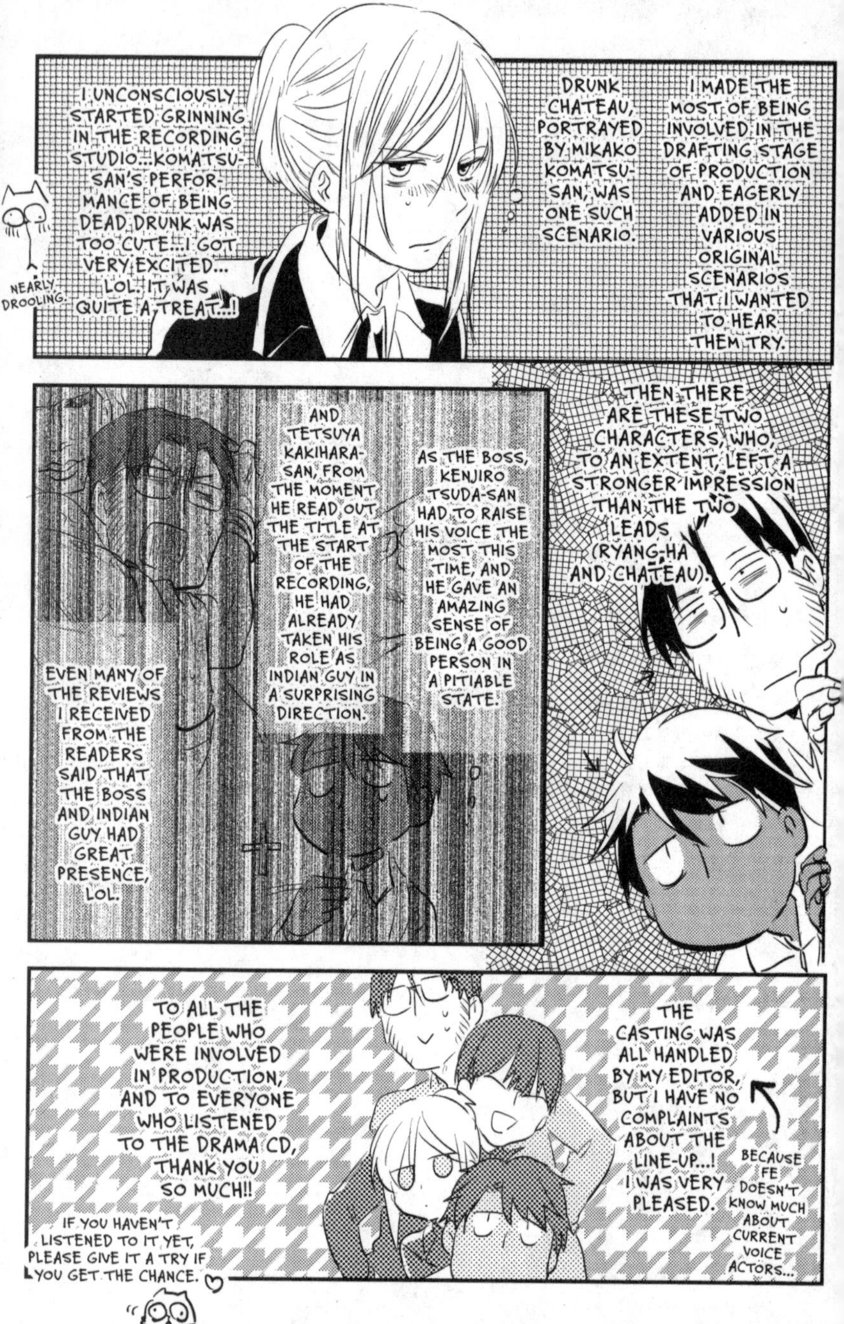

I MADE THE MOST OF BEING INVOLVED IN THE DRAFTING STAGE OF PRODUCTION AND EAGERLY ADDED IN VARIOUS ORIGINAL SCENARIOS THAT I WANTED TO HEAR THEM TRY.
DRUNK CHATEAU, PORTRAYED BY MIKAKO KOMATSU-SAN, WAS ONE SUCH SCENARIO.
I UNCONSCIOUSLY STARTED GRINNING IN THE RECORDING STUDIO...KOMATSU-SAN'S PERFORMANCE OF BEING DEAD DRUNK WAS TOO CUTE...I GOT VERY EXCITED... LOL. IT WAS QUITE A TREAT...!
NEARLY DROOLING.
THEN THERE ARE THESE TWO CHARACTERS, WHO, TO AN EXTENT, LEFT A STRONGER IMPRESSION THAN THE TWO LEADS (RYANG-HA AND CHATEAU).
AS THE BOSS, KENJIRO TSUDA-SAN HAD TO RAISE HIS VOICE THE MOST THIS TIME, AND HE GAVE AN AMAZING SENSE OF BEING A GOOD PERSON IN A PITIABLE STATE.
AND TETSUYA KAKIHARA-SAN, FROM THE MOMENT HE READ OUT THE TITLE AT THE START OF THE RECORDING, HE HAD ALREADY TAKEN HIS ROLE AS INDIAN GUY IN A SURPRISING DIRECTION.
EVEN MANY OF THE REVIEWS I RECEIVED FROM THE READERS SAID THAT THE BOSS AND INDIAN GUY HAD GREAT PRESENCE, LOL.
THE CASTING WAS ALL HANDLED BY MY EDITOR, BUT I HAVE NO COMPLAINTS ABOUT THE LINE-UP...! I WAS VERY PLEASED.
BECAUSE FE DOESN'T KNOW MUCH ABOUT CURRENT VOICE ACTORS...
TO ALL THE PEOPLE WHO WERE INVOLVED IN PRODUCTION, AND TO EVERYONE WHO LISTENED TO THE DRAMA CD, THANK YOU SO MUCH!!
IF YOU HAVEN'T LISTENED TO IT YET, PLEASE GIVE IT A TRY IF YOU GET THE CHANCE.

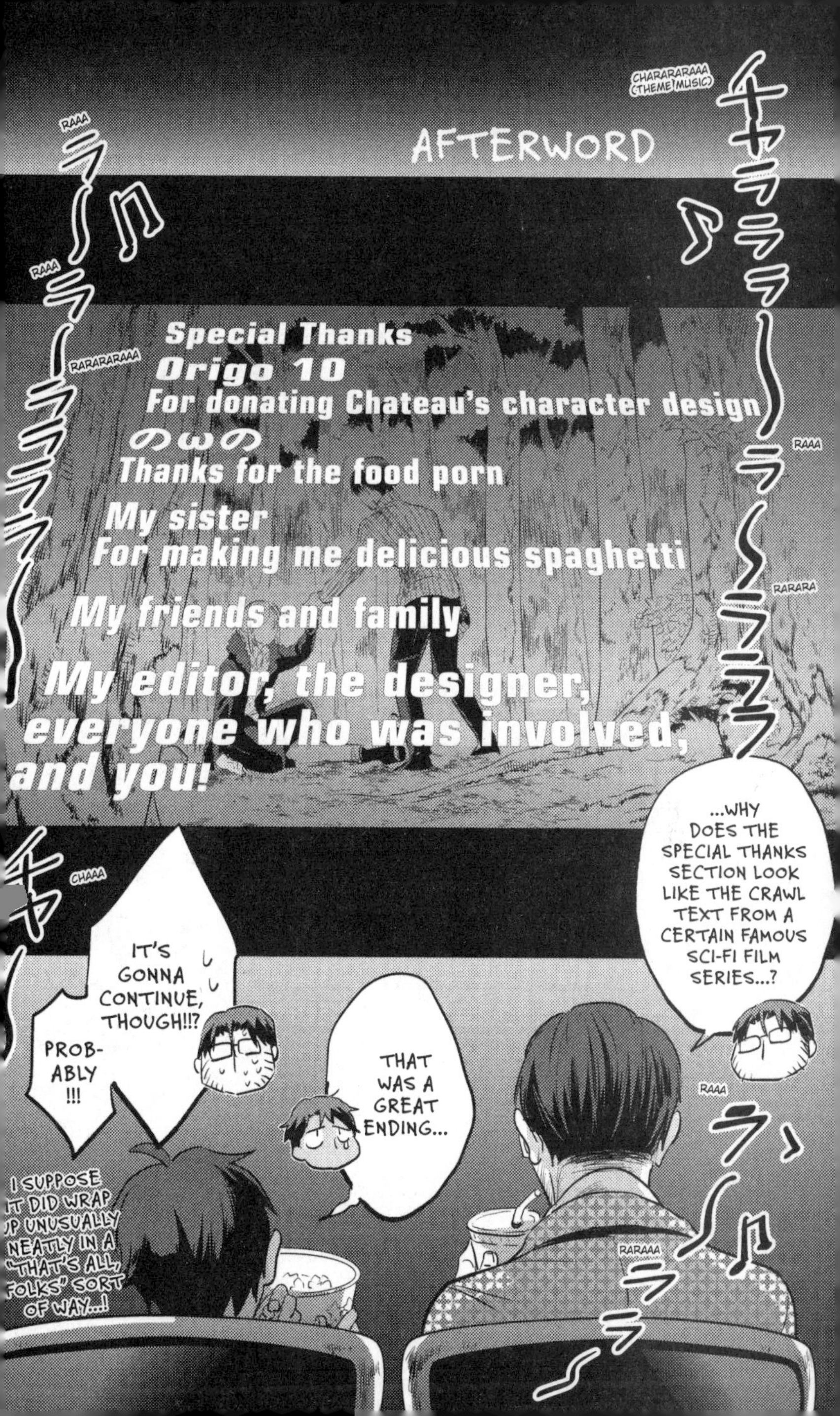
CHARARARAAA (THEME MUSIC)
AFTERWORD
RAAA
RARARA
RAAA
RAAA
RARARARAAA
Special Thanks
Origo 10
For donating Chateau's character design
のωの
Thanks for the food porn
My sister
For making me delicious spaghetti
My friends and family
My editor, the designer, everyone who was involved, and you!
CHAAA
...WHY DOES THE SPECIAL THANKS SECTION LOOK LIKE THE CRAWL TEXT FROM A CERTAIN FAMOUS SCI-FI FILM SERIES...?
RAAA
RARAAA
THAT WAS A GREAT ENDING...
IT'S GONNA CONTINUE, THOUGH!!?
PROB-ABLY!!!
I SUPPOSE IT DID WRAP UP UNUSUALLY NEATLY IN A "THAT'S ALL, FOLKS" SORT OF WAY...!

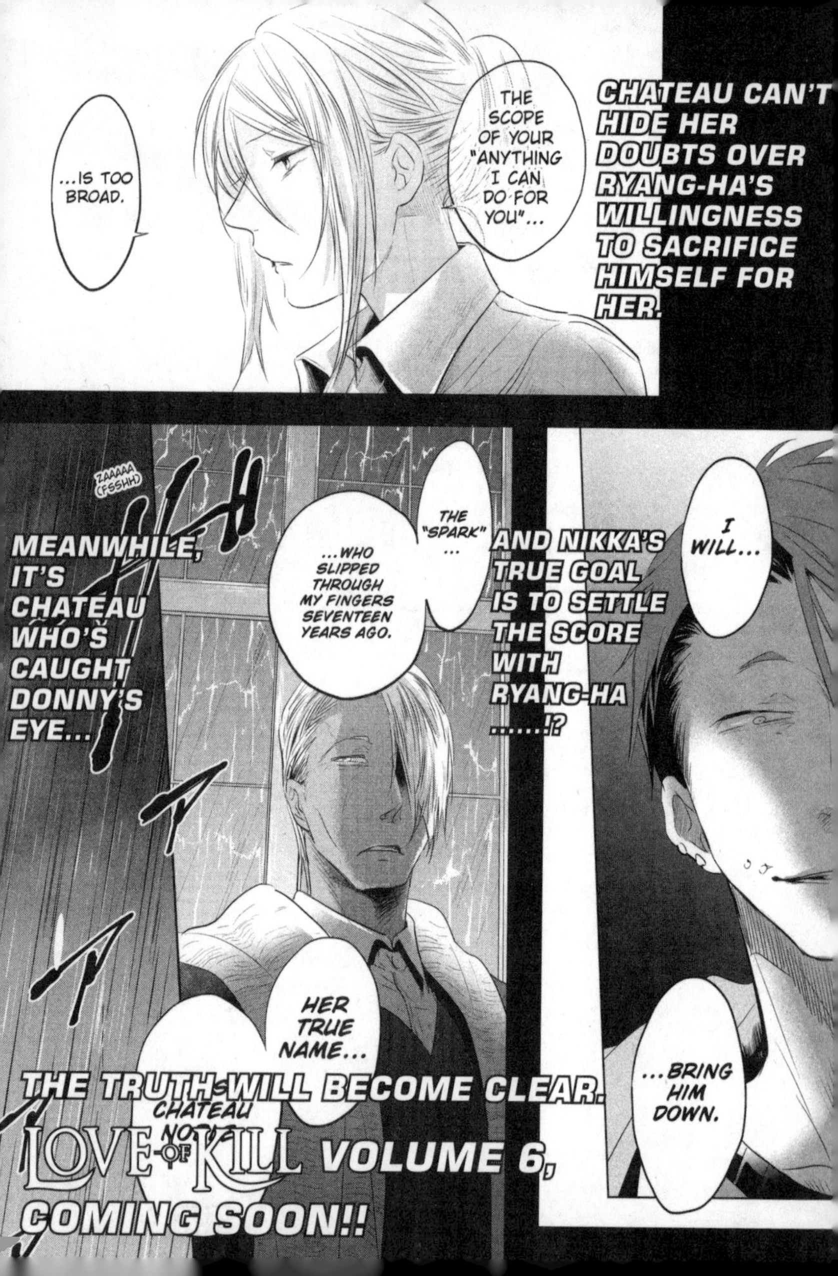
CHATEAU CAN'T HIDE HER DOUBTS OVER RYANG-HA'S WILLINGNESS TO SACRIFICE HIMSELF FOR HER.
THE SCOPE OF YOUR "ANYTHING I CAN DO FOR YOU"...
...IS TOO BROAD.
I WILL...
...BRING HIM DOWN.
AND NIKKA'S TRUE GOAL IS TO SETTLE THE SCORE WITH RYANG-HA ......!?
THE "SPARK"...
...WHO SLIPPED THROUGH MY FINGERS SEVENTEEN YEARS AGO.
HER TRUE NAME...
CHATEAU
ZAAAAA (FSSHH)
MEANWHILE, IT'S CHATEAU WHO'S CAUGHT DONNY'S EYE...
THE TRUTH WILL BECOME CLEAR.
LOVE of KILL VOLUME 6, COMING SOON!!

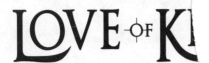

Fe

Translation: Eleanor Ruth Summers   **Lettering: Chiho Christie**

This book is a work of fiction. Names, characters, places, and incidents are the product of the author's imagination or are used fictitiously. Any resemblance to actual events, locales, or persons, living or dead, is coincidental.

KOROSHIAI Vol. 5
© Fe 2018
First published in Japan in 2018 by KADOKAWA CORPORATION, Tokyo.
English translation rights arranged with KADOKAWA CORPORATION, Tokyo, through Tuttle-Mori Agency, Inc., Tokyo.

English translation © 2021 by Yen Press, LLC

Yen Press, LLC supports the right to free expression and the value of copyright. The purpose of copyright is to encourage writers and artists to produce the creative works that enrich our culture.

The scanning, uploading, and distribution of this book without permission is a theft of the author's intellectual property. If you would like permission to use material from the book (other than for review purposes), please contact the publisher. Thank you for your support of the author's rights.

Yen Press
150 West 30th Street, 19th Floor
New York, NY 10001

Visit us at yenpress.com
facebook.com/yenpress
twitter.com/yenpress
yenpress.tumblr.com
instagram.com/yenpress

First Yen Press Edition: November 2021

Yen Press is an imprint of Yen Press, LLC.
The Yen Press name and logo are trademarks of Yen Press, LLC.

The publisher is not responsible for websites (or their content) that are not owned by the publisher.

Library of Congress Control Number: 2020951788

ISBNs: 978-1-9753-2547-3 (paperback)
       978-1-9753-2548-0 (ebook)

10 9 8 7 6 5 4 3 2 1

WOR

Printed in the United States of America